Meat Markets

This work is for
families and such, and friends of all sorts
(particularly animal)

And to Rachel,
You are all and we are one.

I love you

Meat Markets

The Cultural History of Bloody London

Ted Geier

EDINBURGH
University Press

Edinburgh University Press is one of the leading university presses in the UK. We publish academic books and journals in our selected subject areas across the humanities and social sciences, combining cutting-edge scholarship with high editorial and production values to produce academic works of lasting importance. For more information visit our website: edinburghuniversitypress.com

© Ted Geier, 2017

Edinburgh University Press Ltd
The Tun – Holyrood Road
12(2f) Jackson's Entry
Edinburgh EH8 8PJ

Typeset in 10.5/13 pt Sabon by
Servis Filmsetting Ltd, Stockport, Cheshire

A CIP record for this book is available from the British Library

ISBN 978 1 4744 2471 4 (hardback)
ISBN 978 1 4744 2472 1 (webready PDF)
ISBN 978 1 4744 2473 8 (epub)

The right of Ted Geier to be identified as the author of this work has been asserted in accordance with the Copyright, Designs and Patents Act 1988, and the Copyright and Related Rights Regulations 2003 (SI No. 2498).

Contents

List of Figures		vi
Acknowledgements		vii
	Introduction: 'A condition more abject . . .' Meat City and Nonhuman Objects	1
1	A Parliament of Monsters: Romantic Nonhumans and Victorian Erasure	27
2	Meat without Animals: Outcast Objects and the Improvement of London	77
3	Mass Production: Impossible London's Criminal Subjects	119
	Conclusion: Post-meat	168
Index		181

List of Figures

Figure 1	John Tenniel's mutton illustration for *Through the Looking Glass*. Public domain	13
Figure 2	OXO Tower, London. Used by permission of walklondon.com	107
Figure 3	Bovril puts beef into you. Public domain	108
Figure 4	Bovril at the front. Public domain	109
Figure 5	Smithfield Poulters' Company Arms. Photograph by Ted Geier	110
Figure 6	Smithfield commemorative bench (full). Photograph by Ted Geier	110
Figure 7	Smithfield commemorative bench (detail – Smoothe-Field). Photograph by Ted Geier	111
Figure 8	Smithfield commemorative bench (detail – 'The bleating of sheep'). Photograph by Ted Geier	112
Figure 9	*Vanity Fair* whales ball. Public domain	125

Acknowledgements

Having this work with Edinburgh University Press was always my secret wish, not least because Edinburgh students won the commission for the 2006 commemorative bench at Smithfield I photographed for Chapter 2. The bench is its own constellation of cultural history and literary thought, and the Smithfield story is not complete without a sit. John Lawson Johnston, inventor of the Bovril 'fluid meat', had his butcher shop in Edinburgh. Edinburgh also brings my long thinking about national bard Robert Burns and animals home.

Being a part of the Edinburgh Animal Studies' nineteenth-century literature and theory tradition does me great honour that I surely don't deserve. At Edinburgh, I thank Michelle Houston for her wise counsel and passion for the project, and I thank Rebecca Mackenzie for a stunning cover and further confirmation that Edinburgh is the proper, lively home for such work. Adela Rauchova has also been perfect in every way. Throughout the book's completion, James Dale has steered me right, and a brilliant copy editor, Barbara Eastman, made sure I made sense. There are surely others I'm forgetting but to whom I am ever grateful. A note of thanks, as well, to the Walkmaster at walklondon.com for permitting use of the Oxo tower image in Chapter 2.

In developing this work, I owe deep gratitude to the UC Davis Environments & Societies (UCD E&S): History, Literature, and Justice Mellon Research Initiative, and especially to my mentors Julie Sze and Mike Ziser. Julie and Mike supported me amidst their myriad other commitments and taught brilliant seminars. UCD E&S provided research funding for my 2013 London expedition, contributing especially to Chapters 2 and 3 in this work.

I was fortunate to develop portions of this work at several conferences in recent years, and I owe thanks to the UC Davis Office of Graduate Studies and the Graduate Students Association for generous travel awards in addition to my department's unfailing support for my research activity while at Davis. I am grateful to the organisers of these conferences and to the incredible host of key scholars and attendees participating and offering their feedback in those settings. In particular: Miranda Burgess, David L. Clark and Jacques Khalip for the MLA Romantic Period Division Session on 'Nature' in 2014; Kari Weil, Antoine Traisnel, and the excellent 'Traffic in Animals (19th c.)' ACLA 2014 seminar group; Lynn Voskuil, David Thomas and Chris van den Bossche, as well as Joe McLaughlin for excellent feedback and suggestions after my Interdisciplinary Nineteenth Century Studies Conference talk in 2014; Robert McKay and John Miller for the exceptional 'Reading Animals' Conference at Sheffield in 2014, where seemingly everyone wound up for perhaps the finest Animal Studies gathering I've had the privilege to attend in person; and the entire gang at Society for Literature, Science, and the Arts (SLSA) 2012. I must extend a very special thanks to harlan weaver for the 2013 'Funny Kinds of Love' conference at Berkeley and for the chance to connect with Colin Dayan, Carla Freccero, Donna Haraway, Robert C. Jones and a multitude of the very best critters. At Rice, Cymene Howe and Dominic Boyer steward an exceptional set of endeavours, and the Anthropology Department hosted me for a talk on 'Meat Without Animals: The Smithfield System'. Thanks to the Department and to the Colloquium participants, some of whom have since become my very favourite friends-from-afar via social media. Thanks especially to my graduate host (himself an emerging voice of great consequence on these matters), Drew Winter. I also presented more work from the book at SLSA in Houston in 2015, where I got to again see favourites like Lynn Turner (one never really sees enough of her) and Antoine Traisnel, and far too many more to count. I also met Alastair Hunt for the first time, who in fact became the last person I talked at length with about these Romantic animals in a vegan restaurant in Portland in October of 2016. Also from my SLSA connections, thanks to Gregg Lambert for his work and his intellectual generosity, and thanks to Aaron Jaffe, especially for pointing out the Joseph Conrad infatuation with Bovril that I continue to ignore.

I was a privileged participant in the 2015–16 Rice Seminars, 'After Biopolitics', led by Cary Wolfe and Tim Morton and comprised of an exceptional group of rigorous collaborators and special guests including the inimitable David L. Clark (who reminded me to attend to the 'rendering' in Mary Wollstonecraft's *Vindication*, among other endless debts I owe to him). Gregg Flaxman instigated sharp inquiry all year, often gathering our coterie of nineteenth-century specialists (Ryan White, Sophia Hsu and Joe Carson) toward the literary and theoretical stakes of this fraught convention, 'biopolitics', while our guests Wendy

Brown and David Wills, in particular, sparked considerations of the 'creaturely' in neoliberalism and the techniques of death, respectively, that have ended up in here at times.

There is a long list of other folks who were at Rice or with whom I convened during the year, but those closest to this task and to life itself during my year in Houston: along my office hall, I had the privilege of daily chats with Helena Michie and/or Alexander Regier. In the Humanities Research Center (HRC), Farès El-Dahdah and Melissa Bailar kept me in line and supported a summer 2016 London venture so that I could speak at Derrida Today (Lynn Turner again!) but also to revisit some of the key sites in this book, including the British Library for a fresh look at some parchment, that revered form of meat-under-glass. Adriana Chiaramonti keeps the HRC in line. Dear friends and partners in crime Alex Tarr, Carolyn Adams and Rex Troumbley ensured that all went well, even when it didn't, and ensured a sustained discussion of poetry, urban spaces and political forms throughout the year that continues to influence my work. More importantly, we had a community instead of just an office. This is, itself, an unlikely thing that the book reflects deeply upon. It matters.

I got to UC Davis from my beginnings on some of these subjects at San Francisco State University, where Saul Steier, Wai-Leung Kwok, Volker Langbehn, Mary Scott and Rob Thomas were my foremost mentors and supporters. James Martel was a kind and invested supporter of the Master of Arts (MA) project I proposed while there, and perhaps one day we'll get back to it. At Davis, David Simpson was (and is) an especially influential presence, and I would be much less without the intellectual substance he imparts through his own work and teaching, as well as in hosting and enriching scintillating events with, foremost, David L. Clark (yet again!) and James Raven. Mike Martel and I ended up in a two-person Romanticism reading seminar together that remains some of the most generative close reading I have ever been a part of. Tobias Menely, who arrived at Davis as I was leaving, generously shared with me his important work on British animal writing and law, now in the world as *The Animal Claim*. That work has complicated my own considerably by spurring it to be much better than it was. I hope.

Back at Davis some time ago, Allison Coudert hired me as a teaching assistant (TA) for her Ethical Eating course and has been one of my greatest supporters as well as an always-scintillating interlocutor on issues animal, sympathy, eating and more. She also ensured that the UC Davis Animal Studies group would always find its way. There is a litany of incredible graduate students and faculty collaborators in that work that I thank profusely for their ongoing commitment to the field and its futures. Stefan Uhlig helped me along with a good number of issues to do with public literacy and literary production in England, and he continues to support my work on Romanticism and otherwise while also being a very good friend to the newly minted academic. Jaimey Fisher deputised my intellectual explorations and continues to be a stalwart advisor and supporter as well as an incisive collaborator. Jeff Fort's care for language and the precision of critical inquiry remain, for me, the deepest imperative to think. Juliana Schiesari has been, from day one, my rock steady academic guide and my own personal enthusiast. One could not be luckier than to work for her and with her. Thanks to Dr Andy Jones for friendship and guidance.

Tim Morton and I first met before I started my PhD studies. On my way to an environmental philosophy conference at my alma mater, the University of Oregon, I wrote to introduce myself. We went to a little Mediterranean restaurant on the main campus strip after he gave his paper, and he told me to read *Mont Blanc* as I started to talk about animals and poetry with him for the first time. I've lost track of all the time we've spent on these subjects since, only I feel I remember it all at the same time. He and I somehow, magically, wound up on the same London–Houston flight once upon a time in the process of this work, and we talked about things for hours, standing in the aisle while others slept and watched terrible free movies on the backs of each other's heads. This book does not exist without Tim. He will not be held responsible for its deficiencies, which stand out only thanks to the strengths he permitted, over time, through our work together.

Thanks to our tolerant little housemate for many years now, Madeline the Cat, and thanks always and forever to Dr Rachel Taylor Geier (who did not type a single word of this manuscript), without whom I could never be.

Introduction: 'A condition more abject . . .' Meat City and Nonhuman Objects

Alas! Why does man boast of sensibilities superior to those apparent in the brute; it only renders them more necessary beings.[1]

There is a line in Zola's *Pot-Bouille* about a man being killed 'like an animal in an abattoir'. It is a threat from a disturbed man, Saturnin, who has returned from a stay at an asylum in relation to some business with an inheritance. The accompanying woodcut by Georges Bellenger hardly fits the description, but for the gaping skeleton's visage on the man awaiting dispatch by his assailant's long knife. The intruder, who has invaded the condemned man's bedchambers, is in full business attire and sprawls across the man in his nightclothes, in a well-appointed bed chamber, subduing him while holding him by the hair and preparing the final cut. 'I will bleed you like a pig', the assailant tells him before he begins, then twice again in the space of a few lines.[2] Readers of Kafka might already have thought of the famous ending of *The Trial*, when an anonymous dispatch polishes off Josef K. 'like a dog'. Here the parallel of animal slaughter to violent, yet intimately domestic intrusion, remarks – thrice – on the animality of humanity in the new metropolis, where civic space and quotidian compressions produce such figurative violence between men. But this would of course be to undermine the animal of animality, which was already a routinely 'de-animated' market object and administered form of life for killing, for parts, for distribution and for consumption.

The easiest critique of the 'biopolitical' moment in this nineteenth-century context is to lament the force of market expectations thrust upon human bodies in the massive civic space. The far less natural approach, at least outside the Animal Studies approaches that begin 'after' the centripetal pull of humanist analysis, is to catalogue the all-too-natural economisation of life required by such a space and by such a populous. That market logic hardly considers species difference and quite easily subdues individuals, even types, to the will of metropolitan function. Consider Poe's 'Man of the Crowd', in which the barrage of labour-class types culminates in an impossible individual, a singling-out of an inscrutable traveller of the night-time London to which the narrator can only assign 'the type and genius of deep crime', a human and civic text that refuses to be read, as the well-known German quote in the story's opening remarks. In some sense, the city has replaced the human as the individual centre of life and its flourishing, a grand apparatus of fungible, replaceable parts.

This is a key concern of Dickens's *Bleak House* and *Oliver Twist*, both of which consider the force of the city – the civic force of experience – that is a disorienting fog and muck, respectively (at Smithfield specifically, in the latter case). The city is also a mapping of Oliver's narrative progress, yet another figuration of the civic force against humanity and against life, when Oliver travels from east to west across London, through Smithfield at the climax of his disorientation as an appendage of the Dodger, finally arriving within the criminal type at his journey's end. The chapter is called 'The Expedition'. A journey of purpose like this, ending in darkened rooms while respectable types slumber, is the same setting Zola's bleeding pig and business-class butcher inhabit. There are no longer exceptional journeys in the city, despite the pains to recuperate little Oliver by the novel's end ('The Parish Boy's Progress'). There are only anonymous, possibly (or practically) covert, and accelerated trips along arteries and routes that could be mapped, perhaps set along a grid even, but that only sporadically turn up with any public or community identity, and then largely the result of a broken routine and the anti-tragedy of a meaningless, anonymous death: the dispatch.

There would be any number of approaches to the nineteenth-century European slaughterhouse, which 'abattoir' may be translated as, focused on the Parisian contexts of the Zola novel. Paris saw the first public abattoir movement, part of a civic reordering to remove the traffic in animals and the scenes of slaughter from increasingly congested city centres. The idea was, however, also to render more efficient the administration of life, death, disassembly and distribution of the meat object. This concept of a new, mass structure by which to manage lives and contain the threats to hygiene, decency and worse is in fact precisely the target of *Pot-Bouille*, which was part of Zola's massive series, *Les Rougon-Macquart*. The titular object is the new apartment building, the title rendered variously as Piping Hot!, pot luck, melting pot. The subtext is that there are no assurances and no longer any appearances to be kept up beyond the one, homogenising, and erasive appearance of the façade. People in the partitioned stalls of the apartment building are not *like* anything, and the pig is not a base-level poor life; life itself is poor, if the measure could mean anything at all.

Against these social literary modes in the period, the gothic tones of the city butcher, like Sweeney Todd, and the documentary horrors of the urban crime tale or the romanticised yet journalistic highwayman tale, could not care less about the social – the civic – project in Zola or Dickens. If realism had reacted to Romanticism's artifice and dangerous use (consider Twain's satire of the South for its misappropriation of the other target of his satire, Sir Walter Scott), it did so as an attempt to express and negotiate experience through the documentation of social realities or, in the case of naturalism, social determinants. And yet, in an unintended irony, the literary rejection of the individualistic aesthetic in Romanticism is in turn the valorisation of the lost individual in the metropolitan meat grinder that Dickens will strive to recuperate and, perhaps, ultimately abandon when Esther must succumb to narrating her husband's esteem as the good little woman and little else. This turn began out of horror, with little hope of ever accounting for the immensity of that structure, and like the case, never terminates. Meanwhile, the market circuitry churns out more cheap text and meat, reprocessing both at will per market needs.

Dickens and the popular penny fiction of nineteenth-century London, particularly in the case of *Sweeney Todd* and the horrors of new urban market zones replete with mystery meat and bloodthirsty psychopaths privy to all manner of technological methods of atrocity, paint a gruesome and dirty picture of London and the modern consumer society. Population growth and shifting notions of social experience in the nineteenth-century city space had also rendered the Smithfield scene insufficient and inhumane by the changed civic standards. The issues with meat sources, general hygiene and crime had already influenced changes at the site before market removal. Smithfield was horrible yet not anomalous despite its close proximity to the low forms of life that British reform movements would target throughout the century. The depravity of Smithfield was an everyday commonplace, and even when removed from city centre daily encounter, the London reading audience improved through education and literary efforts thirsted for the blood and guts that once ran through the streets and the corpses that once broke the church floorboards.

This imbrication of quotidian intimacies and mundane contact with unspeakable atrocities, disease, and unsavoury characters, including the spectacle of oddities at Bartholomew Fair, were aggressively legislated alongside the animal welfare activism centred on Smithfield. Legal action was meant to right the social wrongs, and faith in the law to do so was largely sincere. Still today, animal law studies begin with English Common Law and the development of chattle (cattle) property law while marking Martin's Act of 1822 as a foundational moment. The law's failure to save animals from slaughter, and animal rights law's outright complicity in the evolution of mass slaughter and meat consumption, is one of a number of such failures. Besides the insufficiency of animal protections and the grim irony of 'humane slaughter' regulations in the meat industry, the meat product industry also exported its work to less-regulated spaces such as the Liebig Meat Extract Company/Oxo's South American meat processing plants. Concentrating 'meat' into a spreadable paste, filled not only with animal bodies but now also producing early versions of the corporate transnational outsourcing mode in the new global industry, makes the regulated and legislated meat object of the nineteenth century an emergent, nascent commodity separate from the animal body and prior geospatial restrictions on care and transport. Smithfield removal was one stage in this evolution, and the popular London literatures expose the cultural consumption tastes attending that progression. In all, the animal question in nineteenth-century London and the Smithfield scene of gruesome narratives and public fears coalesce in the legal addresses, failures and subjections that Dickens would directly address as his Romantic precursors had in literary forms like apostrophe and the other modes explicated in Chapter 1.

Smithfield's legal success in addressing captive suffering and human–nonhuman coexistence ironically intensified (as silence and invisibility) the animal slaughter wrought by that procedural success, a fate in the city shared by humans. In turn, the human meat of *Sweeney Todd*, as discussed in Chapter 3, is the frustrated, at best, form of human life possible in the bureaucratic society. This suspicion shows up in Poe, and certainly in Melville's Bartleby, but was already the stuff of Romanticism's fragmentary interrogations of precarious individuation under the threat of administered life post-enclosure. The human made no sense, a bewildering status that Dickens would transfer to the overwhelming sensory overload of London. This civic history, which I have elsewhere written about as 'anthrozootic social conditions' in the lineage of biopolitical thought and Frankfurt School critique of the World War-era evacuation of life forms, contributes directly to the sense of nonhuman object status that had been highlighted in the Romantic frustrated apostrophic forms and the horror stories of the mass-produced, fungible penny dreadfuls.[3] Chapters 1 and 3, respectively, will address these literary modes.

These conditions were also articulated in the critical theoretical texts of the period itself. Perhaps not incidentally, Karl Marx's thirty-year residency in the British Library's round Reading Room, where he wrote *Das Kapital*, took place about one mostly straight mile down High Holborn from Smithfield Market. Researching the work, the first part of which was published in 1867, would have kept Marx in the library for the entire height of Smithfield reform debates and completion, contending daily with the urban density and homogenising production modes driving the market debates. Marx's primary historical examples were often drawn from English history, and he works at length on the same issues of enclosure the Romantic works herein addressed and the agrarian changes the butchers had complained about in their 1795 petition pamphlet.[4] In the twentieth century, Frankfurt School theorists negotiated the outcome of those modes of production and their attendant social relations in the context of World War-era atrocities including the concentration camps. This critique has now returned to its agrarian origins in the case of, for example, J. M. Coetzee's alignment of the Concentrated Animal Feeding Operation (CAFO) and the camp.[5]

This critique directs once again to the Smithfield condition in nineteenth-century London as the meat production industry undergoes incredible change. Animals had already been run through city streets for centuries by the time, in the early nineteenth century, public outcry about sites like Smithfield Market began to become part and parcel of parliamentary action. The earliest animal rights laws would begin in Parliament as Acts regulating the driving of animals to slaughter and the unlawful slaughter of horses, suggesting from the earliest point that animal rights would have to contend with its welfarist stream to the last. This version of animal rights that permits animal use for human consumption – food, entertainment and display, candles and parchment, clothing, pets – attempts to draw the line of ethical treatment of the animals destined for that life or lack thereof within human culture. The Acts would not be passed on their first tries, generally, though the earliest, the 1786 Knackers Act against unlicensed (and thus, generally cruel and gruesome) horse slaughter was. Subsequent Acts aspiring to go further and ban various forms of cruelty to animals associated with entertainments such as bear-, badger- and bull-baiting would see several defeats before finally passing nearer the middle decades of the nineteenth century. Nevertheless, the social concern backing such action was constant in London, and bodies like the Royal Society for the Prevention of Cruelty to Animals (RSPCA), founded in 1824, are clear markers of the broad concern for animal welfare and rights launched in the century. The literature attending this lengthy period, centred in London, is concretely identified with social concern.

Ascribing a contemporary critical concept like post-humanism to this eighteenth-to-nineteenth century British human–animal context would perform an anachronous sleight of hand: the intersections of technological change and anthropocentricism in the Romantic and Victorian periods are not the same as those motivating Cary Wolfe's or other recent theorists' evaluation of a post-human condition. At the same time, in articulating both the priority and posterity of post-humanism – before and after humanism – Wolfe's post-humanism bears an uncanny resemblance to Romantic social critiques of reflexivity. Wolfe's rubric of technical-cognitive apparatuses of life, unsettled boundary zones and undone binary metanarratives, and a critical, persistent subjectivity against perfectibility and authenticity that tries to contend with its own ossification seem wholly Romantic.[6] Romantic trends such as these will be articulated in Chapter 1. These are also the signs and responses to the atrophy of experience Benjamin writes of, and all of these conditions inflect Adorno's sense of an administered life that subjects life (and non-life) forms, as concrete economic objects (and 'objects of reason' merely avoids that more fundamental reification) to static categories or use values.[7] What seems to occur, and what Dickens especially will investigate in literary form, is a reduction of the very concepts of individuation, life, humanity and wholeness. Authors writing on the 'post-Darwin' context have identified this as a formative indeterminacy in human–animal relations, as well.[8]

The meat markets are easy targets for such critique, as the insensate herding, slaughter, processing, parcelling and vending of bodies are their *raison d'être*. The contemporary theory audience will think immediately, and perhaps decisively, of Foucault's concept of biopower and state apparatuses that 'make live and let die'.[9] Indeed, both Wolfe and Dickens write about the confirmed articulation – the rendering as article – of everything under the sign of progress, technology, civic organisation and so on. Mary Wollstonecraft's repeated articulation of woman as object to manly society follows this fraught verb, 'to render', as well: 'Men are not aware of the misery they cause, and the vicious weakness they cherish, by only inciting women to render themselves pleasing.'[10] Wollstonecraft's 'rendering' becomes Mary Shelley's burden in *Frankenstein*, as well, echoing Wollstonecraft's claim that

> the preposterous distinctions of rank, which render civilization a curse, by dividing the world between voluptuous tyrants, and cunning envious dependents, corrupt, almost equally, every class of people, because respectability is not attached to the discharge of the relative duties of life, but to the station.[11]

This concern for 'station' will also be examined in the case of Bartleby and Poe's businessmen in Chapter 3.

Chapter 2 is an assessment of the Smithfield condition (called the Smithfield System in its heyday) in conjunction with the aesthetic expression of its central objects – nonhumans, all of us – that might lend itself to a stronger critical history and usefulness of the figure, 'post-human'. The Smithfield live animal market made human–animal coexistence a fundamental aspect of London civic development. Authors who published well-known reactions to the writhing, stinking, horrible, anonymous mingling of animals and humans included Swift, Defoe, Dickens and Hardy. Smithfield's removal was a long, arduous process culminating in an even worse outcome: the magnificent, efficient, sparklingly clean and brutally mechanised new Metropolitan Meat Market at Islington. It would carry into the full sense of modernity invoked in twentieth-century social theory on inhuman, bare life and the anonymous devaluation of individual lives wrought by meticulous, clinical administration. The period's slaughter reform produced a concept of meat with all notion of the animal itself – the stinking, noisy, suffering, proximate animal body – erased. Far worse than the preceding cruelty, market removal and slaughter reform/revision quelled middle class animal concern but inflicted the deepest horror of all. Animals were emptied of content by modes of production including the successful practical management of a massive, seething population in a space that already struggled to maintain a hint of human splendour against the backdrop of widespread poverty and disease. Wordsworth's 'Parliament of Monsters', addressed again in Chapter 1, foreshadowed nothing less.

The classist moralising about the cacophony at Smithfield included claims that labour forms, such as butchery and driving, bred morally bankrupt humans while broader social concern produced an animal welfare movement, institutions like the RSPCA, and a series of parliamentary acts banning cruelty. Responses of the day called these objects, this meat that was the product of world-renowned animal husbandry – technology – manufactured articles. The animals were perfectible machines and now the meat that left no trace of the blood, guts and other offal not for eating (maybe for lighting or for washing) was the heart of a humming, thriving and newly self-aware commodity production and distribution system wondered at as any new railway or gas lighting would have been. Not even just a cut, not merely, but totally the thing – some thing – that was not a live animal.

The uncanny recognitions of dehumanised humans in industrial, urban London, and the increasing technicity of biotic and other material administration and ecological risks such as cholera, water supplies and more, led to organised refigurings of the idealised, perfectible human subject. The animal rights debates in Parliament would rail against lower class iniquity to accomplish their ends while, as Dickens lampoons in *Bleak House*, social consciousness, even global awareness, could be properly, hollowly performed by middle and higher class sophisticates while London wallowed in squalor. What such contradictions highlight is an overwhelming sense of performative consumption and of the strange new social life forms challenging constitutive notions of identity and cultural or human substance (to say nothing of conceits of superiority). The humanist subject was a routinely satirised object while paper got cheaper, journalism and popular literatures exploded, and literacy among the working class exponentially rose with the population.

The intense social and animal concern of this period seems, by definition, critical of a coexistence comprised of indistinguishable, unidentifiable nonhumans that could be manipulated, categorised and assembled into uncanny, alien forms. As Dickens and Hardy documented, and as contemporary historians such as Hilda Keane and Robyn Metcalfe confirm, the seething, meaty masses of London urban market space mobilised biological anxieties against an interspecies, material consubstantiality of filth and noise that evacuated humanist concepts of life and value because the consequences for humans near animals at Smithfield were the same as they were for animals near animals through the streets of London and to market: daily shocks, unsettling din and bruisings that damaged the quality of any individual animal as violently as they disrupted any remaining hope that urban life retained a properly 'humane' quality.[12]

These animals were apparently required to feed a massive population, an economic reality with direct effects on the humans and the animals in just the way Burns saw enclosure to assault humans and animals alike. The reduction of life to such modes recalls Adorno's proto-posthumanist assessment of economic forms producing an inhuman subject. This subject is deprived of prior concepts of individual autonomy yet wholly demolished under the same concept of consequential individual life. Smithfield animals and technicised, productive animals and humans become indistinguishable masses, managed as labour and forced into mechanised, calculated deaths that matter so much exactly because of the horror of this total vacancy. The technical improvement, or perfection of the individual, killable animal body amalgamated bodies as one meat population, and thus Adorno and Foucault conjoin in articulating the biopolitical structures motivating the resistant social concerns of the period itself. This mattered enough to reform slaughter techniques in the cruellest irony of welfarist animal protection.[13] And it mattered to anti-slavery reforms, which have been discussed at times in correlation to animal rights rhetoric and literature.

But the sincerity of commitment, the practical reality, could always be freshly negated, and literature especially was preoccupied with the tenuous success of any animal concern or nonhuman thought. Something about the task itself was a destined failure that matched the ironic negations of Romantic literature. A number of examples from Romantic literature suggest a deep and abiding animal concern that also articulates the 'post-human condition' by, quite fittingly, decentring the human in an interspecies community of suffering that eludes communication. What was under review was coexistence and the limits of concern, in all its forms. The deep suspicion of the literature of nonhumans in the period becomes the dominant reality of human and nonhuman experience in the London of the Smithfield era, and this motivates further efforts to 'address' 'real' suffering in civic reorganisation and legal reform, both of which are taken up in Chapter 1. What has happened, when the Romantics already address themselves as nonhumans and then struggle to address anything else, is this: the abject form of coexistent nothingness does not reduce experience or undo the critical vantage at all. It was already thus, and thus cannot be addressed at all, merely expressed.

In the passage just before the provocative 'condition more abject' in the chapter's title, the creature explicates in the famous response to humanity in Volume II of *Frankenstein*, to be base and vicious appears to be worse – more abject – than 'to be a great and virtuous man'. This anthropocentric chauvinism of propriety – of civilisation – grounds the improvement tropes of English society in the same period. The laws against animal abuse, which were the first in modern legal history, generally proceeded as arguments for the improvement of human behaviour including the tempering of alcohol consumption and the Sunday cockfights, with the gambling and cursing that went along with them, keeping men and youths from proper church attendance. Mary Shelley's creature, however, is not referring to law or to London society, but to the status of existence it has been subjected to. The abjected experience outside human society is compared to the 'blind mole' and the 'harmless worm', but the final analysis of the human condition in the work is that these were misconceptions. Humanity, in practice, is a decidedly negative status, capable of every extreme atrocity and not reliably 'humane', and certainly not civilised at all. Saving humanity from itself would seem a reasonable aim, as a result.

While Shelley's speculative, would-be-social nonhuman in *Frankenstein* invites thinking on the anxieties of sociation as well as on genetics and biopolitical structures of life and society, it is also part of a dense Romantic interrogation and address of nonhumans of diverse sorts. The all-too-human yet tragically nonhuman creature learns of humanity through a fortunate accident: a satchel with three books in it provides an education while it learns to speak and yearn for community by watching the DeLacey family through the window of a cottage in the woods. Thus, as the comparison to mole and worm confirms, Frankenstein's framed, constructed monstrosity is capable of analogising his predicament outside human society with the nonhuman status of, well, nonhumans. This is because his aesthetic distance – outside the domestic space he romanticises, where things seem to be – is also his ontological distance. The demands of performing and verbalising community participation he can meet; the task of appearing to be human, he cannot. Other Romantics, as I'll discuss in Chapter 1, found all manner of nonhuman address besides these deeply human existential concerns.[14] The comparative logic – animals to humans, humans to animals – grounds the 'apparent' and deeply ironic definition and evaluation of humanity in the passages from *Frankenstein*.

The insufficiency of that comparison and the ways in which 'brute' analogies impede empathy and sincerity are part of broader London conditions at the Smithfield Market. The nonhuman coexistence of humans and animals, diseases and filth, water and corpses leads to civic reforms on the heels of animal concern. The meat factory status of urban life also impels the gory serial fiction of the penny presses being consumed by the London mass audience that had already proven to have a taste for death, if not the blood itself, in popular cultural modes and amusements like the public hanging. It would seem that, in the age of 'Humanity Dick', there was very little humanity to go around. This curious tension, to borrow Lewis Carroll's adjective for the intimate strangeness of coexistence, resembles an agonistic cultural history now. The fiercest animal rights achievements of the period attend the certain increase in animal deaths – and their invisible process – as Smithfield Market is kicked out of the city centre on the heels of Martin's Act while British consumers eat ever more meat, ever more quickly, ever more humanely, as discussed in Chapter 2. How to equally represent such divided concerns?

As it turns out, the democratic consideration of nonhumans, including meat, is waged in early Romantic works. Consider Robert Burns's 'To a Haggis.' The haggis becomes a heroic actor, addressed in a spirited ritual ode. The speaker says O twice, in both instances addressing the speaker's own aesthetic experience: 'O what a glorious sight' and 'O how unfit!'[15] The haggis is, however, directly addressed and interpellated as a royal coexistent via direct address: 'Great Chieftain o' the Puddin-race!'[16] The meat object, an assemblage of oats, sheep's organs, onions and spices encased in a sheep's stomach, is the occasion for the ode on national identity. The closing asserts the rich, savoury haggis's role in national pride:

> Auld Scotland wants nae skinking ware
> > That jaups in luggies;
> But, if ye wish her gratefu' pray'r,
> > Gie her a *Haggis!*[17]

Here 'skinking ware that jaups in luggies' refers to vibrant, sugary foodstuffs (skinking ware) rolling or sloshing around (jauping) in formal vessels (luggies – handled bowls one can 'lug' food about in), bereft of filling proteins and the hearty, savoury, irony, salted tastes of the haggis mix. 'Auld Scotland' prefers something of more character, and if you want 'her' to respond to your address, best gie her a haggis.

Burns's 1787 poem suggests the weighty role of meat and meat consumption that will be further examined in Chapter 2 through what is the key formal concern in Chapter 1, the apostrophe, yet it also resists the full anthropomorphic turn in Lewis Carroll's 1865 and 1871 works on Alice. Carroll animates impossible and everyday objects throughout the works. The riotous banquet scene when Alice is queen, just before waking, also mocks the formality of address and decorum that subtends the reflexive apostrophe of Romanticism and the hopeless social concern of Dickens's idiosyncratic realism. The Red Queen's sulking adherence to etiquette and formality as Alice meets the meal proceeds thusly:

> 'You look a little shy: let me introduce you to that leg of mutton,' said the Red Queen. 'Alice – Mutton: Mutton – Alice.' The leg of mutton got up in the dish and made a little bow to Alice: and Alice returned the bow, not knowing whether to be frightened or amused.[18]

Next, the Red Queen refuses Alice's offer to cut her a slice, saying 'it isn't etiquette to cut any one you've been introduced to'.[19] And later, after Alice tries her hand at sovereignty and recalls a pudding dismissed by the Red Queen after another 'Alice – [object] : [Object] – Alice' introduction, she cuts a slice, less shy now about her address of foodstuffs. The pudding is, naturally, not amused:

> 'What impertinence!' said the pudding. 'I wonder how you'd like it, if I were to cut a slice out of *you*, you creature!'
> It spoke in a thick, suety sort of voice, and Alice hadn't a word to say in reply: she could only sit and look at it and gasp.
> 'Make a remark,' said the Red Queen: 'it's ridiculous to leave all the conversation to the pudding!'[20]

This mute wonder or bewilderment will trouble most of the characters and works under consideration here. The raucous nonsense of Carroll's children's literature, whatever 'children's literature' is to suggest in the case of such a dexterous, rich experiment in literary imagination, formal and linguistic play, lacks the seriousness of the canonical Romantic works. Burns is every bit as playful and ridiculous in his patriotic lauding of the haggis. What Burns and Carroll assert, and what I include at the outset as a sort of friendly gesture before what is, frankly, a gruesome tale, is the spirited heart about which so many of the works and concerns examined revolve and upon which they all depend (Figure 1).

This study will at times address institutionalised legal addresses of nonhumans, moving ultimately to a markedly different context by implicating the legal fiction of Dickens in the tasks of interrogating and salvaging nonhuman forms of life from the ravages of the human forms and structures by which the abjected remainders show up – appear – as lesser life forms fit to be tied, beaten, enslaved, slaughtered, eaten and worse. It will also examine the ways in which the live animal is summarily erased from London city space in the nineteenth century, and the meat animal – whatever that is to mean – is erased twice over in being produced and processed in the shimmering efficiencies of the massive public slaughterhouses that develop by the latter half of the century. No one encounters the animal that gave the food in the city as the city itself copes with its new intensities of population, technology and, as I'll also suggest in the course of this study, literacy.

The meat of London, like the pulp of its most popular cultural forms in the nineteenth century, is a form that complicates the notion of life and not-life in the husbandry and labour division rhetorics underpinning meat industry developments leading to a major civic reform, the Smithfield Removal Act of 1852. There is a strong rhetorical lineage from apostrophe and the broad social concern of the period that also produced England's well-known early animal rights. This, in turn, inflected Smithfield removal debates with an apparent logic of sympathy and animal rights even as the operative causes were vastly more complex and economically motivated. The Smithfield meat form, already established as a manufactured meat article or object form long before in English animal husbandry and distribution systems in London, paralleled London civic experience reflected in the gruesome, dangerous, bloody tales driving much literary production in cheap serials. Animal rights, which contributed to human slaughter reforms, led only to the easier, more efficient systematisation of meat animal production and disassembly. Animal rights thus contributed to mass, technological animal slaughter. This is the curious industrial parallel – again, not so

Figure 1 John Tenniel's mutton illustration for *Through the Looking Glass*. Public domain.

surprising at all – of mass production, distribution and consumption of cheap literature and meat in nineteenth-century London. The legal forms that bred the erasure of life in the evolved slaughter practice had their counterpart in an equally butchered penny blood and dreadful literary form defined by mass, anonymous production, fungible characters and storylines, sensationalism, and general butchery and criminal types in the dark, dirty London city centre.

This comparison shows precisely how futile those practical reform efforts and bureaucratic reorganisations of civic life were and how decisively aesthetic expression from Romanticism through modernism, and beyond, returns as a necessary, if troubled, address of deep social concerns. The nineteenth-century revision of human chauvinisms through literary form relies upon gruesome themes and is routinely rendered mute by other material forms. This implies a corpus of nonhuman aesthetics in Romantic literature that then must be read as an historical precursor to a still-progressing cultural project, directly related to the early animal rights movement and other social reforms including public education and literacy that produced the massive new reading public the pennies fed.[21] This curious melding of market invention and mechanisms of social concern – the humanist improvement trope, specifically – requires the pulp fiction machinery as naturally as the market for meat requires the invisible meat machinery ushered in on the heels of an improved, 'humane' slaughter etiquette achieved by the world's foundational animal rights movement.

This casting of nonhumans, if it is intent upon a successful or coherent expression, then might also be said to express how very unwell humans had become, were still becoming and perhaps were always going to be. This implies a concern for the subjects of literary expression, in the case of the animals and nonhumans in Romantic literature. Certainly, the social novels of Dickens reflect intense practical concern with the London he confronted. They are called 'social' novels because of their social critique, after all.[22] Even in a gruesome popular story like *Sweeney Todd*, the actions of the demon barber are presented as scintillating criminal mysteries to be solved, stopped and punished. The resolution of the story, however, does not condone murder or cannibalism, though both are crucial, so to speak, to the story's vibrancy. While the penny dreadfuls and bloods deal in horror and savage butchery, they do so generally in a build up to horrible climax, discovery, and resolution of the dangerous criminal element. And so the literatures attending Smithfield Market share a social ethics and a lineage of animal concern.

Romantic nonhuman thought presciently attempts to negotiate the rigours of nonhuman conditions in reflexive formal modes such as apostrophe. After Romanticism, Victorian period literatures such as the realist social novel and the penny serials employ techniques such as the objective documentary form of print journalism and the prose of Dickens. The pennies, like Dickens, were published in serial form but were much cheaper than the works of Dickens and printed on cheaper paper, besides. This penny serial form was thus an inherently disposable form, and the works themselves were often shared by multiple readers in local reading communities.[23] Penny press serials also traded in equally cheap, disposable literary techniques and devices, and even outright plagiarism of Dickens and others. These Victorian forms in turn amplify the objective and clinical yet grotesque, nonhuman conditions of city life and meat production. These London conditions formally undo narrative authority and subjective consistency.

Smithfield, as the stand-in for this literary–cultural constellation, produces a sterile, invisible, meaty object in the spaces something that could be called 'animal' or 'human' once populated. The literary and economic forms of this nexus produce the abjected other precisely at the points that most aggressively employ the philosophical and legal rhetorics meant to preserve individual lives against such exclusionary, horrifying logics. The most forcefully argued legal accomplishments in animal rights, which were clearly addressed to human interlocutors as calls for the reformed treatment of animals and the improvement of human behaviour, were simultaneously an anthropocentric moralist discourse and a set of material welfare outcomes borne by sincere animal concern. This legal and civic history at Smithfield, in particular, shows a clear success for the animal rights activists but an atrocious failure for the broader project of improving animals' chances at life – the reform of meat production and slaughter practices constitute the welfarist approach to animals that maintains the anthropocentric entitlement to using and killing animals while attempting also to assert a claim on humane treatment of those objects of use. The fact of the animal's death, in this form, is thus ruled out a priori as a relevant consideration. It is assured. The death of the animal is the guarantee that renders life irrelevant through the welfarist position, in which the focus on treatment before the unceremonious and perfunctory death enables meat to become meat.

While the legal history of animal rights at Smithfield and in other contexts is fraught with repeated failures and impediments, there is rarely such a thing as a negative history of animal rights like this synopsis of Smithfield suggests. Martin's Act remains a pivotal moment in a long march to animal rights not only in British contexts but also in the United States, and, as historian Hilda Kean notes, Martin's work to clear the city centre of the public spectacle of animal cruelty was seen as part of 'a modern, city-based society disengaging itself from a former barbarity'.[24] That work was a successful relocation of the sites of cruelty as part of a broader civic reorganisation. Market reforms including the transition from open air street markets to controlled, enclosed spaces across the city regulated public space, as Robyn Metcalfe has documented in her history of Smithfield, in 'a growing acknowledgment of the government's duty to protect public interests such as free trade, public safety, access to food and public health'.[25] As Metcalfe also notes, however, the city's residents were already reacting to a constant sense of upheaval amidst rampant civic construction and restructuring projects, and the activity in the first half of the nineteenth century 'eroded any sense of permanence in the neighborhood and portended a questionable future that prevented new businesses and tenants from putting down roots in Smithfield'.[26] The increased density of urban population and the impacted spaces of city life had already begun to negatively affect people's sense of their own existence and future status. The city's administrative tendencies now also threatened the sense of life in the city, and Metcalfe reveals the entrenched modes of biopower in the Smithfield case.

Thus it is that the fate of animal lives protected by some parts of early animal law was that they were never saved from their fate as meat for human consumption – quite the contrary, in fact. Smithfield reform debates and the eventual removal of the market were precisely directed toward improving meat production efficiency for an increased demand for meat from an exponentially increasing urban population.[27] At the time of the Smithfield debates, widespread criticism of the cruelty of cattle drovers, butchers and other agents at the market fuelled public sentiment and parliamentary action to reform Smithfield. Martin and the RSPCA, in the pages of the periodical *The Animal's Friend* as well as in pamphlets distributed in London, ultimately abetted civic interests the butchers opposed, leading to the smooth-running, centralised and institutionalised administration of the meat industry. Martin and other animal cruelty activists, in presenting individual agents such as cabbies and butchers as the villains in the plight of animals at Smithfield, succeeded in taking the public spectacles of cruelty out of the public domain and hiding them away in the gleaming new Metropolitan slaughter works at Islington.

This gruesome irony of the Smithfield debate animal rights activism was prefigured in the Romantic fixation on frustrated yet intricate addresses of animals. Romantic authors, however, were more sceptical about the effectiveness of rational administrative authority than London civic planners and Parliament would be later in the nineteenth century.

They incorporated their critiques of the instability of human representations and addresses of animal suffering in their work. Burns's poetics attempt to address, represent or advocate for animals but risk regular failure. The form of address itself, as a human construction, may well be the primary cause of such failure. Nevertheless, Burns's speaker attempts to protect the mother mouse turned up by his plough in the poem from the cruelty of human society:

> Still thou art blest, compar'd wi'me
> The present only touches thee:
> But och! I backward cast my e'e.
> On prospects drear!

Burns's articulation of the human–nonhuman relation and the governing differences between species is also aware of its articulating habit, as will be addressed further in Chapter 1.

This difference, and any adherence to its ontological primacy in considerations of the animal, may not measure up to contemporary Animal Studies frameworks and certainly is a reminder of Martin Heidegger's 'poor in world' – *weltarm* – animals from *The Fundamental Concepts of Metaphysics: World, Finitude, Solitude*.[28] In 'To a Mouse', Burns expresses the shared economic subjection of a human and a mouse. The agrarian ploughman speaker has lost the British commons to enclosure and expanded private property concepts in the early Romantic period. In *The Making of the English Working Class*, E. P. Thompson discusses the period of 1790–1830 as the period in which field workers were the largest single working class in England. Between 1780 and 1840, public land rights are lost to private land title and fenced off agricultural land, resulting in massive waves of migration from the country to city centres.[29] In Burns's Scotland, Highland Clearance enclosure was especially brutal. Removing tenants from land that had been consolidated under the title of wealthy landowners was often violent and came on little – if any – notice. This is reflected directly in 'To a Mouse', and resonates deeply with the later urban afflictions that dominate Victorian-era literature also commenting on new, alienating life forms. Burns's speaker also considers the insufficiency of human/animal or town/country divisions in the poem, as reflected in the poem's meditation on the circumstances that have found him in his country home but that show precisely how entangled all nodes of the British economic and legal communities were.

In comparison with Burns's 'To a Mouse', Wordsworth's 'There was a Boy' seems to lack such direct political engagement. The poem discloses the boy's death and constructs a final stanza of mourning. The mute fact of his death and the strong effect that death had on the speaker is punctuated by the speaker's final disclosure that, in the churchyard where the grave is,

> A long half-hour together I have stood
> Mute – looking at the grave in which he lies![30]

Wordsworth thus constructs a personal, individuated suffering in reflective remembrance. In Burns's precise political aspect, the speaker and the mouse in the poem are separated, like the speaker from his object of address, the natural world in 'There was a Boy'. The deep sadness of Burns's speaker recognising the inevitable fate mice and men share is similar to the harrowing conclusion of the Wordsworth poem. Burns's poem expresses an excruciating condition of coexistence in mutual suffering – the mouse due to human agrarian use of land and the ploughman under enclosure. Wordsworth's poem is not immediately concerned with the material forces afflicting humans and animals with precise forms of economic subjection, and so belies activist critique. And yet, Wordsworth's speaker performs a sort of self-abjection, stopping the poem in its closing stanza with an aggressive volta to the post-mortem, staged 'muteness'. Chapter 1 will consider Wordsworth's uncanny politics further and the anthropocentric chauvinism of Burns's speaker as it attempts a related recuperation of circumstances, telling the mouse that she is lucky to not have history and memory.

Burns's ploughman labourer and mouse provide a counterpoint to any moralising abjection of the butcher class at Smithfield. The literature examined throughout this book wonders at the uncanny solidarity called for by the weird coexistence they interrogate. The butchers were the villains in much anti-Smithfield narrative, but they are also a well-organised and long-standing trade guild in London that had its own complaints to enter in the debate. The discourse against cruelty employed in a variety of new animal laws and reiterated as part of Smithfield Market removal advocacy focused primarily on the depraved cruelty and the low society that congregated around Smithfield and its labouring ranks. The butchers, however, in fact developed the 'humane' killing methods themselves and took great pride in their efficient dispatch. 'Management' remains a technical achievement, as does the rumoured skill of the hunt and the art of the dressing. The rhetoric of morality and decency in parliamentary debates on the side of anti-cruelty legislature suggest a civic programme that merely reiterates a brand of human concern focused on treating animals a certain way insofar as that treatment breeds a more ideal human comportment and welfare. All of these claims to human decency make the butchers and drivers less than human, in no uncertain terms. That discourse on improvement is also clear in the thriving vegetarianism of the period, which more closely resembles religious temperance than it does any contemporary form of animal liberation ideology it might otherwise be a precursor to.[31]

Smithfield as a historical negotiation for nineteenth-century London mobilises all of the period's rampant fears of disease, of gruesome and murderous depravity in dark, uncontrolled, labyrinth urban spaces, and of the shock of urban anonymity in massive and deterministic economic systems. While this last condition has clearly mapped literary consequences in naturalism and social realism, and this same milieu has no small role in the Marxian analysis that breeds later cultural theory closely related to some of the usual approaches to the 'post-human' condition, in fact it is Romanticism and the less-frequently considered popular penny presses that best articulate the formal consequences of such conditions. By the time the popular presses are feeding a massive, newly literate working class English audience, the rampant interest in their bloody details and themes of adventure, danger, murder, mystery and liminal transgressions reflect the day's cultural condition. Londoners, as it turns out, had a well-developed taste for blood, cheaply produced.

The case cracking resolutions in the pennies, as in Bram Stoker's *Dracula* or Poe's tales, neatly capped the bloody, depraved, sensational escapades of the pennies, but this reliably perfunctory narrative form, much like reliable meat, demands little critical or moral consideration of consequence. This was precisely their soiled reputation. Romanticism formally surmised that successful address and resolution of political or economic concerns might be unlikely; the mass popular fiction never even considered it. In fact, a popular story might go on indefinitely according to demand, and popular characters killed in one volume might turn up later in another with no discussion at all.[32] Stoker himself was a voracious consumer of the penny dreadful, and even plagiarised scenes of Lucy in the coffin from *Varney the Vampyre*. The pennies, before Stoker, had plagiarised the more expensive Dickens novels, and so the genre presents not only a crucial material consumption study in direct parallel with forms of meat production and consumption efficiency, but also a vital and 'contaminated' intersectional genre between canonical nineteenth-century literatures, reflecting as well the general anxieties about physical contamination and permeation in the London city space.

The food history attending Smithfield has surprisingly strong parallel technical developments. For example, the complex Oxo company story begins with Justus von Liebig, the scientist who invented modern industrial agriculture by developing an artificial nitrogen-fixing process and who devised a way to concentrate 30 kg of beef into 1 kg of extract, then expected it to be consumed by those too poor to afford the real thing in nineteenth-century London. From this starting point, the Bovril/Oxo extract production was exported to southern Uruguay.[33] There, meat production ran one third the cost it did in England at the time because the company was able to exploit an animal-use economy focused on hide processing and not on meat production. Hence, the cattle could be purchased at much cheaper rates, rather than bred directly. But once this mystery meat form, from mysterious foreign origins, was inserted back into the London consumer economy, it was yet another strange, disorienting evolution of food that fed an increasingly vivid urban imagination of insidious foreign agents in water, air and everything else. As will be discussed further in Chapter 2, Bovril becomes a pure emblem of national substance. Bovril and the Oxo brand have been wildly popular, and, like the pennies, they are also indicative of the sinewy intersections of nonhuman conditions in the London city space and the material adaptations of consumption and animal (or literary) use: the beef had been distilled to its pure, portable 'beefiness', and this commodity extraction was part of the total annihilation of the animal in the period that Smithfield removal and slaughter revision achieved through erasure of the animal bodies from the civic space. It was indeterminate and perfunctory.

The condensed meatiness of a spreadable, portable paste form ironises material consumption, and penny dreadfuls might more properly be called an 'extractive' literature. The pennies stand between and against the political commitments of Romantics like Burns and later realists like Dickens. Romantic presentations of the forms of subjection and abjection begin in the robust expressions of animal suffering, inhuman conditions and measured cross-species empathy in works such as Mary Shelley's *Frankenstein*. The anxieties about anonymity in such works manifest in the interchangeable and hardly nourishing portable narratives of the pennies. The pennies were produced at new speeds, using new technologies, and the reading public that consumed them was, likewise, new and massive. The pennies plagiarised Dickens to make those popular works even more accessible to the new lower class reading public. They were liberally borrowed from.

The material conditions of penny literary production and consumption in London thus parallel the Smithfield Market conditions. The narrative content, such as the case of the mystery meats and bloody technologies in proximity to the meat market in *Sweeney Todd*, are precisely the conditions documented by the comprehensive social presentations in Dickens. Engaging these literary modes in a cross-study of the Smithfield case and examples such as the Bovril/Oxo company, as well as their respective roles in reinforcing the subjection and abjection of nonhumans for meat and pulp, builds a literary heritage of nonhuman thought and amplifies these authors' conviction that human society had already made literature into non-literature (and back again), humans into nonhumans, nonhumans into worse than not-humans or even not-animals. The bloody serial fiction fed a rampant new reading population in a mass-production market model, not always with clear origins. They relied heavily upon reliable, modular narrative formulae that focused on sensational suspense, horror or adventure with predictable payoffs and descriptive, gory language.

This inaugurates a prolific popular culture, and select streams in the serial fiction output were also extremely preoccupied with the terrifying, gruesome dangers of the outskirts of the city and the highwaymen and murdering marauders one might encounter in those liminal social spaces as in the dark and horrible spaces of the urban centre that so fascinates Dickens. But where Dickens's descriptions of the urban mazes in an increasingly crowded London space often worked to make a coherent, controlled point about those spaces, the penny dreadfuls were much more focused on heightening – perhaps simply hyping – the threat and the mystery of the dark corners of both town and country.[34] This sets up simple revelations and solutions. The basic narrative recycling fed habit, not edification. The overriding aesthetic investment in such works is in the 'unspeakable', the ghastly, the denouement of the criminals and the momentary resolution – typically after their death or, as in one vital and wildly popular work, *Sweeney Todd*, their arrest – of the culture of fear their crimes produced.

Immediately, such concerns suggest the works of Poe, and, to be sure, Poe's expressions of a similar urban horror and the captivating, relentless pursuit of discovery must be compared to the penny dreadful genre. There is also a vast body of bloody crime consumption back to Daniel Defoe and in the incredibly well-attended public hangings of criminals like Jack Sheppard, as discussed in Chapter 3. Sheppard is caught and hung in the early eighteenth century, but he then becomes one of the most famous characters in the penny dreadfuls of the mid-nineteenth century. Dickens also wrote on the ongoing public executions in his London. The criminal heritage in the pennies and in Dickens thus reflects the public taste for gruesome spectacle, be it individual civic experiences in the dark spaces that remind of basement abattoirs and dark butchers' alleys or the mass event of the execution. Dickens's rebuke of the public hanging in periodicals of the day, also discussed in Chapter 3, further demonstrates the tension of committed social concern and the ubiquity and popularity of horrible forms of entertainment.

In the case of the Smithfield Market removal debates through this same period, proposals to reform Smithfield and do away with seemingly unnecessary animal suffering suggested that those public scenes of suffering were not as entertaining. The primary arguments for removal, like the animal welfare legislature they were related to and drew upon after 1822, matched the social concern and improvement rhetoric of Dickens on the public hanging. Market noise and impaction were damaging consumer attitudes and the quality of the meat, and the problem had thus become an economic one, not a moral one. The hygiene issues were real, but then those too could be effectively mobilised to systematise London meat production and commercial networks, in the process threatening the small business sorts running the market and the nearby butchers' abattoirs and cut meat shops. Any arguments to keep not only the mass live animal market in place, but also these established private abattoirs and commercial networks, met with a strong opposition in the form of a sympathetic cultural climate focused intently on the tropes of improvement and civic reform. That some of the strongest and most organised voices for a market status quo were also the most readily demonised animal abusers, like the Worshipful Company of Butchers, only ensured their failure. Market removal was a paramount achievement of what today proceeds within industrial agriculture, albeit with some exceptions and with significant accomplishments in real animal welfare even in agricultural applications that still end in meat consumption: the animals are articles and objects, and their silent, efficient, mass killing was not only authorised by the tropes of animal welfare canonised in nineteenth-century England, but in fact desired by the anthropocentric tones of civilising social reform in the period that wanted, more than anything else, to quell the neurosis of known horrors underpinning the social architecture of London.

This, to be sure, departs in important ways from another version of British cultural moods in the period that has been widely discussed. The incredible rise in vegetarianism in the period also has literary roots and prominent exponents such as Percy Shelley, but then the work of influential contemporaries like Joseph Ritson on the natural diet and on the barbarous consequences of meat eating still have a strong sense of human improvement and not of animal welfare. Shelley and Ritson probably more closely resemble religious temperance advocates than they do contemporary ethical vegetarianism focused on animal liberation. And, in fact, the Vegetarian Society in England was founded by the temperance advocate Reverend William Cowherd. Byron also acted out of dietary austerity, turning to vegetarianism for its health effects. While all of these examples certainly suggest hope for the poor creatures humans might otherwise eat, they might also belie any coherent mode of animal concern. The individuated austerity of dietary regimes seem much more reminiscent of the anthropocentric conceit of self-control and singularity a poet like Walt Whitman both espouses and explodes in his unruly – but thus unfettered and manly – verse style across the Atlantic later in the nineteenth century. That comportment works as well for a vegetarian vigilance as it does for a meat-eating vigilance in self-cultivation. At the heart of early nineteenth-century British vegetarianism was an ascetic, 'natural' diet in response to the growing concerns about food with a history of processing. This concern melded neatly, soon enough, with animal concern in the period more troubled by the history of violence, and so Victorian vegetarianism might more closely resemble the contemporary disciplinary motifs of vegan abstention and the holistic consumer politics of food justice movements.

Ultimately, this is an archaeology of thinking nonhumans through a dense, foundational history and a recognition of collective suffering, animal concern, and meat production/consumption that somehow fails to mitigate any of the most aggressively documented horrors. The literary arc of this archaeology includes canonical evolutions and the intersectional genre of the penny dreadful. This shows how literary form engages with the cultural history at Smithfield and the excruciating irony of an animal rights movement that produces even more unspeakable, more insufferable, less articulate but brutally articulating nonhuman conditions. Against the cultural history of Smithfield, oscillation between literary strategies appears as a technique of resistance. Meat City names an abiding conceptualisation of nonhuman conditions to express the horror and, perhaps, the inexpressibility of vacant coexistence. Meat City, with its nonhuman objects, is the excruciating totality and the inarticulate nothing of modern life.

Notes

1. Shelley, Mary. *Frankenstein; Or, the Modern Prometheus*. 1818 text, ed. D. L. Macdonald and Kathleen Scherf. Broadview, 2012, p. 116. The opening 'condition more abject' is also taken form *Frankenstein* and spoken by the creature: 'To be a great and virtuous man appeared the highest honour that can befall a sensitive being; to be base and vicious, as many on record have been, appeared the lowest degradation, a condition more abject than that of the blind mole or the harmless worm', p. 135.

2. Zola, Emile. *Piping Hot! A Realistic Novel*. Vizetelly & Co., 1887, pp. 318–19.
3. See: Geier, Ted. *Kafka's Nonhuman Form: Troubling the Boundaries of the Kafkaesque*. Palgrave Macmillan, 2016.
4. Marx, Karl. 'Chapter 27: Expropriation of the Agricultural Population from the Land', *Capital, Volume I*, trans. Ben Fowkes. Penguin, 1992.
5. See: Coetzee, J. M. *Elizabeth Costello*. Penguin, 2004.
6. See: Wolfe, Cary. *What is Posthumanism?* University of Minnesota Press, 2010.
7. See: Benjamin, Walter. 'On Some Motifs in Baudelaire', in *Selected Writings, Volume 4: 1938-1940*, trans. Edmund Jephcott, ed. Howard Eiland and Michael W. Jennings. Belknap/Harvard University Press, 2003, pp. 313–55. I am thinking here also of Adorno's *Metaphysics: Concept and Problems*, ed. Rolph Tiedemann, trans. Edmund Jephcott. Stanford University Press, 2001.
8. See, for example: Richter, Virginia. *Literature after Darwin: Human Beasts in Western Fiction, 1859-1939*. Palgrave Macmillan, 2011. See especially: Ritvo, Harriet. *The Animal Estate: The English and Other Creatures in Victorian England*. Harvard University Press, 1987.
9. See especially: Foucault, Michel. *The History of Sexuality: An Introduction*, Vol. I. Vintage, 1990. Foucault's development of the concept in lectures at the Collège de France is well documented. Select lectures of particular import have been published as: *Security, Territory, Population*. Palgrave Macmillan, 2004. See also: *Society Must Be Defended*. Picador, 2003.
10. Wollstonecraft, Mary. *A Vindication of the Rights of Woman*, Ch. IX. Available at: <www.bartleby.com/144/9.html> (last accessed 1 December 2016).
11. Ibid.
12. See: Kean, Hilda. *Animal Rights: Political and Social Change in Britain since 1800*. Reaktion, 1998. See also: Metcalfe, Robyn. *Meat, Commerce, and the City: The London Food Market, 1800–1855*. Pickering & Chatto, 2012.
13. See: Lee, Paula Young, ed. *Meat, Modernity, and the Rise of the Slaughterhouse*. University of New Hampshire Press, 2008.
14. Two important volumes consider formal aesthetic addresses of the question of animal life and of life, more generally, as they turn up in Romantic period works. On species indeterminacy in literature 'pre-Darwin', for example, see: Heymans, Peter. *Animality in British Romanticism: The Aesthetics of Species*. Routledge, 2012. See also: Wilson, Ross, ed. *The Concept of 'Life' in Romantic Poetry and Poetics*. Routledge, 2009.
15. Burns, 'To a Haggis', ll. 17 and 36, *Selected Poems and Songs*. Oxford University Press, pp. 134–5. The Oxford edition notes deem the poem 'mock-heroic' at points, but the heroic ode form, ironic or not, is clearly employed in the task. See: Burns, p. 335.
16. Burns, l.2, p. 134.
17. Burns, ll.45–8, p. 135.
18. Carroll, Lewis. *Alice's Adventures in Wonderland* and *Through the Looking Glass*. Penguin, 1998, p. 229.
19. Carroll, pp. 229–30.

20. Carroll, p. 230.
21. There is a robust literature on literacy rates and reading publics leading up to and through the nineteenth century. See: Altick, Richard D. *The English Common Reader: A Social History of the Mass Reading Public, 1800–1900*. Ohio State University Press, 1957; Klancher, Jon. *The Making of English Reading Audiences, 1790–1832*. University of Wisconsin Press, 1987; and Hunter, J. Paul. *Before Novels: The Cultural Contexts of Eighteenth Century English Fiction*. Norton, 1990. There is some debate on the methods used to ascertain literacy rates. Louis James, for example, refers to the use of marriage certificate signatures no longer considered to be conclusive bases, but there is general agreement on the rapid and massive increase in literacy. James, *Fiction for the Working Man, 1830-1850: A Study of the Literature Produced for the Working Classes in Early Victorian Urban England*. Oxford University Press, 1963.
22. One comprehensive study of the social novel and Dickens's development of the genre: Cazamian, Louis. *The Social Novel in England: 1830–1850*. Routledge, 1973.
23. Scholarship on the pennies is a developing field, and the excellent new digital project and collaborative work group, Price One Penny, has gathered several extant overviews of this and other aspects of period audience practices: available at: <www.priceonepenny.info> (last accessed 1 December 2016). See especially: James, Louis. *Fiction for the Working Man 1830–1850*. Oxford University Press, 1963. See also: James, Elizabeth and Helen R. Smith. *Penny Dreadfuls and Boys' Adventures: The Barry Ono Collection of Victorian Popular Literature in the British Library*. British Library, 1998.
24. Kean, p. 61.
25. Metcalfe, Robyn. *Meat, Commerce, and the City: The London Food Market, 1800–1855*. Pickering & Chatto, 2012, p. 84.
26. Metcalfe, p. 83.
27. Metcalfe often invoking the singular work of Richard Perren in tracking meat animal transport and meat consumption numbers in the period. See: Metcalfe, pp. 33–47 and Perren, Richard. *The Meat Trade in Britain, 1840-1914*. Routledge, 1978. See also: Rixson, Derrick. *The History of Meat Trading*. Nottingham University Press, 2000, pp. 279–84.
28. Heidegger, Martin. *The Fundamental Concepts of Metaphysics: World, Finitude, Solitude*, trans. William McNeill and Nicholas Walker. Indiana University Press, 2001, p. 177.
29. See in particular 'The Field Labourers', in Thompson, E. P. *The Making of the English Working Class*. Vintage, 1963, pp. 213–33. See as well John Barrell's study of Clare's poetry, which includes essential discussions of enclosure: *The Idea of Landscape and the Sense of Place 1730-1840: An Approach to the Poetry of John Clare*. Cambridge University Press, 1972. Thanks to David Simpson for a nod toward this text, and more, in his comments on one of my first papers on Romantic literature and meat production/consumption.
30. Wordsworth, William. 'There was a Boy', in Wordsworth and Samuel Taylor Coleridge. *Lyrical Ballads: 1798 and 1800*, ed. Michael Gamer and Dahlia Porter. Broadview, 2008. 1800 edition, Vol. II, ll.33–4, p. 299.

31. See, in particular, Kenyon-Jones, Christine. *Kindred Brutes: Animals in Romantic Period Writing*. Ashgate, 2001, pp. 109–34.
32. See here again James, *Fiction for the Working Man 1830–1850*.
33. Specifically, to the town of Fray Bentos, which would also be the international trade name outside England. Borges sets his 1942 short story, 'Funes the Memorious' here.
34. In an essay on *Bleak House*, J. Hillis Miller makes an important point about Dickens's specific brand of symbolic realism: '[S]cenes in Dickens which are initially merely narrative realism are transformed into symbolic expressions of the entire destiny of a character.' In Korg, Jacob, ed. *Twentieth Century Interpretations of Bleak House*. Prentice Hall, 1968, p. 84.

Chapter 1

A Parliament of Monsters: Romantic Nonhumans and Victorian Erasure

All out-o'th'-way, far-fetched, perverted things,
All freaks of Nature, all Promethean thoughts
Of man; his dullness, madness, and their feats,
All jumbled up together, to compose
A Parliament of Monsters. Tents and Booths,
Meanwhile, as if the whole were one vast mill,
Are vomiting, receiving, on all sides,
Men, Women, three-years' Children, Babes in arms.
      Oh blank confusion! True epitome
Of what the mighty City is herself
To thousands upon thousands of her Sons,
Living amid the same perpetual whirl
Of trivial objects, melted and reduced
To one identity, by differences
That have no law, no meaning, and no end;
Oppression under which even the highest minds
Must labour, whence the strongest are not free![1]

An excruciating, vacant ecology and a frustrated human experience dominate works like Mary Shelley's *Frankenstein* or William Blake's *Book of Thel*. Anxieties about the trouble with human/nonhuman intercourse also show up in less unnatural figures of animals, inhuman conditions and mass vacancy in works such as Burns's 'To a Mouse'. And we might say that Samuel Taylor Coleridge's 'Rime' and 'To a Young Ass' join two poles of nonhuman thought in the period within one *oeuvre*. Animals and the nonhuman return again and again as targets of thought in British Romantic literature. This incorporation of animals includes domestic and agricultural modes, wilderness motifs, hunting, and meditations on less defined nonhuman modes include the quasi-scientific assemblage of dead body parts in *Frankenstein*, Coleridge's weird, possibly supernatural mariner, and the inescapable dark spirits of Robert Burns's 'Tam o' Shanter'.

Wordsworth and Coleridge craft *Lyrical Ballads* in 1797 as part of a broad, public social critique of the Poor Laws, and the poems include multiple engagements of animals and other nonhumans. Coleridge's separate poem, 'To a Young Ass', is about an abused, labouring animal, and Wordsworth's animals include owls, harts, heifers and many more. Burns and John Clare spend the majority of their poetic lives lamenting enclosure, cultural disruption, and the suffering of birds, badgers and others, and they narrate sentimental and non-sentimental losses of places that seem to ruin things for all critters equally. As David Perkins has noted, Clare writes 'The Badger' as bans on badger-baiting, bull-baiting and cockfighting pass thru British Parliament in 1835.[2] Writers throughout the Romantic period, regardless of direct political interests such as Wordsworth and Coleridge's or circumstantial overlap such as 'The Badger' and parliamentary developments in bull-baiting that Lord Byron may have been present for, articulate interspecies community at the formal level.[3]

This only scratches the surface of the deep nonhuman engagements in the literature. Burns and Clare both often seem to fit an ideal peasant poet role that could materially inhabit the marginalised agrarian subject position to articulate a consubstantiality of human and nonhuman experience. Burns, for one, seems anything but idealistic as his plough digs up a mouse and her nest, and although the general themes of uprooting and disappointment (for mice and men alike) dominate the piece, the narrator's 'union' with an affectionately hailed 'mousie' opens up a space for shared suffering and mediation of collective disenfranchisement. This intersectional mode also inflects texts on other nonhumans such as spirits and angels, creatures like Frankenstein's monster, plants, worms, insects, the celestial orbs of works reflecting on the universe and more. Throughout British Romantic literature, nonhumans, humans and the nonhuman humans at the heart of Romantic critiques of subject position and anthropocentric hubris are all negotiated as intermingling and potentially at risk.

In many cases, the notion of risk or of cross-species threat is negotiated as a further conceit of the human subject. This can seem especially true in the most directly sympathetic works like 'To a Mouse.' A certain Romantic 'interspeciesism' takes multiple forms as failed encounter, failed critique, sincere sympathy, sadistic pity, empathic consideration and more. British Romantic literature is also often read as a proto-environmentalist movement that looks beyond negotiations of the individual or the human to address the natural world, thus espousing a form of social concern similar to the operative improvement and civility tones behind animal rights debates. This presents Romantic literature as part of or as a precursor to the Victorian self-improvement project that attempts to build a more perfect human subject in a more organised human city.

Jonathan Bate's study of the period, *Romantic Ecology*, and later works such as James McKusick's *Green Writing: Romanticism and Ecology*, claim an inherent environmentalism in Romantic literature by tracking connections between Romantic literature and the North American conservationist rhetoric of John Muir and others.[4] Nature, in such readings, is a sublime refuge from an urbanising modernity, a green container for escapist human thought. This of course overlooks deeper political concerns, such as Coleridge and Wordsworth's poetic assault on the Removal Act of 1795 and the archaic poor laws of the day.[5] The proto-environmentalist interpretation of Romantic literature does not always perform a rigorous social critique of Romantic literature – including animal concern – focusing as it does on a sort of transcendental misanthropy that is surely performed in a great many Romantic works but that ends up isolating the human subject as the only consequential subject of analysis. Nevertheless, this oft-documented aspect of Romantic literature's social consciousness carries through to the broader cultural programmes of Victorian England, including the slaughter reform and market removal documented in Chapter 2.

In considering Romantic literature's social awareness, one must also consider the Romantic address of audience. This can be interior to the poem in clear ways, as in the case of Romantic apostrophe. However, the Romantic period also opens a decisive consideration of the public as an entity to be addressed and, more importantly, to be persuaded on social reform and political issues.[6] Romantic authors are not simply writing works about animals, with animals or even for animals and other nonhumans in an expressive vacuum. When Romantic authors address clouds, clods of dirt, animals, ghosts and others, the work expressing such apparently vacuous apostrophic endeavours highlights the comportment of the speaker while also presuming, perhaps even designing, a reading audience capable of reflecting upon that reflexivity. Poems and novels striving to express and negotiate interspecies and nonhuman communities through formal experimentation, thematic details, or with the outright demonstration of animal concern in the animal rights era 'Badger' poem by Clare thus work on the speaker, the reading public and then on nothing at all.

This 'nothing at all' is a persistent potentiality of the Romantic work, one that Marjorie Levinson's poetic theory of the fragment may be best suited to.[7] Levinson's intensive study of Romantic poems that were incomplete or fragmentary by apparent design, including the 'deliberate fragment', Coleridge's 'Kubla Khan'. The idea that the works might either frame a sense of incompletion in their completion or, on the other hand, fail to address their audience, which is also a frequent narrative aspect of works like *Frankenstein* or Wordsworth's 'There was a Boy', ultimately reframes the stakes of the work of art altogether. I will examine *Frankenstein* later in this chapter to consider both the play on apostrophe and the more common concerns about techno-biological effects upon life, human or otherwise. Pure expression, 'perhaps' expression that has no audience, ironically dominates literary production in the early era of its mass publicity.[8]

Percy Shelley's 'Ozymandias' features a relatively successful work weathered by time and then removed from its disintegrated context in a violent assertion of finitude:

> I met a traveller from an antique land,
> Who said – 'Two vast and trunkless legs of stone
> Stand in the desert. . . . Near them, on the sand,
> Half sunk a shattered visage lies, whose frown,
> And wrinkled lip, and sneer of cold command,
> Tell that its sculptor well those passions read
> Which yet survive, stamped on these lifeless things,
> The hand that mocked them, and the heart that fed;
> And on the pedestal, these words appear:
> My name is Ozymandias, King of Kings;
> Look on my Works, ye Mighty, and despair!
> Nothing beside remains. Round the decay
> Of that colossal Wreck, boundless and bare
> The lone and level sands stretch far away.'[9]

The aperture of the poem is a first person address that immediately unravels the artifice of report or documentation, for within the reported report are myriad questions about authorship and record. The 'hand that mocked them' and 'the heart that fed' could be the same artist or scribe, carver or sculptor. The poem's volta unmistakably contrasts human monument and accomplishment with nonhuman timescale and coexistent indifference, but then it is also a melancholy, even melodramatically anthropocentric lament. The poem's speaker has only quoted this response to all that is contained within. No critical marks dictate a perspective outside the socio-global remark 'I met a traveller' besides the fascinating ellipses inserted early, as if to remind of the material quotation in hand. This 'as if' returns frequently in Romantic irony and simulacrous expression.

Ultimately, the constructed object accomplishes all and more that any authentic nonhuman object could for aesthetic experience and deep thinking, as perhaps demonstrated again in the reflexive genre modes in the Ozymandias sonnet. Shelley's revision of the sonnet form relies upon the stability of the sonnet form – and, presumably, an audience's recognition of that form – to achieve its experimental ends. Instead of the rote three-quatrain, one couplet pattern in ABAB, CDCD, EFEF, GG scheme, 'Ozymandias' follows an ABAB ACDC EDEF EF pattern. One of the obvious consequences of this innovation is that the words 'things' and 'kings' are paired in a glaring instance of formal anomaly. On the other hand, 'read' and 'fed' and the triplet rhymes produced by the other variations – 'land sand command' and 'appear despair bare' – invoke mockery and mimesis, fallen tyrants and the dust of empires, and forgotten artists lingering in the artefacts of conquest. The rhyme pairs themselves are just a shade off in most spots besides the kings–things and the evacuated property triplet of land-sand-command. The enjambment amplifies the sense of 'lifeless things' in an unsettling critique of rote rhyme, an encroaching, quaint lineation and unsatisfying resolutions.

I focus on the line endings because the poem is so very concerned with the play on endings and non-endings itself, and perhaps no clue better assures of this interpretation than the only open phonemics in the poem, 'decay' and 'away'. The punctuation throughout, and the frequent stoppages with hard, terminal closure on consonants disrupted by the slippery, would-be inanimacy of 'stone', plays on endings. When the end is reached, however, Shelley's speaker(s) save the worst for last: decay and away, which settle the mouth on no certain task until the next line is taken up, are paired in the only timeless certainty of the poem and its subjects. In the graphic novel *Watchmen*, Alan Moore fixed on this sense of ending and persistence with his character, Adrian Veidt/Ozymandias, whose question 'I did the right thing, didn't I? It all worked out in the end', is answered by science, in the form of the nuclear superman, Dr Manhattan, in two separate speech bubbles, one with repeated speech ironised in quotation marks, as though the question were human, all too human: '*Nothing* ends, Adrian. Nothing *ever* ends.'[10] The hand that mocked, and the heart that fed. Jon (Dr Manhattan) disappears immediately after this, leaving Adrian/Ozymandias to stew alone after his own ellipses: 'What do you mean by . . .'

This trouble with audience and expectation in Romantic literature on the failed human or the 'post-human', as in 'Ozymandias', and on animals in other poems is part of a broader self-consciousness. Romantic literature in England ushers itself in as a direct address of public audience, and of an audience with a prior sense of poetry that may condition them to resist these new strains of common speech and 'radical' writing.

The Advertisement to the 1798 edition of *Lyrical Ballads* includes the admonition:

> Readers accustomed to the gaudiness and inane phraseology of many modern writers, if they persist in reading this book to its conclusion, will perhaps frequently have to struggle with feelings of strangeness and awkwardness: they will look round for poetry, and will be induced to enquire by what species of courtesy these attempts can be permitted to assume that title.[11]

Even this non-literary Advertisement performs the role, through sarcasm and mockery, of social catalyst; it interpellates a readership that will mark the text's failure, and so the text prefigures not the accuracy of judgment on that count but the affective strangeness – the alienation and resistance – produced in the interaction of text and audience. The poetry – any text whatever – is insufficient before it has even been read. As an act of aperture, the Advertisement ensures a didactic experience and simultaneously brings into question the presumptions of the educators. In conjunction with the social concern and political engagement of the text, this suggests another way to consider Wordsworth and Coleridge's *Lyrical Ballads*: as marking the insufficiency of law and social concern to address their purported objects, in this case on the issue of the new Poor Laws and in the wake of several modes of the Corn Laws, and all of this after the primary documents of enclosure.[12]

David Simpson has perhaps remarked most conclusively on this strange tension between authorship, audience, 'concern' and effect:

> In using the word *concern* in my subtitle, I intend to capture the unresolved nature of the questions Wordsworth raises about suffering and sympathy. To be concerned usually means not having finished with an issue, being in a state of suspended attention that may produce a resolution but has not done so yet. The word also usefully signals the reflexive component of Wordsworth's poetry, which is so often about itself and its own making.[13]

Apostrophe is such a suspended or incomplete address, a determinate failure exhibiting the mutual abjection of human and nonhuman. Simpson's uncommitted 'may produce' figure is instructive. Simpson goes on, in a later passage, to discuss the 'spectral figure' of the soldier encountered in the summer vacation episode of Book IV of the *Prelude*. Simpson uses instead a 1798 fragment from an edition of *Lyrical Ballads* that, indeed, suggests an even more extraordinary 'deformity' he associates with the figure of the *Muselmann* and thereby with the walking dead and the debris of modern industrial administration.[14] This bridges the atrocities of the world wars already inflicted in the eighteenth century, long before their more recent philosophical articulation in twentieth and twenty-first century works by Giorgio Agamben, Theodor Adorno and others, with the World Wars and technological shifts operative in those latter expressions. The interminable persistence of such figures, which may produce – or may be produced – also gathers liminal conceptions in *Frankenstein* with other threats to humanity.

The version of the lines in *The Prelude* emphasise the word 'common'. Simpson does not dwell on the figure's solitude, expressed as '[c]ompanionless, no dog attending, and by no staff sustained he stood'.[15] Simpson notes the narrator's 'animal delight', which is 'countered by this vision of animal insensibility, as his self-possessed silence is displaced by the soldier's "murmuring sounds"'.[16]

> [He was in stature tall,]
> A foot above man's common measure tall,
> And lank, and upright. There was in his form
> A meager stiffness. You might almost think
> That his bones wounded him. His legs were long,
> So long and shapeless that I looked at them
> Forgetful of the body they sustained.
> His arms were long and lean; his hands were bare;
> [His visage, wasted though it seem'd, was large
> In feature, his cheeks sunken, and his mouth]
> Shewed ghastly in the moonlight . . .[17]

The 'visage' foreshadows the half sunk, shattered visage of a former greatness, or terribleness, in Shelley's 'Ozymandias'. Wordsworth, in *The Prelude*, goes on to write that 'yet still his form kept the same awful steadiness', and this steady form, along with the soldier's 'stately air of mild indifference', both monumentalise and demolish the human in nonhuman form, which Simpson's version denotes as the soldier being 'scarcely "akin to man"'.

Simpson also discusses Wordsworth's poetry on poverty – and certainly also on impoverished experience – and considers the difficulty of political address under the sign of poetic expression and the performance of abjection:

> Making decisions between these options is made all the harder because it is not absolutely clear that Wordsworth approves of himself here: he could be retrospectively casting himself as a rather pompous young man endorsing the views of a figure whom he admires while adding in his own limiting conditions drawn from the British poor law debates of the time . . . What does it mean to be 'lowly'? Does this simply mean near the bottom of the socioeconomic order, or does one have to demonstrate abjection as well?[18]

The 'legalized exclusion' of human objects already rendered nonhuman – foreclosing the assertion of humanity altogether in the 'steady form' of abject individuals – takes shape not merely in value and commodity forms, the subject of Simpson's book; not merely in the killable animal body at times protected by the new laws of the Romantic period and at times rendered even more monumentally disposable; not merely in the atrocity of war and exhausted, spectral soldiers defined by 'ghastly mildness' as in *The Prelude*:

> ... Yet not the less
> Hatred of absolute rule, where will of One
> Is law for all, and of that barren pride
> In them who, by immunities unjust,
> Between the Sovereign and the People stand,
> His helper and not theirs, laid stronger hold
> Daily upon me, mixed with pity too
> And love; for where hope is, there love will be
> For the abject multitude. And when we chanced
> One day to meet a hunger-bitten Girl
> Who crept along fitting her languid gait
> Unto a heifer's motion, by a cord
> Tied to her arm, and picking thus from the lane
> Its sustenance, while the Girl with pallid hands
> Was busy knitting in a heartless mood
> Of solitude, and at the sight my Friend
> In agitation said, ''Tis against *that*,
> That we are fighting', I with him believed
> That a benignant Spirit was abroad
> Which might not be withstood, that poverty,
> Abject as this, would in a little time
> Be found no more, that we should see the earth
> Unthwarted in her wish to recompence
> The meek, the lowly, patient Child of Toil,
> All institutes forever blotted out
> That legalized exclusion, empty pomp
> Abolished, sensual State and cruel Power,
> Whether by edict of the One or few;
> And finally, as sum and crown of all,
> Should see the People having a strong hand
> In framing their own Laws, whence better days
> To all mankind.[19]

The Girl at the heart of this meditation on poverty, sovereignty and law is bound and indelibly paired, like kings and lifeless things, to the heifer. The proper noun capitalisation suggests a categorical hierarchy between human and animal at first glance, and Wordsworth does not openly consider the matter here. On the other hand, the trouble with capitalised, singular subjects and diminished, modular objects under the sign of species is of vital 'concern', to borrow the term, to many

Romantic works. 'Heifer' marks specificities besides a merely killable 'chattle' object: this is, at least, an identifiably female cow. These are not the firmest indicators of the poem's potential for an interspecies reading, however. The

> Girl
> Who crept along fitting her languid gait
> Unto a heifer's motion, by a cord
> Tied to her arm, and picking thus from the lane
> Its sustenance, while the Girl with pallid hands
> Was busy knitting in a heartless mood
> Of solitude

is not alone. The 'heartless mood' is perhaps due to her lot amongst the bovine, but the unity of these 'lifeless objects' seems total here. Her 'languid gait' and the clear contrast of a 'hunger-bitten' girl tied to a cow mundanely feeding itself with no apparent trouble surely induce a perspective – perhaps an activism – on the human-induced poverty of humans. The cows, after all, appear to have it better. Reading the poem against the grain a bit to suggest a lock step coexistence of girl cow and girl human, of human and nonhuman, risks precisely Wordsworth's object here: the girl is rendered inhuman. The figure engages both the animal fate and the precarity of an impoverished humanity to articulate the proximity of inhuman to nonhuman, of the evacuation of the concept founding his critique of war, its ghastly atrocities and the post-war ghastliness one can measure in one substantial post-man, as Simpson documents in his study of the earlier fragment. As such, the unified form here is nonhuman–nonhuman and not Girl–heifer, when we reflect successfully on the suffering and the abjection inflicted by modern society. Wordsworth further troubles – considers and mitigates – the social force of such critiques as he revises and reissues these lines in *The Prelude*. Zachary Leader, in his comprehensive study of Romantic authorship and the phenomenon of revision in the period, remarks on Wordsworth's editorial longevity, 'Where Wordsworth differs from many other poets is in his refusal, with rare exceptions, to recognize earlier work as the work of an earlier self, insisting instead on "affinities preserved | Between all stages of the life of man", and constantly returning to the past to test and confirm personal identity.'[20] Wordsworth's editorial energies reiterate the gravity of critique.

I mention Wordsworth's biography in relation to literary influence and cultural history in this case only to contextualise the concern with audience and reception and also any would-be theoretical interest in figures such as 'post-human' or in the thicker historical concern with abjected bodies damaged by war and riven with disease and hunger.

Connecting this broader cultural historical aspect to his particular practices of revision and his authoritative editorial role in literary development through the turn from the long eighteenth to long nineteenth century is another way of addressing the very same human status Shelley questions in 'Ozymandias'. Charlotte Smith, an author Wordsworth was an early champion of at least in writing, was no less concerned with the violence of category, the equivalence of war and the differentiation of species that motivate so much of the other Romantics' works.

Felicity Nussbaum has addressed these limits of the human in long eighteenth-century literature, discussing precursors to the vital matter of life that Romantic authors take up again and again in blank verse, epistolary and other forms. In her study, which considers tropes of deformity and defectiveness in literatures that link race and gender in mutually bolstered, abject status, Nussbaum discusses a 1774 account of a shipwrecked girl:

> [S]he allegedly inspired those who first saw her to shout, '*Voilà le Diable!*' The savage white child, feeding on roots and raw game, lives as a weasel-like amphibious creature until she is captured and integrated into gentility in a nunnery. Her life, lived at the limits of the human, extends beyond Eve's defective duplicity or Desdemona's fanciful romance to suggest an alternative narrative that would enable incorporating the untamable feminized primitive into civility through education and religious instruction.[21]

Nussbaum does examine the categorical violence of abjecting animals from social experience and the status of autonomous life, focusing here on abjected classes of human species. Nussbaum plumbs the atrocious limits of the civilising imagination.[22] Nussbaum thus establishes some of the discourses on nonhuman abjection and on the London socius before and immediately into the nineteenth century, including the social interactions of Samuel Johnson and Elizabeth Montagu on the issues of national literary and linguistic heritage, class and civilisation. Montagu ridiculed Johnson's 'deformity', his effeminacy, and his general behaviour.[23] Nussbaum contends that Montagu's aggressive assessments of good taste in fashion, writing and more, produced her violent rebukes of Johnson and more than just his verbose written style. Perhaps the most curious example of Montagu's anti-Johnson streak is the analogy she draws from Johnson's style to the savages who throng at oddity markets like Bartholomew and Haymarket or the 'barbarous and uncultivated' coal miners she oversees upon the death of her husband, the owner of coal mines. Nussbaum unearths a telling, if conventional, link between ornament, classification and nonhuman objects subjected to cultural politics. Nussbaum writes of Montagu:

She characterizes overwrought ornamentation as an exotic strangeness that is attractive to a mob mentality and uses as an example a Haymarket mob's admiring the sea monsters that adorned the King's coach: 'False thoughts & grotesque ornaments may please & surprise but it is only the just, the natural, & the proper, that can engage. The mob indeed are attracted by the exhibition of monsters . . .' In this passage Montagu reveals her belief that a class association exists between the unruly and the unlettered, and that the grotesque, the monstrous, the rare, and the foreign especially allure the mob and inspire lawlessness . . . Savages are especially vulnerable to this kind of show since they 'still decorate their persons with shells, feathers, skins of beasts, & c'.[24]

Here Nussbaum has located an incriminating bit of classist, colonial chauvinism. The unity of lifeless things that so severely piques Montagu's contempt is another conjoining of abjected human–nonhuman lowness, as in the Wordsworth passages.

Wordsworth was also interested in the marketspace, as Paul Youngquist documents in his study of Romantic literature and its fascinations with bodies, which also includes a lengthy historical review of the audience for anomalies at Bartholomew Fair at West Smithfield. Youngquist deems Wordsworth as 'the poet laureate of the proper body'.[25] Wordsworth writes of Bartholomew Fair in *The Prelude*, and his withdrawal from the horrors of the site and the city in general fuel Youngquist's critique of the 'normalizing force of his poetry': 'Wordsworth confronts flesh and blood en masse and retreats in mild disgust to the cleaner consolations of the proper body.'[26] As I will also discuss in greater detail in Chapter 2, Smithfield Market was also the site of Bartholomew Fair. As I will discuss in subsequent chapters, this location inspired a dazzling assortment of such anxieties leading eventually to the market's removal and relocation, yet not quelling the popular cultural and literary fascination with the depraved, bloody atrocities of dark Smithfield alleys and urban butchery in the new, criminal district not so far from the Fleet Street barber shop where Sweeney Todd's meat pies will be made under the sign of suspicious meat products of unknown origins at the heart of the city.

The Smithfield scene, a literary fascination well before Wordsworth and well after Dickens, includes the intensity of the animal masses and comingling of all sorts, breeds, humans and otherwise in this space, dictating a particular aspect of the London literature in the period that is not defined by the typical urban, technological and business motifs but by meat, animals, and then also by the common concern with hygiene and contamination in a changing London ecology. However, as we shall see, business class concerns are immediately related, perhaps even operative, in the forms of life under duress and negotiation across these literatures. In the passage that began the chapter, Wordsworth responds directly to this concoction of urban coexistence with many of the same civilising tones of the Montagu class, foreshadowing the utter incapacity of the structuring, authoritative rationality in legal and civic administration of social and animal ills to resolve these perceived privations. As Nussbaum writes to close her study of the eighteenth century:

> In fact, of course, the multiple ways of being human undermine any single subject of modernity. White women's sexuality becomes the carefully guarded line between the infected and uninfected spaces of racial and cultural contagion as an intact normative femininity and a bolstered masculinity free of defect serve as signs of successfully fending off contaminated forms. The black shadow harbored now *within* the country, the potential pollution that blackness brings to that femininity, comes to signify the menace of impurity and degeneration looming over and within an increasingly imperial England in the long eighteenth century.[27]

Wordsworth's anxiety at muddled masses in an unruly city space is echoed in the sweeping fear of invasion and contamination from the inside-out in the England Nussbaum articulates. Wordsworth's reaction must also be considered a racist, classist abhorrence of the full scope of Bartholomew Fair.[28]

Crowds and assemblages, especially the 'mobs' in England and other metropolises in the wake of the French and American Revolutions, were legislated against as a means of political control that only reiterated these chauvinistic classifications.[29] 'Trivial objects, melted and reduced to one identity, by differences that have no law, no meaning, and no end' expresses the animal fate at Smithfield just as forcefully, in fact. The interminable sense of London's crowded coexistence called for laws, and laws and other municipal measures were soon passed to manage a number of emergent civic problems including traffic, health and hygiene, and of discriminatory social abuses like slavery. Recalling here the way in which Wordsworth's ghastly soldier helps to undo the hard divisions between human–nonhuman, however, the 'trivial objects, melted and reduced', besides its invocation of rendering down bodies, is a proposition immediately rejected by 'differences that have no law, no meaning, and no end'. 'End' as purpose, as well as termination, would both lead to Wordsworth undoing himself if his object is to lament the coexistence at Smithfield on the grounds of inauthentic, oppressed and decaying experience. In the case of the London Dickens writes about, as well, the massive unity of the place still does not overrule the concern for individuation even as the potency of individual experience is undone by the irrational sensorium afoot. These texts, like Burns's 'To a Mouse', interrogate the trouble with coexistence, with individuation and with consubstantiality, and they negotiate in an increasingly open, inquisitive way in the wake of Wordsworth's categorical aggressions.

This reinvigorates object status, opening onto the examination of mutual abjection and object experience. Furthermore, the turn to address and the limits of coexistence – what can humans even say to nonhumans, once humans are under interrogation? – manifests in a series of experiments with apostrophe, linking formal study to nonhuman thought. Another consequence of the redress of address in Romantic works in the afterlife of the animal rights that begin in the Romantic period, right in the heart of London on the Parliament floor, is that apostrophe and Romantic expression, in general, negotiate a failed legal encounter of nonhumans and an insufficient legal and social redress of human ills. This will be clear as an extension of the recurring failure of human address of nonhumans in Romantic literature, a considerate failure based on the mutual demolition of subject and object, human and animal, in the sometimes hopeful, sometimes disaffected 'Parliament of Monsters' in the works here examined.

Michael Macovski writes, in the introduction to his study of apostrophe in Romantic literature, on the discursive reach of literature

> as a composite of voices – interactive personae that not only are contained within the literary text but extend beyond it, to other works, authors, and interpretations. Within this schema, literary characters interact not only with individual voices but also with other discourses themselves – political, religious, and historical.[30]

This approach to literature seems brazenly associative, but then it also draws heavily on the suggestion of Wordsworth in the Advertisement and, further, the figures of bare life, animal suffering and racial abuse documented in the literature before, during and after Romanticism. He writes of apostrophe:

> The recurrence of the apostrophized listener in these poems thus begins to suggest a rhetoric of Romanticism. It is this rhetoric that first led M.H. Abrams to define the Romantic lyric as a 'sustained colloquy, sometimes with himself or with the outer scene, but more frequently with a silent human auditor, present or absent' ('Lyric' 527). For Abrams, such an apostrophe 'captures remarkably the qualities of the intimate speaking voice' within the 'dramatic mode of address to an unanswering listener' (531, 533; cf. 533–56). Yet this 'silent human authority' suggests not only a rhetoric of 'address' but a poetics of dialogue – a poetics in which a speaker's words are actually constructed in relation to proleptic repose. As Paul Magnuson has noted, such a poetics emerges from the 'vital and dynamic relationship

between speaker and auditor' – the sense that there 'cannot be segregated and isolated utterances.' Generally speaking, the rhetorical inclusion of even a mute listener implies the form of a dialogue, with its attendant notions of reception, affect, and potential for response. Indeed, the incorporation of the Romantic addressee as a metonymic listener within the text sets up the formal configuration of a 'co-respondence' – the structure, at least, of a communication. Romantic apostrophe accordingly becomes a rhetorical synecdoche or figure for dialogue – even if this form remains vestigial or unspoken.[31]

Surprisingly, Poe's notion of the self-determined poetic in *The Poetic Principle* (1850) might suggest this same figuration, or situation: 'this poem *per se* – this poem which is a poem and nothing more, this poem written solely for the poem's sake'.[32] Poe produces here a nonhuman poetics by attending to the poem's singularity outside human aesthetic economies even as he invokes classic humanist aesthetics in implicit apostrophe. He discusses 'Truth', labelling it a 'she' with 'severe demands' and calls upon fine categories such as Pure Intellect, Taste and Moral Sense. But Poe's narrator, as will be especially clear in the case of 'The Man of the Crowd', routinely fails to prove the authority of a human sphere in which such virtues, comportments and faculties subsist. To the contrary, London undoes the rational ground.

This tension between social figuration and civic sociation is the veritable method of Romanticism. Kevin Gilmartin has written that 'early nineteenth century radicals were prepared to theorize the terms of the public debate, and to deploy those theories (including the idea of a single public) as political weapons'.[33] Andrew Franta has recently written on what Jeremy Bentham called the 'regime of publicity', suggesting that the term publicity 'transforms "public" into a set of practices or mode of action' that British Romantics were constantly negotiating in their poetry.[34] This, Franta argues, was a continuance of the period's political endeavours, which also developed as part of a burgeoning mass periodical system. The gathering sense of Romantic address, audience and effect here, taking Poe as a supervenient voice on the matter, maintains the reflexive concern for discursive coexistence and the complex, thick entanglements of form and social context. This seems to be Marcovski's object, as well, and while I will focus most intently on the effects of apostrophe in Romantic works on, with, to, from – however and whatever – animals, this larger interaction of literature and culture marks the intensification of the interactions between public literacy, mass production (of literature and of animals) and social concern through the long nineteenth century.

In particular, I will question the engagement with animal welfare and the relation to developments in animal law, at times, in what follows.

The roles of mass public literacy and revolutions in publication technologies will be considered in the case of the most popular, most widely read literatures of the period, the penny fictions that produced serial works like *Sweeney Todd* and other horrific narratives. In the case of Romantic literature, however, the intersection of this new concept of publicity with social and political expectations for published literature precedes the bare fact of a mass public. It may prove to be the case that the massive public literature of the penny fictions follows after the great political period of British literature, or that, at best, the mass fungibility of the literary form circulated in penny editions reveals something intractably determinate about the social conditions and political prospects of the period. That is to say, cheap, replaceable works match the modes of life in their period of great industrial productivity. If without political projects, the works might at least express social conditions.

Romantic literature may be taken to express social forms in more overtly effective ways. The literary form, at the level of sentence construction or a device like apostrophe, addresses these matters directly, whereas a text like *Sweeney Todd* might employ irony, sarcasm, wit and the classic narrative arc along with character development, and so on, yet its object is certainly not vocation, expression and address – the successes and the limitations of each, as well. They are not reflexive works. Likewise, the politics of *Todd* and the pennies do not suggest the commitments of the Romantics, even where they inflect political discourse and cultural theory with themes and problems.

I take up a relatively standard stance on Romantic literature as more or less an activist literature concerned with a variety of social projects of the day, and yet I examine apostrophe and the animal concern in these works not so much as a bookend to the animal law also being waged in the period but as instead an attempt to properly consider and include nonhumans that are improperly separated from the human community via the hubris of human exceptionalism.[35] As the authors discussed to this point have surely shown, being suspicious of this foundational division of human and animal is the starting point to articulating the lingering senses of community, coexistence and even difference – which will still matter, at the end of the day – precluded by prior structures of the human–nonhuman divide.

Apostrophe is surely a speaking to oneself, and potentially an egotistical bout of staged melancholy. But the impulse itself is not necessarily always reflexive and ironic. Levinson's discussion of Romantic literature as an emphatically fragmentary genre is again useful here. Even when the poems themselves are not aggressively performing framed, epistolary or multiple forms that resist total articulation, failed expression becomes the theme of much Romantic literature, but then also a remarkable success. This theme can stand out as it does, for example, in the ruined monuments in Shelley's 'Ozymandias', that yet communicate and interpellate. And in the course of this, Shelley also manages to critique the imperial removal of objects from colonised lands for leisurely consumption at the British Museum. This is a strong version of the multiple discursive zones, I think, Marcovski is after and that I will also be sketching through readings of several canonical poems on animals – *real* animals, so to speak, for the most part – and then a few creatures for good measure.

John Clare's works are routinely held up as the ideal realisation of the peasant poet motif other Romantics portray. Elizabeth Helsinger, among others, has pinpointed the class distinction between a Wordsworth and Clare, noting the 'middle class fantasy' of landscape Wordsworth enacts in his peasant aspirations. But 'Clare – like Burns or Bloomfield before him – was identified with the social as well as the geographical place that was his subject.'[36] Clare's own biography is perhaps most responsible for this important tension between the *real* peasant poet and the staged peasant ideal of other Romantics. Born to a farmer in rural England, Clare did not go to college like other Romantic poets and he did not have literary or politically connected parentage like a Mary Shelley or a Lord Byron. Clare was of the British country and remained a labouring class poet. He had a brief military career before beginning his major poetic activity and, later in life, would be committed to an asylum, where he lived from 1841 until his death. His poems themselves track the displacement and alienation of English agriculturalists as enclosure of the commons dramatically revised the economic relations of labouring humans to the new notion of real property and to the agricultural land they worked for others under that property system. Clare's poems also tracked the human alienation from self in the modern industrial age, but without any significant attention to the city or to technology.

Clare wrote extensively on what David Perkins calls 'endangered nests'.[37] Clare's poems often address birds, threatened homes and the remaining havens, such as flooded marshes, in which 'security pervades' and animals can hide from destructive humans.[38] Humans also hide from other humans in the country, and humans and animals also convene in old age and death:

> And this is nought but common life, what everybody finds
> As well as I, or more's the luck of those that better speed
> I'll mete my lot to bear with the lot of kindred minds
> And grudge not those who say they for sorrow have no need
> Why should I, when I know that it will not aid a nay?

> For Summer is the season; even then the little fly
> Finds friends enow, indeed, both for leisure and for play;
> But on the winter window it must crawl alone to die:
> Such is life, and such am I–a wounded, stricken flie[39]

Clare goes a rung lower than Burns's mouse, opening his sympathetic community to the fly where Burns, perhaps because the plough directed it so, unearthed 'only' a mouse. If Wordsworth versus Clare comes out on Clare's side for peasantry, then Burns versus Clare is another win for Clare as the lowlier than thou expresser of supreme interspecies empathy. This empathic mode, as Christine Kenyon-Jones and Perkins acknowledge, was not only a hallmark Romantic style but also an influence on social concern and, ultimately, parliamentary debate and legislation. Clare's poem to the badger on the eve of parliamentary bans on badger-baiting reminds, happily, of Kenneth Grahame's anti-social, anthropomorphised Badger in *The Wind in the Willows* while skipping over anthropomorphism quite a bit more convincingly; the poem breeds empathy via competitive opposition of human society, with domesticated dogs as foe to an inscrutable badger.[40]

Clare's investigations of alienation and displacement could be considered, for lack of a better word, organic in their themes. Animals and humans on the land were not yet subjected to the technological compressions of urban life or the mechanised mass slaughter awaiting meat animals. Clare, when he wrote of cattle or sheep, could certainly have been thinking of their lot and their future destination in London, however, and Chapter 2 will discuss some of that animal traffic in further detail. Although life in the country was disrupted in different ways and at different intensities, Clare's explorations of displacement and anonymity in 'organic' spaces are as terrifying as the urban spaces and technological horrors when they articulate the disarming sadness of nonhuman life influenced by seasons and other 'natural' forces. Clare's works struggled, to the end, to negotiate the valueless existence they inaugurate in all sorts of things.

Clare's figure of alienation is an ontological displacement, at times brought by winter and solitude, at other times by the violence of humans abusing animals as in the later 'Badger'. Regarding an 'organic' alienation in Clare's poetry, his poem 'The Nightingale's Nest' probes the general irrelevance of life while cradling life as the dearest thing at the same time. This proceeds as a fascination with delicate nonhuman minutiae that then refract the human subject position and narrative role:

> Up this green woodland-ride let's softly rove,
> And list the nightingale – she dwells just here.

> Hush ! let the wood-gate softly clap, for fear
> The noise might drive her from her home of love[41]

The opening establishes a surreptitious management of the nonhuman but also a careful, sincere appreciation of its proximity. The 'wood-gate' implies that the bird has made a nest in a human structure. The poem's aperture, as a whole, thus amplifies the sense of quiet entry into a world constructed by humans – as a poem or as a space called 'nature'. Clare's entry point also opens the narrator's company to the nightingale's space and to nonhuman space in general. Even if humans built the gate, 'Hush!' and the imploration against driving the bird away usher in care and concern. The poem's narrative opening into a bounded space of observation is matched by the entry into a gated space in the poem's narrative world and reiterates the aesthetic experience Clare's narrator is after, as the next lines show:

> For here I've heard her many a merry year -
> At morn, at eve, nay, all the live-long day,
> As though she lived on song. This very spot,
> Just where that old-man's-beard all wildly trails
> Rude arbours o'er the road, and stops the way -
> And where that child its blue-bell flowers hath got,
> Laughing and creeping through the mossy rails -
> There have I hunted like a very boy,
> Creeping on hands and knees through matted thorn
> To find her nest, and see her feed her young.
> And vainly did I many hours employ:
> All seemed as hidden as a thought unborn.[42]

The sense of surreptitious, ineffective snooping – vainly, all seemed hidden – and the willingness to acknowledge failure in sincerity and toil preserve the nightingale's autonomy despite its status as an object of study.

Clare's poem on the badger is sometimes called 'The Badger', sometimes simply 'Badger'. Sometimes it is published starting in narrative pronouncement at 'When midnight comes a host of dogs and men/Go out and track the badger to his den.' Other editions begin, in media res, with a proto-modernist 'The badger grunting on its woodland track'. The poem would not be published in Clare's lifetime, first appearing in 1920.[43] In the edition edited by Merryn and Raymond Williams, it is 'The Badger' and it begins with 'The badger grunting ...'[44] In this volume, the poem is followed by 'The Hedgehog'. The hedgehog poem includes particularly gruesome commentaries on the state of human affairs as they encroach ever more on the nonhuman world. It is clear, upon reading both poems, why Merryn and Raymond Williams placed them adjacent to one another:

> The hedgehog hides beneath the rotten hedge
> And makes a great round nest of grass and sedge
> Or in a bush or in a hollow tree
> And many often stops and say they see
> Him roll and fill his prickles full of crabs
> And creep away and where the magpie dabs
> His wing at muddy dyke in aged root
> He makes a nest and fills it full of fruit
> On the hedge bottom hunts for crabs and sloes
> And whistles like a cricket as he goes
> It rolls up like a ball or shapeless hog
> When gipseys hunt it with their noisey dogs
> I've seen it in their camps they call it sweet
> Though black and bitter and unsavoury meat
>
> But they who hunt the field for rotten meat
> And wash in muddy dyke and call it sweet
> And eat what dogs refuse wheree'er they dwell
> Care little either for the taste or smell
> They say they milk the cows and when they lye
> Nibble their fleshy teats and make them dry
> But they who've seen the small head like a hog
> Rolled up to meet the savage of a dog
> With mouth scarce big enough to hold a straw
> Will ne'er believe what no one ever saw
> But still they hunt the hedges all about
> And shepherd dogs are trained to hunt them out
> They hurl with savage force the stick and stone
> And no one cares and still the strife goes on[45]

The badger poem details the hunting expedition more but lacks some of the nose for the inscrutability of the nonhuman world; at the same time it offers that more intricate detail of the human–nonhuman relation. After various tortures and assaults, celebrations and 'hollos' by boys, men and bulldogs,

> He falls as dead ... and kicked by boys and men,
> Then starts and grins and drives the crowd again;
> Till kicked and torn and beaten out he lies
> And leaves his hold and crackles, groans, and dies.[46]

The badger was taken from his home and forced to perform as Badger – the constructed terrible beast but also, in Clare's words, vital and noble and clever and in charge of the action in important ways, latent and manifest:

> The badger grunting on his woodland track
> With shaggy hide and sharp nose scrowed with black
> Roots in the bushes and the woods and makes
> A great high burrow in the ferns and brakes
> With nose on ground he runs a awkward pace
> And anything will beat him in the race
> The shepherds dog will run him to his den
> Followed and hooted by the dogs and men
> The woodman when the hunting comes about
> Go round at night to stop the foxes out
> And hurrying through the bushes ferns and brakes
> Nor sees the many holes the badger makes
> And often through the bushes to the chin
> Breaks the old holes and tumbles headlong in[47]

Next, the poem introduces the covert midnight operation and a brief bestiary of fox, goose, poacher, hare flees the scene as the posse captures the baiting badger. The poem ends with something more unsettling than the death of the single badger:

> Some keep a baited badger tame as hog
> And tame him till he follows like the dog
> They urge him on like dogs and show fair play
> He beats and scarcely wounded goes away
> Lapt up as if asleep he scorns to fly
> And seizes any dog that ventures nigh
> Clapt like a dog he never bites the men
> But worrys dogs and hurrys to his den
> They let him out and turn a harrow down
> And there he fights the host of all the town
> He licks the patting hand and trys to play
> And never trys to bite or run away
> And runs away from noise in hollow trees
> Burnt by the boys to get a swarm of bees[48]

Clare's poem presents the domesticated 'wild' badger for sport. This is the precarious status of the badger when the badger-baiting laws passed in England: a sort of manufactured article for entertainment not at the level of test tubes and hybridities, but age-old husbandry techniques that were highly developed in England for horses, dogs and meat livestock in the century before and during Clare's poem. I will discuss aspects of husbandry and 'manufactured articles' (otherwise known as animals) in Chapter 2, but for now this sense of the performing, captive animal that is also expected to represent a wild foe for pursuit, capture and abuse (the dogs are also in a precarious game position) is presented as a discursive theme of animality in Romantic works without the formal play of apostrophe interior to the poem. Clare's works stand as relatively sincere complaints on human behaviour relative to, certainly, a privileged animal. And yet, this is not to say that Clare's animals are decidedly de-animalised. He attempts to retain animal identities with verbs like 'roots', and this contrasts the anthropomorphism of the tame badger when 'he trys to fight'. Clare is onto something here. Clare's poetry is not dominated by the trope of apostrophe in the way several other poets' works are, and so he may also offer more on the suffering of animals than the controlled reflexes of other Romantics.

Burns's narrator in 'To a Mouse' struggles to equate the mother mouse's behaviour with his own language of suffering even as the poem suggests both have suffered from the breakdown of 'Nature's social union' that separates them and then further oppresses them individually. The ploughman narrator is cast off the commons and labouring under private property systems that developed in the decades immediately preceding the 1785 poem and the mouse's nest was destroyed by his plough. Burns seemingly assigns human behaviour to the mother mouse, saying 'panic's in they breastie': the narration classifies the emotion as 'panic' even while foregrounding bodily reactions to the shock of a demolished home space. The truer form of pathetic fallacy is in 'Nature's social union', which is capitalised in the middle of the line and, thus, anthropomorphised by the violence of the same proper noun system William Blake ironises in *The Book of Thel*, which I will discuss in the subsequent section. But in both cases, Burns's attempt to express interspecies conviviality – and its rupture when Nature's social union is broken – retains a de-anthropocentric impulse.

This impulse does not successfully drive the narrator's later pontification on the mouse's superior, less-encumbered relation to being and time:

> Still, thou art blest, compared wi'me!
> The present only touches thee:
> But och! I backward cast cast my e'e,
>   On prospects drear!
> An' forward tho I canna see,
>   I guess an' fear![49]

There is no 'I' there, nor an 'eye', and the object 'me' galvanises the failed rhyme of 'I' and 'eye' both in formal rhyme prospects and the narrative content of the mutually abjected human and mouse. The aesthetic subject position is annihilated yet mandatory in formal redresses of literary modes like the pastoral and consistent in portable categories of human/nonhuman. Burns here pre-iterates the differentiating animality (poorness in world) that Martin Heidegger would later impose in his twentieth-century philosophical work on finitude and human exceptionalism.[50] The mouse is without memory and history but also incapable of prospect view and, thus, any aesthetics of experience: the mouse is not the same subject, and hence not the same sufferer, as the ploughman who knows of the past and can then be depressed about the future. For Burns's narrator, this is the preferred situation.

There is a curious connection between this salvational world-poverty and Heidegger's later claims on the lack of world in a stone. Heidegger's pathetic fallacy/anthropocentric anthropomorphism runs rampant where art can open a world of agrarian labour and humble suffering in an inanimate object (a painting of peasant's shoes), and he also invokes Jakob von Uexküll's concept of Umwelt to discuss immanent experience and responsiveness to environment.[51] For Heidegger, Umwelt and the evidence from animal science on bees and others von Uexküll draws together presents a crucial sense of life. Nonhumans with a 'life-world' that makes sense or operates according to the modes these other species exist in the world ought to not suffer a renewed categorical violence like the one Heidegger inflicts with his 'poor in world' dictum. The difference for Burns is that his narrator is not outside the scene of suffering as Heidegger's philosophical voice is. Burns well might be, but then the phatic attention to the Scots language disrupts any quick assessment of authorial intention and objectivity by reminding his reader of the governing cultural forms. Again, this is Marcovski's claim on apostrophe.

The reference to Heidegger here is cursory, and included only to draw attention to the central place Burns's question of animal experience and human articulation thereof retains in subsequent theoretical addresses. The imperative to address abjection and to voice concern dominates philosophical inquiry into the hallmark atrocities of the twentieth century World War period, as reflected in the emergence of a critical theory interrogating human suffering under the anti-Semitic strains of organised, teleological industrial violence. The seemingly anachronous association here posits enclosure, for Burns, as a parallel motivating atrocity. In his late lectures, Adorno would note the unsettling blankness of death in contradistinction to Heidegger's philosophy, and the nothingness Burns's ploughman shares with a mouse he cannot properly address suggests that he is in fact abjected in ways the mouse is not:

> The so-called epic death, which is presented in Heidegger's doctrine of death as a necessary moment of the 'wholeness of existence', and which is really at the root of all these death metaphysics, is no longer possible, because such a wholeness of life no longer exists. . . .

If mortally weary people take an affirmative view of death, it is most likely the case that death relieves them of a burden. The reason for the allegedly positive relationship to death taught by these metaphysics is none other than . . .: that the life in question amounted to so little that there was little resistance to its ending.[52]

The pastoral motif makes its mark in 'To a Mouse' by impeding direct comprehension and communication, but not quiet and rich coexistence as interaction and recognition. This absence of an unsettling gesture may be even worse than the horrors of the more grotesque examples. As Adorno writes, 'because the individual actually no longer exists, death has become something wholly incommensurable, the annihilation of a nothing'.[53] It must be allowed – indeed, it was never to be allowed or disallowed at all – that Adorno's intended context has no parallel, and further that to loosely suggest extending the camp logic to the abuse and displacement of animals or even humans under a separate historical administration of life under enclosure commits an unconscionable offense. But it also must be the case that the question of whether or not one can write poetry or live 'after Auschwitz', which Adorno returns to in these late lectures as he strives also to articulate a philosophy after Auschwitz and, indeed, an aesthetic theory in the wake of the end of experience and of expression, is precisely the limit concept of an age that has occluded the limit concept altogether. The world and all of its objects have come under the sign of human domination and annihilation, such that suffering can be excluded from the calculus of extermination on the basis that the deaths are not deaths, the objects erased not lives. This is the same concern Burns shares with the mouse that, truly, cannot comprehend that diminution of its life even as it suffers under the fact. This is parallel atrocity, the figuration of life that undoes the narrative conceit while still never achieving a governing meta-language outside such lexicons.

'To a Mouse . . .' marks the rapid enclosure of the British commons and the increasing violence to the ways of life of both the tilling peasant and the burrowing mouse. The narrator discovers the mother mouse trembling and frightened when his till unearths her nest. The poem's famous 'best laid plans of mice and men' realises a deep coexistent suffering, sharing life and its disruption across species lines. Both the individual labouring on the land and the individual making any other form of home of that land – animal or otherwise – are losing the space of those existences in an uninterrupted coexistence now defined precisely by disruptive displacement and potential evacuation of their life forms. The poem critically addresses these pre-existent articulations of individual labouring life or discrete animal family (mother mouse and baby mice, for example), and also applies its critique to the Scottish national identity fractured by British sovereignty. Instead of a terminal lament on a lost reality or authenticity, the poem's overbearing existential mode rules out reifications of status or existence. As seasonal variance threatens even well sown plants, radical coexistence eradicates categorical precision and dominion: the narrator can notice and describe the trembling and apparent emotions of the mother mouse, but cannot articulate its experience or define his own in the traumatic setting of the poem. But despite clear markers of enclosure and incidental yet total interspecies violence, the narrator gathers coexistent suffering under a measured form in the poem's pastoral mode. Burns has found a way to articulate suffering yet resist prescriptive ontological claims for justice, equality or revolution. This effects an ineffectual elegiac mode in a way, and one that will not satisfy the impulses of 'concern', but the narrator's reflective authority, even where synthesis of the presented scenarios is ruled out, resists submission to catastrophic, anonymous coexistence in bare life at the same time. Mourning cannot be inaugurated even as the speaker stops work to mark the violence of coexistent displacement. The poem's political content works in the absence of a call to arms. Conversely, in Coleridge, according to Perkins and Kenyon-Jones, the political project of interspecies community results in insecure 'burlesque' or self-satire. Clare, perhaps, could not hold up against such competing threads.

Burns does not seem burdened by commitment here, yet is deeply committed, for example, in the case of the sovereign parallel lingualism of 'Tam o'Shanter'. 'To a Mouse ...' is narrated 'chiefly in the Scottish dialect' that is both estranged from an English milieu while also in agreement with other English narrations: the narrator cannot quite appropriate and articulate the clear behaviour of suffering on the part of a mother mouse turned up in a field the tiller/narrator is working, but stops everything in the place of agrarian dailiness to mark it, to address it, to mourn it and attend to the trouble with agriculture and landed economies none in the poem can ameliorate or negotiate beyond attention and testimonial. The apology:

> I'm truly sorry man's dominion
> had broken Nature's social union.

That the narrator cannot narrate the mouse's suffering or explain that failure is a gripping human suffering in the poem as well. The mouse is a narrated object in total terror, but the narrator marks the impeded sharing and cannot imagine 'what it's like to be a mouse' before simply ploughing ahead and gathering mice and men in shared suffering. Burns's diminutive phrases in the poem are worth evaluating, but the primary impulse and general theme of frustrated human endeavour, in conjunction with Burns's lifelong resistance to English linguistic and cultural hegemony, strike a measured blow against a too-quickly flattened space of inclusion that elides or erases Scottish and animal places alike.

In another version of this impulse, Charlotte Smith critiques the prospect view and scientific catalogues of natural history in 'Beachy Head', and all those human efforts to lay hands on nature and critters wash away with the tide or are forgotten in an unapproachable (though narrated) place: a watery cave at the foot of the Beachy Head cliff. Smith's poem includes reflexive address of aesthetic experience and expression, and a more direct lament on the shortcomings of the poet than Burns's speaker allows in 'To a Mouse . . .'

> Ah! hills so early loved! In fancy still
> I breathe your keen air; and still behold
> Those widely spreading views, mocking alike
> The Poet and the Painter's utmost art.
> And still, observing objects more minute,
> Wondering remark the strange and foreign forms
> Of sea-shells; with the pale calcareous soil
> Mingled, and seeming of resembling substance.[54]

Burns's figuration of frustrated yet somehow full interspecies thought aspires to interspecies community while resisting categorical inventories of objects and species. Romantic efforts to address nonhumans while evaluating the violence and hubris of address recurs as radical unreliability in literary frame structures like that of *Frankenstein*, or even in the much later *Dracula*. Theme and mood, such as the misanthropic epic wanderer of a Byron pilgrimage or a Wordsworth excursion, also ensure that the human is always somehow in question. Romantic authors were thus generally concerned with practical social change and experimented in their literature with formal modes of critique that both supported calls for social concern and complicated defences of humans – and their concerns – altogether.

Apostrophe tends to be closed with exclamation marks. In Blake's *Book of Thel*, a young girl addresses cloud, worm and finally Clod of Dirt, and these address her, as well, with the characteristic 'O' aperture – Blake gathers humanoids and nonhumanoids together in their clunky, mannered addresses to things that are not there. Thel is seeking answers to her questions about finitude. Thel is a virginal angeloid, but at least humanoid against nonhumanoid before a weird levelling in the poem's final stanza when Thel is in her grave in the ground. The human form she represents is humiliated and runs home to her mother and a social life she is accustomed to, away from terrible places she is not at home in. What Thel refuses here is the more properly interspecies coexistence Blake wages, an uncanny, weird and unsettling mingling that produces abject horror at the bare, indeterminate state of life. Thel succumbs to this evacuated ontology, which must be what the monster imposes upon the complacent, horrified Victor Frankenstein.

Blake thinks the strange coexistence of humans and nonhumans as a flattened ontology, nodding heavily to the figure of worms Milton, Shakespeare and myriad others employ to decentre the human form. This produces a de-individuated process or no-thing-ness of existence and redresses particular human activities and historicises ambition, domination and suffering as a body of references that go on despite the impossible problem of meaningless coexistence. Thel gets to approach and encounter the nonhuman and the anonymous 'somewhere' on the precipice of her own grave, but she has first encountered a worm beloved as a thing, simply, by some God, and only thought to ask if this was in fact a worm at all. As a sourceless voice emanating from Thel's could-be grave asks, why an ear? Why any fleshiness at all covering up any impulse or any contemplative comportment? Each sense is registered but none is valorised besides the sublime fear that enables Thel to escape back to the social realm of un-strange substance.

Blake's version of the supernatural – and the intensity of human–nonhuman contact in Thel drains the titular (supernatural) character of her capacity to even entertain supernatural interactions – is not the same as Mary Shelley's technical supernatural, in which the same anxiety of contact infests every enframed encounter perhaps especially when the creature closes impossible distance in a literary zoom atop the mountains and annihilates Victor's authority in that particularly meaty encounter. Burns's poem, in contrast, seems simpler, more organic. This claim mounts a deep irony considering the source of the creature and the location of Thel's fit at the end of the poem. She stands by her own grave as she apostrophises the worm. Few objects would seem more organic than the loamy burial site and the lowly worm. When Thel addresses the cloud in equally reverent, humbly beseeching tones a bit earlier, 'O Cloud', her tone makes sense. But when her address turns to the clod of dirt and the worm, Blake seems to have accomplished a humiliation of the human. Blake's literary use of the clod of clay, the worm and the cloud employ nonhumans in direct distinction to a human, reiterating a species difference in the process. But, of course, Thel is not entirely human.

What Blake achieves is a diminishment of all subject positions. The cloud, clod of clay, and worm function as a satire of formal apostrophe. So, too, does Thel herself, for these objects, and the Lily of the Valley, all address her in various ways including 'Queen of the vales' and 'virgin'. But Thel first 'charges' the Cloud to tell her something, and Thel doubts the Worm's authority ('Image of weakness, art thou but a Worm?'). The satire begins with the Lily of the Valley, proceeds to the Cloud and on to the Worm and then the Worm's mother, the Clod of Clay. Blake traces all life back to an original organic mother material, and the Clod of Clay invites Thel into her world thusly: 'Wilt thou, O Queen, enter my house?' This show of hospitality is the Clod's response to overhearing Thel's interrogation of the 'helpless worm'. Blake capitalises the objects when they are speaking subjects, but in the narrator's description of the worm in this case, he does not.

When any of the poem's speaking subjects address one another, or merely pontificate, the others are capitalised. But in the narrator's description, it is a 'helpless worm', not capitalised: this worm is an anonymous object. And so in this case, Blake's emphasis on the capitalisation draws attention to the irony of proper names, and the resulting satire of both subjective propriety and of formal apostrophe matches the poem's thematic and narrative content as Thel descends through two examples apiece of the parallel categories of life and non-life that yet have various poetic and taxonomic roles (clouds and flowers at the top, worms and dirt at the bottom). What ends up only ironically or performatively at the bottom is Thel in her own future-imaginary grave, posing as a version of the tree of knowledge in an unnatural yet organic Eden. She escapes, albeit horrified, 'with a shriek', and racing away from the Clod of Clay, the helpless worm. Where she approached the Lily and the Cloud in extravagant apostrophic humility, she doubted the Worm and both reader and Clod of Clay recognised her conceit.

Thel reveals her conceit and the limitations subject position imposes on thought. Thel is captivated, captured, subjected by the Clod of Clay and goes exactly where she is told. The Worm, as it turns out, could not speak, only weep. Only its presumed show of suffering marked its identity, and this was what the Clod responded to out of pity. The earth punishes Thel, in this revenge fantasy, for all of Thel's abuses of the helpless, including when she continues to apostrophise the Worm only to ask if it is a Worm at all and to wonder aloud, in patronising tones, at its lameness. Blake's Clod of Clay attempts to rescue the abjected and speechless from the iterative subject position altogether, and does so in the narrative through an eradicating horror. Thel is overcome by the horror of this moment and flees to her semi-human counterparts, away from the decidedly nonhumans she had been communing with, after coming face to face with her own grave and the reality of her finitude. For an angel like Thel, this is also an empty encounter, and so Thel leaves fanciful discursive play in the 'unknown lands' of death only to return to untroubled Elysian lightness and play.

The didactic lesson of the earth is an abject failure. Thel cannot be contained despite the record of her exchanges suggesting clearly that her choice, in and of itself, to stay with these nonhuman objects or return to the vales of Har reiterates the inequality of what appears to be an anthropocentric anthropomorphism. Thel's anthropocentric anthropomorphism meant that she assigned human characteristics to nonhumans she had already relegated to subhuman status. Thel, in other words, has a centrism. A device closely related to anthropomorphism, perhaps even identical, is John Ruskin's 'pathetic fallacy' ('affective' fallacy in recent literary theory).[55] Both terms denote that a work of art bestows human characteristics upon nonhumans. But Romantics, writing before Ruskin coins the term 'pathetic fallacy', were already suspicious of anthropomorphism, as Blake's Thel and other examples show clearly.

The titular character of Poe's 'Man of the Crowd' fervently seeks out contact and unbroken urban experience to sustain constant sensation, in case solitude and quiet might demolish him in a hail of self-contemplation instead of sensory coexistence.[56] Poe's narrator, the observing agent in a story begun with a German quote that roughly means 'it refuses to allow itself to be read', is completely stymied in his obsessive, analytic pursuit of one man's class and mode. Whereas every other urban denizen proved legible and reducible to group or species, class or category, this singularly illegible specimen refuses analysis and will not be erased. The frustrated narrator thus becomes the object of analysis and the bounded but unmarked space of the narrative becomes a sheer environmentality, the man of the crowd is sheer sociality. Like the sea space of Coleridge's narrated narration in 'The Rime of the Ancient Mariner', nature in such an urban coexistence precludes Nature if 'Hey! I'm having an Experience!' is the only demarcation of environmentality required. This is how Baudelaire can lampoon Landscape, the eclogue, and calm repose in nature in 'Paysage', and can in turn mark the pastoral as an artificial mode while also lambasting the use of imagination.[57] This revises one Romantic mode to reveal that those contemplative, imaginary modes that articulate a specific shape of Nature as the container of their activity are in fact the phenomenal grounds of an environmentality that precedes thinking environment or environmentality at all. The logic of environment the pastoral presumes would seem to build the environmental degradation and domination demanding recovery and escape for the poet's subjects into its structure before the process of repose and recovery is ever begun. Recovery, as such, can never take place at all. The performance will always be a failure of contemplative objectification unless it embraces the deeper strangeness of constant contact and uncanny coexistence that dominates the forms of environmentality in *Frankenstein* and other Romantic texts.

Romantic texts also forego modes of community or consubstantiality, even when their authors are among the era's fiercest political critics, in order to probe human experience, contact and intimacy, horror and strangeness, and the generally elided critical distances between objects and subjects in a dysfunctional aesthetic-experiential economy that proposes the subject always-already as an object of thinking within an unproblematic thinking. This latter problematic has been worked on by Paul Hamilton and others, and one schematic version of the periods' characters might present the Romantic anti-subject as a bit of stylish, erudite misanthropy wandering the truer wilds and communing directly with the remnants of reality outside the commercial centres of human (and object) dissolution while constantly dealing in an 'as if' irony of such performances.[58] The period, in effect, launches a much broader ongoing analysis of life/nonlife (and the likely failure of such division). Two works at the heart of this investigation are *Frankenstein* and Coleridge's 'Rime of the Ancient Mariner'.

Coleridge in particular works through some of the 'aesthetic' hang-ups in any consubstantiality project by negotiating the weird, dark coexistence and interpenetration of objects that horrify and terrify human subjects unawares. The famous 'all creatures great and small' at the end is preceded only a bit by a cacophony of owls and wolves. What has been taken often as an earnest, sober community of coexistents is also terrifying and humiliating. The terrible encounters with ghastly objects like Wordsworth's soldier and Coleridge's characters rupture and captivate because of the essential mundaneness and constancy of uncanny contact and not, echoing again Adorno's critique of Heidegger, a more epic (and thus articulable) singularity.

Mary Shelley, in *Frankenstein*, is especially attuned to this uncanny coexistence, for example when the creature bounds impossibly across a full mountainscape, impeding Victor Frankenstein's recuperative contemplation and escapism. Shelley's text is, throughout, pontificating on the business of being human and repeats figures of observing life through window frames and, of course, through the frame of the constructed life form itself. One of its central revelations is that bringing unlife to life is not more horrible than bringing life to unlife. Both seem a form of murder, if murder is the sovereign negation of the life status of another object. The horror rehearsed again and again, and that the monster's consciousness ultimately imposes on the doctor once it realises the stakes and the potential of the game, is that humans can and do (or do not) wield sovereign power over any other being at all. The text constructs a thinking, feeling nonhuman human with interiority and rampant rational power. But this enframing cannot push the monster through the frame (window, narrative, other). Despite a horrible intimacy in many scenes with Victor, it does not enjoy intimacy with them and is never acknowledged as a coexistent. The play on apostrophe here is not subtle: the nonliving assemblage of dead meat addresses, is addressed and craves a partner creature to address authentically and intimately. By the time the monster is aboard the ship in the novel's close, wishing intimacy with the dead body and also, perhaps, with the bride one dead body had refused to animate when still able to, the sheer excess, the overload of humanity the monster embodies is too much for the ship's crew. The monster occupies the ship's cabin holding the dead body as an inaccessible, unapproachable horror of intimate desire. As in the cabin in the woods, first communing with the blind musician but subsequently eradicating human intimacy and community when the terrified family flees the area, the monster now wages the full human anxiety of impossible intimacy and contact and stands in for the full flattening of life to a mechanical but valueless assemblage of nonspecific atoms. The human is meaningless in *Frankenstein*'s final calculus.

What both Coleridge and Shelley uncover is that, impossibly, coexistence itself is the alienating experience. One always-already coexists with the objects of one's thought, and objects are inaccessible in fundamental ways that not even the most contrived naive realism can bracket out of the recognition of total coexistence and interpenetration between things. The framed being of *Frankenstein*, like the wedding guest of the Rime, horrified at its own position and at the encroaching old mariner's verses, is no-thing but is with everything. Sense is impossible yet total, crucial yet wholly without force. The culminating artefact of this radical strangeness of sensation is not merely a blank nihilism. This, returned to the feedback loop of human comportment, shows that all of the un-suspended human endeavours that coexist with such reflective or frustrated-reflective thinking can carry on regardless of such discoveries. Fittingly, this sublime renovation of human as in-'human' means nothing and has no bearing except for the potential to reinscribe enframed existence with such attitude and comportment as results from this terrible, horrible, dark mode of thinking. Thinking is not for humans and is not about humans and nonhumans. As such, thinking must have alternative ends, if it has any ends at all. This returns us to the earlier Wordsworth problematic.

Frankenstein revises apostrophe almost constantly, waging a prolonged meditation on the radical strangeness of the iterative 'I' in discourse. The book frustrates the interpersonal, interspecies and the interobjective as creatures interpellate a speechless horror reduced time and again to baseless, empty frames like 'devil' and 'evil', 'vile beast', 'infernal', but never accomplishing the intimacy all forms seem intensely to desire and seek out throughout the written work. It thereby exposes the vacancy of the terminological frameworks these characters assert upon worlds they struggle to attend to. The impossible apostrophe might be the full aspect of a Romantic interspeciesism that cannot be, but must be done. The expression of shared suffering, which is a failure the moment it supposes total articulation and presentation of its concept, is really in the ellipses in 'Ozymandias'. Such a Romantic interspeciesism is not failed address but constant addresses to the fact that address can never thoroughly appropriate or access. The sense of reflexive materiality in this mode seems of particular interest to the modernist or postmodernist, if not also being the dominant impetus for a realist or a naturalist's exhaustive efforts to catalogue and report on suffering or on determinate impossibility in the hopes that the message will get across somehow. Romanticism's position is far less certain, even when it is far more assertive.

Romantic authors have other strategies that resist categorical inventories of objects and species – think of the violence of taxonomy Charlotte Smith negotiates from prospect position to sea cave grave at the base of Beachy Head. Through multiple instances of apostrophic, direct address of nonhumans in Romantic works, authors try everywhere to adequately attend to nonhumans while simultaneously evaluating the violence, or merely the irony, of address. At the formal level, authors on either end of the Victorian period explore radical unreliability in literary frame structures like those of *Frankenstein* or *Dracula* and unsettle human authority at the very heart of literary production.

Coleridge's 1794 poem, 'To a Young Ass', clarifies the animal concern of the nineteenth century while also explicating the trouble with apostrophe. This is a poem often discussed in relation to Coleridge and Southey's political ideals for an egalitarian commune in North America. Coleridge's recognition of animal suffering here denotes his broad sympathy within an interspecies community, as in the closing of the Rime. The ass's chief pains are domination by human masters and hunger, combining the concerns of Wordsworth's 'hunger-bitten Girl', and the narrator also wonders at the suffering of the ass's mother tethered nearby:

> Or is thy sad heart thrill'd with filial pain
> To see thy wretched mother's shorten'd chain?
> And truly, very piteous is her lot–
> Chain'd to a log within a narrow spot,
> Where the close-eaten grass is scarcely seen,
> While sweet around her waves the tempting green!⁵⁹

These family ties are echoed in the politically charged 'Brother' in the poem, and Coleridge thus invites the nonhuman directly into political affiliation on the basis of recognised and, ostensibly, shared suffering under the whip of economic subjection.

The ass was laughed out of court, so to speak, when Parliament considered extending horse protection measures to donkeys during the 1821 cruelty act debates. Surely, it could not function as a target of compassion. Kenyon-Jones and Perkins consider Coleridge's revisions and hedging an authorial gap that threatens a true compassion. Perkins seems to make the alluring claim that Coleridge experienced the full crisis of his utopian ideals while attempting to get this brief poem 'just right'.⁶⁰ The ass, both honourable and ridiculous, fails to measure up, risking the entire objective of flourishing interspecies community if that is the point.

If there is something like a Romantic post-humanism, it would have to include these ironic failures of humans on the precipice of nonhuman thought. Such thinking on nonhumans, a figure including anything (including humans) hits its mark by exploding revision and social reform, in a mouse's shudder or an ass's dull, lifeless persistence tethered to an empty, grassless circle of grass. This expression is quite confident of the inescapable reality of mute, anonymous coexistence that escapes articulation or, quite worse, as in the case of administered, nonhuman meat, organises life best when authorising its evacuation. There is surely a marked frustration in attempts at interspecies communication and redresses of authority, as Burns perhaps shows best despite stunted, anthropocentric surrender. In many ways, this finely wrought programme of thought goes hand in hand with the vibrant escapism of penny fiction, which will be examined in Chapter 3, but it would not be quite fair to say that the Romantic interspecies impulse always ends in total frustration, even as the crafty forms of apostrophic de-anthropocentrism the period spawns build an impressive case against general human hubris. There is also the fact of communities of non-suffering. The owls in Wordsworth's canonical 'There was a Boy' don't need to be responding directly in the dead boy's narrated past to be being themselves and also to be being past, possibly dead. The failed 'mimic hootings' are an ironic valence of interspecies, nonhuman consubstantiality.⁶¹

There was a Boy; ye knew him well, ye cliffs
And islands of Winander! many a time,
At evening, when the earliest stars began
To move along the edges of the hills,
Rising or setting, would he stand alone,
Beneath the trees, or by the glimmering lake;
And there, with fingers interwoven, both hands
Pressed closely palm to palm and to his mouth
Uplifted, he, as through an instrument,
Blew mimic hootings to the silent owls
That they might answer him. – And they would shout
Across the watery vale, and shout again,
Responsive to his call, – with quivering peals,
And long halloos, and screams, and echoes loud
Redoubled and redoubled; concourse wild
Of jocund din! And, when there came a pause
Of silence such as baffled his best skill:
Then, sometimes, in that silence, while he hung
Listening, a gentle shock of mild surprise
Has carried far into his heart the voice
Of mountain-torrents; or the visible scene
Would enter unawares into his mind
With all its solemn imagery, its rocks,
Its woods, and that uncertain heaven received
Into the bosom of the steady lake.

    This boy was taken from his mates, and died
In childhood, ere he was full twelve years old.
Pre-eminent in beauty is the vale
Where he was born and bred: the churchyard hangs
Upon a slope above the village-school;
And through that churchyard when my way has led
On summer-evenings, I believe that there
A long half-hour together I have stood
Mute – looking at the grave in which he lies!

The narrator begins with formal apostrophe: 'There was a boy; ye knew him well, ye cliffs and islands of Winander!' Already, in a personifying trope of address to a so-called inanimate object, humans are considering their place in an act of mourning, at a funereal. The poem closes with the narrator standing next to the grave of the boy after narrating his life and interspecies, interobjective nature romps and efforts at interspecies communication. Wordsworth narrates a non-thing or non-place in regimented blank verse. The ghostly 'long halloos' of the owls/boy are the imaginative non-thing. The onomatopoeia in a recollection/speculative narration of the boy's interspecies intercourse with the watery, rocky place was a seductive excursion into what interspecies intercourse would be 'as if' it were possible. What is really dominant in the work after the fact of reading outside the space of the poem is the fruitless, hollow apostrophe of the (presumably older, wizened) narrator in address to the remaining cliffs and islands.

If literary culture develops unimpeded throughout the century – and the myriad technical accelerations of nineteenth-century life threatening the thought of life is surely also the acceleration of serial literary production and circulation – what is the shape of such reflexive narration in the work that abhors the fragmentary, ironic expressions of Romantic apostrophe? Dickens emerges, in *Bleak House* especially, with parallel social concerns formed as massive, completed, practical satire. *Bleak House*, perhaps like any other work, renders inanimate characters and types as mobile yet inanimate objects beholden to social forms. Dickens's narrative technique and formal play critique of the violent effect the law and London have on the subject. The form and the content – narrative authority and legal subjection – of *Bleak House* operates on at least three critical registers: practical/legal; formal/narrative; and philosophical/theoretical. Together, these critiques implicate literary form and social structure in an interrogation of administered life and the potential nonlife – the nonhuman forms of life – that results from the machinery of modern (and decidedly urban) society.

Before assessing these threads in *Bleak House*, however, it will be important to link the nonhuman concern of Romantic fragmentary forms to Dickens's mass forms in the London urban and animal contexts. One approach would be to consider the legal history of animals and Smithfield in Chapter 2 and the London occupations examined in the literary examples in Chapter 3, such as Bartleby or Poe's 'Man of the Crowd', as a lineage of class and category critique. Recall as well Peter Singer's analogy of speciesism to racism or classism – and the argument that it thus cannot rightly found discriminatory treatment – is the direct heritage of liberal social critiques such as those found in Dickens's London novels and the broader English reform movement era of the long nineteenth century. This notion of an improvable subject and society – the 'beautiful soul' itself – would then bridge the case of animal rights, public literacy improvements and education reform to the realist's social consciousness and Romantic era social activism. Dickens also has a massive journalistic output in which he defends the butchers at Smithfield as abjected London actors, as discussed in Chapter 2, and his expression of the Smithfield scene in *Oliver Twist* shows his broader concern for suffering, in itself.

Oliver is the precarious life in the Expedition chapter, and in *Great Expectations*, Pip arrives first to the Smithfield scene in the customary Arrival scene in Dickens's London social novels. The passage in *Oliver*

Twist shows the distortion of human and animal figures alike in the market commerce context:

> Countrymen, butchers, drovers, hawkers, boys, thieves, idlers, and vagabonds of every low grade, were mingled together in a mass; the whistling of drovers, the barking dogs, the bellowing and plunging of the oxen, the bleating of sheep, the grunting and squeaking of pigs, the cries of hawkers, the shouts, oaths, and quarrelling on all sides; the ringing of bells and roar of voices, that issued from every public-house; the crowding, pushing, driving, beating, whooping and yelling; the hideous and discordant dim that resounded from every corner of the market; and the unwashed, unshaven, squalid, and dirty figures constantly running to and fro, and bursting in and out of the throng; rendered it a stunning and bewildering scene, which quite confounded the senses.[62]

In *Oliver Twist*, Smithfield is a recurring point of progress for young Oliver that amplifies his uncertainty and unhappiness:

> It was Smithfield that they were crossing, although it might have been Grosvenor Square, for anything Oliver knew to the contrary. The night was dark and foggy. The lights in the shops could scarcely struggle through the heavy mist, which thickened every moment and shrouded the streets and houses in gloom; rendering the strange place still stranger in Oliver's eyes; and making his uncertainty the more dismal and depressing.[63]

As the long section on the Market highlights, and as the earlier and subsequent literary comments on the space also confirm, the mass of live animals at the heart of the city was an immediately recognisable aspect of London that motivated public debate about the fate of this historic site of revelry and spectacle. The Smithfield scene inscribed on daily London life a unique brand of the gathering knowledge that the Market space, like London at large, asserted a consubstantial intermingling of human and nonhuman in a time that Dickens and others also considered one of deep social hypocrisy as millions languished in abject poverty in the world's great metropolis and world power. Smithfield produced the vibrant, paradoxical crises of sociation and Society Dickens documented in meditations on family, work and law. The law had not corrected the conditions Smithfield, as emblematic of London's gathering modernity, inflicted. It had merely served to erase them in facilitating a welfarist censure and removal of the market from city centre space, as will be examined in Chapter 2. Here Oliver is the cypher of the Smithfield scene and, as he is processed by the city works as the object of London and the Smithfield system. People are material for consumption, and this humanist recognition motivates social concern in Dickens as it did in Wordsworth. This concern becomes an exponential failure.

Once removed to less-frequented thoroughfares, the invisible business of slaughter proceeded at an increased rate. Dickens had chronicled the butchers' union fight against the Smithfield reformers in his journalism, addressing the butchers and other meat tradesmen also in less glowing tones through the Market removal period in later instalments of *Household Words*. His targets were often the unnamed civic managers motivating London's reforms, including Parliament, and so the turn to the gears of the Chancery Court in *Bleak House* satirises the formal administration of rules and law in the (as always) foggy, dingy, noisy city that as easily hosts the meat market as the high courts. The law, like the teeming meat market, is ridiculous and uncertain. Dickens's various London works articulate the trouble with the law that had seemed a legitimate remedy to the suffering of animals, humans and anything else in the long nineteenth-century metropolitan meat grinder. The dense, bad air that hangs as a fog over London's Chancery Court in Dickens at the opening of *Bleak House* is another register of the stagnant, oppressive institutional form fixed upon the city's very being. This is Dickens's opening gesture in a massive, practically interminable interrogation of narrative technique as an expression of thematic, historical and ontological forms of life under the sign of law.

The damaging but also ridiculous influence of London civic space and social structures in *Bleak House*, also seen in other Dickens novels, is ambiguously disorienting in ways Dickens's specific London and laboriously intricate depictions of legal disorientation are not. The strangeness of legal procedure and its liminal social forms parallel Dickens's intent focus on London as a source of confusion to the individual. Esther in *Bleak House*, like Oliver, arrives in London but then loses all bearings amidst the mess of it all and the 'distracting state of confusion' only to then be administratively subdued, though no less lost, by the Kenge and Carboy law offices overseeing the Jarndyce and Jarndyce case (apparently located on an old church grounds). The never-ending legal affair Esther is party to concerns a large inheritance she will never receive. She and her siblings are suspended as potential inheritors, and then of course the inheritance is lost to the costs of its legal administration by the novel's close. The laborious performance of the law's entangled meanderings and immense structure consumes the inheritance, burnt up like old Krook, and the money's consumption in legal process is no less ridiculous, in retrospect, than Krook's spontaneous combustion.[64]

Dickens's consideration of legal structures and their rituals as revised social forms marks a broader shift to secular, legal administrations of life. Buildings, such as the converted church that becomes law offices, continue to be repurposed, if not demolished outright, in London –

Smithfield Market is soon to the London Museum, for example, as I will discuss again in Chapter 2. What Dickens's chosen architectural and social symbols here denote is the general shift in London civic space in the period, down to the most hallowed halls. And so institutional form floating upon material civic space is the full target of Dickens's satire in *Bleak House*. This institutional satire blames London's inscrutable immensity for the fate of the individual lost amidst, and processed by, that development. This individual no longer exists as a whole, consistent subject and a status Dickens interrogates alongside his interrogations of the reconfigured London.

Esther is twenty when the novel begins, and her blank naivety remains at least a partial identifying quality to the last. She becomes a potential, peripheral wife-object to Dr Allan Woodcourt while also remaining a focal point of the story and its frequent narrative voice. Esther's peripheral vision (as it were – her narration is as an outsider arriving at the centre of the universe, London) reiterates the coeval disorientation of the law and the city that opened the novel before Esther's first episode of narration. The 'childlike' outlook, for example, can resist some of the ossified tropes of adult behaviour like the bureaucratic procedures of court and business alike. Then again, Jarndyce and Jarndyce, as a case and as a symbol of London in general, confounds all of the adults in the novel as well. Before Esther ever arrives to mark a crisis of faith or a religious lapse, Dickens begins subsequent paragraphs of the opening establishing shot of London and the Law thusly:

'Jarndyce and Jarndyce drones on.'
'Jarndyce and Jarndyce has passed into a joke.'
'How many people out of the suit, Jarndyce and Jarndyce has stretched forth its unwholesome hand to spoil and corrupt, would be a very wide question.'[65]

The punctuation of this third sentence is itself disruptive and resistant on a procedural level the narrative will foreground. The novel thus begins with a premise about the ubiquitous presence of the case and about the law in general and with Jarndyce and Jarndyce also the stand-in for London and the way it incessantly churns around anyone and anything, ubiquitous in its inane yet dreadful effects. A reflective appreciation of the law's substance (or lack thereof, in this case) is marked by the second passage, and then overruled by the curious, staggering sentence about quantities 'touched' by an anthropomorphised, corrupting law. The law is already an elaborate metonymy, for it is its own proper name at the same time as it stands in for the dense nexus of actors and brokered systems that cannot possibly be summarised in only three letters.

The 'unwholesome' broken hand is the corrupting and spoiling influence of an inhumane administrative structure, but it is also the insufficiency of representation. This is a bit of social realist humour, given both Dickens's own ineffective legal representation in his *Christmas Carol* case and the stooges in *Bleak House*, but the deeper stakes for the precarious subject are clear. 'Jarndyce and Jarndyce has stretched forth its unwholesome hand to spoil and corrupt' punctuates the more unsettling, alienating figure it inhabits: 'How many people out of the suit / would be a very wide question.' Dickens reiterates the performativity of sociation and legal process, the demolition of individual identity through occupation and the nonhuman condition under the law. What follows these three simple topic sentences is the clue to the social distortions Dickens demarcates with the strange punctuation stations of the third.

The various office clerks, and folks like 'Mr. Chizzle, Mizzle, or otherwise' are interpellated through the case and, if fortunate, 'may shuffle into themselves out of Jarndyce and Jarndyce'.[66] Dickens repeats the words mud and fog relentlessly in these same opening salvos, culminating in a self-same London mire as earlier described in the Smithfield passages from *Oliver Twist* until, in this precise reiteration in the paragraph-sentence introducing the head of the courts in the thick of London: 'Thus, in the midst of the mud and at the heart of the fog, sits the Lord High Chancellor in his High Court of Chancery.'[67] Mr Tangle, who knows more than anyone else about the case and has the appropriately symbolic name to prove it, addresses the mired Chancellor several times over in a colloquial voice as 'Mlud . . .' Naturally, more than once, the Chancellor responds to Tangle with the fully articulated 'My lord!' as Tangle dazzles and confounds him with the earliest parcels of the ridiculous case and its entanglements.[68]

Dickens, the former court reporter, had a further bone to pick with the law in the case of his own Chancery experience: his *A Christmas Carol* was famously plagiarised and redistributed upon its incredible popularity after the original 1843 printing. He had five separate bills against individual publishing houses all at once at the Old Bailey, the London court. He had already lambasted American presses for distributing his works in the United States but not paying him even one pence. *A Christmas Carol* had been reprinted and sold for a penny in England in the time leading up to his 8 January 1844 suit against the publishing houses. He won his suit, technically, but then the primary target of his charges declared bankruptcy and Dickens was left to pay his own court and attorney's fees while receiving in settlement far less than those costs amounted to. Not only had his works been successfully reduced to popular penny press status, he then was subsidising that reduction out of his own pocket despite the principle of his complaint having been fully upheld – the presses stopped.

Perhaps the most illuminating and thorough account of Dickens's bout with the procedural idiocy and the economic ironies of legal proceedings on financial matters is E. T. Jacques's *Charles Dickens in Chancery, being an account of his proceedings in respect of the "Christmas Carol" with some gossip in relation to the old law courts at Westminster*.[69] Jacques, a Supreme Court solicitor, reminds his reader of Sir Walter Scott's similar troubles with profit on his work and late-in-life destitution, which Dickens pointed to as a cause for his own complaint. Jacques even dabbles in literary criticism and his own bout with ironic Education Law approval before properly returning to his legal review: 'For present purposes I am not concerned with Dickens's merits; and as regards his influence, I think it will be admitted on all hands that no one, literate or illiterate, can read him without being the better for it.'[70] His mention of Education Acts does not specify which; as discussed in the chapter on penny serials (Chapter 3), public literacy rates had exponentially improved starting one hundred years before Jacques wrote. There was a series of new laws relating to education passed throughout the nineteenth century in England and schools for children, slight in existence before the nineteenth century, were being built at incredible rates as well. An 1833 Act provided fee remission for poor parents. It is possible he speaks here specifically of the 1870 Forster Elementary Education Act making school attendance compulsory and establishing government support for school construction where means were lacking. His sense of 'improvement' in the passage would at least suggest an affinity for reform movements. There is no shortage of Dickens characters, incidentally, to inspire such social concern. Dickens's ridiculous, interminable Jarndyce and Jarndyce case in *Bleak House*, while modelled on a different brand of legalities than the copyright case he suffered at Chancery, thus has at least some biographical impetus but then serves a vaster social critique that the legal record itself invokes: literature was firmly anointed as social concern by the judge. The punch line, as even contemporary members of the legal trade writing on Dickens are quick to note, is that court cases seemed then and seem still 'to have no purpose but to line the pockets of lawyers'.[71] Dickens's legal novel is simultaneously an interrogation of the structures of sociation and the prospects of the self down to the very material of selfhood, the individuating narrative voice and legal claimant that, as it turns out, has no claim beyond the letter of the law.

This anxiety can also be examined in terms of domesticity and the family structure. Kieran Dolin, in a chapter on 'Reformist critique in the mid-Victorian "legal novel"' that discusses *Bleak House* at length, notes the symmetry of fractured families and permeable domestic spaces – 'precarious dwellings' – and the insecurity of lower economic classes, children and women. Dickens's 'decaying houses', Dolin writes, are the same as 'the rotting structure of chancery'. Dolin begins this consideration by meditating on the stakes of legal procedure and domestic estate. As Dolin writes,

> If, according to the mythology of English law, an Englishman's home is his castle, then the novel's imagery of homes vulnerable to invasion and of 'decaying houses' in Chancery forces a reconsideration of the security afforded by the law. In consequence, the decrepit slum of Tom-All-Alone's comes to stand not only for the deranged obsession of Tom Jarndyce, but for the rotting structure of Chancery.[72]

At the same time, this apparent focus on domestic forms is really, throughout Dickens, a preoccupation with violable spaces of life. The conditions of life are 'rotting' and Dolin invokes 'security' and 'invasion' themes.

As will be clear in Chapter 2, nineteenth-century 'improvement' tropes mark a broadly ecological crisis in London life. The dark depths of London's ecology unsettle *nomos*, *logos*, *oikos*: structure, governance and space. And so in Dickens, the interminable capture in the London fog, the mucky din of Smithfield Market in *Oliver Twist*, and the legal fog of *Bleak House* denote an interminable coexistence and disruptive levelling. This theme links Dickens and the Romantic interspeciesists, of course, with a striking shift in Dickens away from performative reflexivity and fragmentation. Yet across genre and period, such atmospheres, literal or figural, proceed as a circus of documents – procedures, literally – that are also peripheral – marginal time and again – recordings but not real events at the same time. They cost money, indeed all of the money in *Bleak House*, and the sole *raison d'être* is this sustained consumption. It would not matter when the accounts hit zero, they were always already oriented toward that zero sum subjection of the object–subject, Esther or anyone, to the reality of the city. In the Romantic works considered earlier in the chapter, these gears were in motion, the writing on the wall.

Despite the magic of Krook's combustion, *Bleak House* is conventionally realist in many ways, and so perhaps it cannot always be so neatly fit to an ironic reflexivity on the matter of life's undoing. As a social novel working to enact concern, it would seem endangered by narrative experimentation, marked most clearly by the multiple narrators that many readers are well aware of. Fredric Jameson's recent work on affect in the realist novel reveals the struggle with an impulse to documentation that approaches no truer reality, only a more thorough account of the bodies and feelings of the metropolis and the global populous. This presumes a massive object of experience somehow. Yet even in Jameson's calculus, something called affect – already a refined sense of 'emotion' and 'common sense' according to Jameson – something resists linguistic documentation and perhaps must do so to be the thing in question – 'affect'. It is as if whatever 'affect' is matters little, and this is why taking Jameson's turn to affect on the matter of, for example, 'nineteenth-century boredom' framed concretely as the thing *'ennui'*, reveals precisely the trouble with realism in delineating the bodies, experiences, feelings, sufferings and potentials of the very same life it is at such great pains to document and, according to the broader force of literature, ameliorate through presenting such 'reality' to the reading public that might initiate the change that must come.[73]

Nevertheless, Dickens does not at all reject the equally didactic force of the magical, the mysterious, the dark and doubtful. London, perhaps, requires a fine sense of these virtues. As I will discuss further in the case of the penny press and, for example, the *Sweeney Todd* tale, London's very real disaster became a very desirable entertainment, and eating the terror of bloody murder has been among the foremost public pastimes. Jack the Ripper sent newspapers flying off the stands just as everyone came to see Jack Sheppard hang. One could read about both or those like them in the bloody dreadfuls at a price that invited eating habits as ravenous as the scarfing of convenient, unidentifiable meat stuffs at the finest fast food establishments. There are more 'supernatural' elements in *A Christmas Carol*, a work eerily reminiscent of Blake's *Book of Thel* thanks to protagonists' intercourse with spiritual worlds on the way to truth, salvation or worse. This work's exploration of human intimacy and the loss of humanity – inflicted by greed, if not overt capitalism – matches it precisely with the bureaucratic horrors in *Bleak House* and the nonhuman abjections of Romantic literature.

Dickens also wields the formal frame techniques Stoker after him or Mary Shelley before him did, inserting texts-within-texts, constant concern for handwriting and material documents, and shifting narrative positions throughout *Bleak House*. Dickens's early postmodernism includes the epistolary metafiction techniques of inserting would-be handwritten letters as objects against the typeface narrative, opening onto the persistent concern with writing and interpretation in the book. His narrative style in such cases is not so meddlesome as Sterne's, for example, and the story gets told in the end, as when Esther receives the letter from the law firm 'removing' her from the Greenleaf boarding house and into London to commence the book's, and the case's, full proceedings. The technique is more archival collage, perhaps a precursor to film editing in its arrangement of documentary artefacts, but also a critique of the subjective hand and the institutional force wielded by an anonymous, mass, invisible hand across the structures and spaces called London or Law. As will be the case in Chapter 2, this is likewise the invisible hand of the market, converted to the invisible hand of slaughter techniques that produce an invisible meat. Law as an abominable nonhuman actor in *Bleak House*, and the bureaucratic expectations of society, conjoin and subject the narrator Esther to her own erasure as the good wife in the end, lauding her husband, situating herself.

Aside from the legal structure in Dickens's *Bleak House*, London is also an organising mass object through which the characters and transactions of the story communicate (in the sense Dickens would use himself in identifying the connection of and passage through rooms in a house). London also seethes as an inescapable assortment of objects, objects that Dickens, in chapter after chapter, lists in dazzling series including candlesticks and other household objects. He will also include from time to time the tools of the trade for a particular character's workspace, an accounting that is condensed as an expression of the habit and style of office life in *Bartleby*, for example, and which will further discussed in Chapter 3. Dickens amplifies the overbearing sense of lists and accumulations – piles, really, matching London's rampant development and impaction in Dickens's historical context – by listing much more.

For example, in a satirical passage invoking King George IV's dandyism in order to criticise characters' vacuous, artificial aristocratic airs at Bleak House, Dickens list the virtues his characters lack:

> The brilliant and distinguished circle comprehends within it, no contracted amount of education, sense, courage, honor, beauty, and virtue. Yet there is something alittle wrong about it, in despite of its immense advantages. What can it be?
> Dandyism? There is no King George the Fourth now (more's the pity!) to set the dandy fashion; there are no clear-starched jack-towel neckcloths, no short-waisted coats, no false calves, no stays. There are no caricatures, now, of effeminate Exquisites so arrayed, swooning in opera houses with excess of delight, and being revived by other dainty creatures, poking long-necked scent-bottles at their noses. There is no beau whom it takes four men at once to shake into his buckskins, or who goes to see all the Executions, or who is troubled with the self-reproach of having once consumed a pea.[74]

The party in question is at least one level of substance removed from the real thing, posturing and pretending but missing even the most easily lambasted signals and objects of the original aristocratic performance of excess. Yet Dickens lists virtues beside accessories, feigning real critique only to break the model of performance as well. The virtues themselves can be performed, put on as clothing it would seem, and the lack of these is no more or less conclusive than the missing fashionable object. Anything in such lists, though broken by paragraph gap as if to suggest a difference, is emptied of content as a mere mode of consumption.

The Jarndyce and Jarndyce case is also a costume of sorts, and another link to the real social concern of satire. Dickens may have based the case on a real case that had begun in 1798 and would not actually end until 1915. *Jenners* v *Jenners* did end because the estate ran out of funds through legal costs. Jacqueline Labbe, in her introduction to Charlotte Smith's *The Old Manour House*, has also suggested that Dickens based the case on Smith's father-in-law's Chancery case of more than thirty years.[75] There are further mock engagements. For example, amidst the above lists of objects, Dickens includes an anecdote about Beau Brummel (1778–1840), a real fashion maven who also had the famous one-liner when asked whether he ate vegetables, 'I once ate a pea.' Here the fashion of meat consumption is aligned with consumption of virtuous performance and clothing. Dickens doubles up on animal consumption in the passage, at the least: Beau wears buckskins and boasts at an exclusively carnivorous existence.

He may have tripled up, in fact. Beau also consumes death spectacles, which would have likely been hangings but also immediately recalls the old Smithfield role, parallel to its time as the 'Smoothe-Field' animal market site, as public execution site for religious heretics and enemies of state such as William Wallace. Beau not only attends them, he attends all of them to keep up his proper consuming display. Two chapters later, Dickens uses London's animal marketways, including Mile End, Spitalfields and without question the seething, teeming animal currents to and from the Smithfield Market he writes on in *Oliver Twist* and *Great Expectations*, to punctuate the wayward son Peepy's itinerant, filthy personage:

> As I had not seen Peepy on the occasion of our last call, I now enquired for him again (when he was not to be found with the dustman's cart), I now enquired for him again ... the cook supposed that he had 'gone after the sheep.' When we repeated, with some surprise, 'The sheep?' she said, O yes, on market days he sometimes followed them quite out of town, and came back in such a state as never was![76]

When he finally arrives, he is a dirty mess, and Dickens uses the same listing technique here as what seems to be simple descriptive exposition. He collects all the clothing articles and their condition, including his 'deficient buttons' now replaced by some from Mr Jellyby's coat to paint the proper picture of a degenerate Mrs Jellyby, off to mile end and 'some Borrioboolan business, arising out of a Society called the East London Branch Aid Ramification' (backward r.a.b.l.e.s., with perhaps the extra b stressed in the made up Borrioboolan before) is improving the little man for public consumption and yet not terribly concerned with her own as she works on African relief efforts and, generally, performs as a false aristocrat of character and substance.

Dickens's target is clear, if perhaps hemmed closely to the homeland despite satirical barbs against colonisation's forgotten double-sided consequence: exported improvement as domestic consumption mode. Consciousness is here, in the political sense, a conspicuous consumption fashion statement. Peepy is more or less neglected by much of the family, though here the narrative certainly notices his animality as he 'flows' with and floats on the river of sheep through the London streets. The animal traffic through London was noticed by human denizens, such that it would be removed by Parliamentary Act shortly after the publication of *Bleak House*, and here Dickens includes one of the markets' strongest urban characteristics as a traffic flow linking city nodes in coherent channels.

Dickens's dense historical references and name-drops lead naturally to historicist evaluations of his practical social critique. One quickly deems Dickens's literature didactic or even practical as a result. His cataloguing impulses can also be clearly related to his near-constant journalistic activity. Much like Sir Walter Scott, Dickens was writing all days and seemingly at all hours – Defoe was another public intellectual of this type, and Defoe's connection to the London crime scene and Smithfield record will be further addressed in subsequent chapters. Dickens's vast journalistic output exceeds an already massive novelistic production, and few if any writers of the day chronicled Victorian material life in London more exhaustively. His reportage mode communicates the intensity and monstrous size but still feigns a critical distance. Satire, in this case, seems capable of collecting the facts of oppression and bureaucratic alienation. But Dickens rarely seems convinced that the product of the legal society is so manageable. There is a real sadness and abjection to the characters, and the biting rebukes of fashionable material consumption may be a last resort.

The damaging weight of dispassionate yet obsessive reportage bears down upon the self-reflexive hollowness of Esther's closing entries to the novel. Here the coordinating conjunctions and formal rhythm both drive the magnanimous stoicism Esther idealises and also smuggles in the spirit of protest without literally claiming discontent. The oppositional coordinating conjunction 'but' recurs while the pleasing parallel constructions transport the stylishness of her husband's good works and her own performance of proper feminine absence – her authority is based on the hearsay of his works and this is allowed because she is the good woman of society by her very absence from the outward exercises of moral authority she reports and promotes:

> We are not rich in the bank, but we have always prospered, and we have quite enough. I never walk out with my husband, but I hear the people bless him. I never go into a house of any degree, but I hear his praises, or see them in grateful eyes. I never lie down at night, but I know that in the course of that day he has alleviated pain, and soothed some fellow-creature in the time of need. I know that from the beds of those who were past recovery, thanks have often, often gone up, in the last hour, for his patient ministration. Is this not to be rich?
> The people even praise Me as the doctor's wife . . . [77]

The paragraph break seems to kick Esther out of her report on Allan's excellence, and the deep affectation of the good woman follows immediately after:

> The people even like Me as I go about, and make so much of me that I am quite abashed. I owe it all to him, my love, my pride! They like me for his sake, as I do everything in life for his sake.

Allan then arrives and asks 'My precious little woman, what are you doing here?' (she is on the porch). He asks what Esther is thinking about and she replies that she has been thinking about her 'old looks'. Allan calls her his 'busy bee'. The reporter is marginalised in this closing, despite Allan's surely magnanimous and soothingly positive '(a)nd don't you know that you are prettier than you ever were?' Esther is immediately erased – effaced – by the courtesy of expectation, both hers and Allan's preceding formality, and the novel ends with a rushing list and formally open closure:

> I did not know that; I am not certain that I know it now. But I know that my dearest little pets are very pretty, and that my darling is very beautiful, and that my husband is very handsome, and that my guardian has the brightest and most benevolent face that ever was seen; and that they can very well do without much beauty in me – even supposing – .
> THE END.[78]

The closing editorial remark on the beauty Esther is not allowed to claim and yet cannot forsake revises the dire subservience – the domestic suspension, abjected in the very home she founds – of her performances and narrations. Dickens supposedly held little patience for would-be feminist resistance to domestic modes expecting women to support the well-being of home totally and before any other ventures. The ridiculous tone of the colonising socialites' busy work 'saving' Africans, for example, suggests both a national-level domestic violation and a much simpler, more fundamental dereliction of domestic duties the conspicuous consumer commits in Dickens's eyes. And yet Esther the cataloguer, Esther the journalist, Esther the narrator and Esther the wife and mother is broken by the expectations and roles of Society, the capital-S machine of custom and propriety that yet neglects its London citizens throughout both Dickens's historical milieu and his social novels.

Dickens's target here might still be middle class social climbers and fashionable consumption. Esther could simply be a didactic character sacrifice. But the formal result is an unreliable yet reliable narrator of precisely the damaged life London consumerism and class aspirations – consumerist logic, fashionable name-dropping – inflicts upon everyone. If Esther is not qualified to self-critique, then Esther is not qualified to evaluate the situations she reveals in her narrative. If Dickens's satires of the legal structure and Society succeed due to the formal immensity of their idiocy in narrative length and form in the epic *Bleak House*, then the simultaneous wasting of their reporter is at least a parallel 'success' in this sense. Esther's emptiness is an atrocity of the system as much because of the rambling politeness of her entries as the final mark of vanity when she/the narrator stops the last indelible listing with the long dash stops and the aperture to indeterminate 'supposing'.

The struggle to narrate the 'end' in *Bleak House* is the fragmentary performance of nonhuman concern. Esther has been properly domesticated into a desirable home with no need for the inheritance she would otherwise have received in a cheerful closure to the grand affair. This of course forgets the self-effacement, the narrative erasure of Esther as she continues to hold first person perspective yet narrates the greatness of the husband she is so, so lucky to have landed – captured, by another turn of phrase. Esther is the captive in this case, though, and she resembles a bit too much the captive meat animal spared jostling, striking and other blows from the traffickers that might diminish her quality and her value to the end consumer. Esther's good and lucky wife is the truth of life in the new civic meat space.

Dickens features questionable narrative perspectives and thereby, in the London novels, an experiment in articulating uncertain urban experience through literary form akin to Poe's efforts in 'The Man of the Crowd'. In *Bleak House*, the immensity of social documentation, though in Dickens's unmistakable authorial tones, to be sure, and the frivolity of legal process and documentation coalesce in an insurmountable, idiotic cacophony that the conventional interpretation would suggest is abated by the closure of the case with a found will and the exhausted resources. Dickens exceeds that interpretation, however, in Esther's self-erasure as a lucky, redeemed woman now 'happily' drafting new documents on the social structure she inhabits. The narrative obsession with construction threatens the would-be subject of a secure domestic space. In *Bleak House*, Esther, the would-be protagonist-narrator and also the hero whose 'progress' could successfully achieve catharsis, is limited in the end and is a sort of transient first person narrator to begin with given the chapter shifts between her perspective and another narrator's. The work ends in the punctuation marks that denote not closure or termination but aperture. This terminal suspension, as in the Romantic 'as if' reflexivity, maintains the fragility of social concern as both a committed marking of shared suffering and a staged failure to mitigate that suffering.

Notes

1. Wordsworth, William. *The Fourteen Book Prelude*, ed. W. J. B. Owen. Cornell University Press, 1985, Book VII: 714–30, pp. 156–7.
2. Perkins, David. *Romanticism and Animal Rights*. Cambridge University Press, 2007.
3. Kenyon-Jones, Christine. *Kindred Brutes: Animals in Romantic-period Writing*. Ashgate, 2001, p. 80.
4. See: Bate, Jonathan. *Romantic Ecology: Wordsworth and the Environmental Tradition*. Routledge, 1991, and McKusick, James. *Green Writing: Romanticism and Ecology*. Palgrave, 2000.
5. See: Harrison, Gary Lee. *Wordsworth's Vagrant Muse: Poetry, Poverty, Power*. Wayne State University Press, 1994.
6. For more on this, see: Franta, Andrew. *Romanticism and the Rise of the Mass Public*. Cambridge University Press, 2009.
7. Levinson, Marjorie. *The Romantic Fragment Poem: A Critique of a Form*. University of North Carolina Press, 1986.
8. See again Franta.
9. Available at: <www.poets.org/poetsorg/poem/ozymandias> (last accessed 1 December 2016).
10. Moore, Alan and Dave Gibbons, illustrator. *Watchmen*. DC Comics, 2005, XII: 27.
11. Coleridge, Samuel Taylor and William Wordsworth. *Lyrical Ballads: 1798 and 1800*, ed. Michael Gamer and Dahlia Porter. Broadview, 2008, p. 47.
12. Scott Boehnen addresses poetry and politics in *Lyrical Ballads* by cross-referencing the new sociological 'taxonomy' of poor classes in Jeremy Bentham's 1797 *Annals of Agriculture and Other Useful Arts* (noting as well that Wordsworth read the text in question and suggesting that Wordsworth in fact responds directly to it, perhaps by 1798 and certainly by 1835). See: Boehnen, Scott. 'The Preface to *Lyrical Ballads*: Poetics,

Poor Laws, and the Bold Experiments of 1797–1802', *Nineteenth-Century Contexts: An Interdisciplinary Journal*, 20:3 (1997), pp. 287–311.
13. Simpson, David. *Wordsworth, Commodification and Social Concern.* Cambridge University Press, 2009, p. 5.
14. Simpson, pp. 92–3.
15. Wordsworth, *The Fourteen Book Prelude*, ed. W. J. B. Owen. Cornell University Press, 1985, Book IV: 415–16, p. 90
16. Simpson, p. 92.
17. *'Lyrical Ballads', and Other Poems, 1797-1802*, ed. James Butler and Karen Green. Cornell University Press, 1992, pp. 277–82. Quoted in Simpson, p. 92.
18. Simpson, p. 18.
19. Wordsworth, *The Fourteen Book Prelude*, Book IX: 501–32, p. 193. Simpson quotes in this case from *The Thirteen Book Prelude*, ed. Mark L. Reed, 2 vols. Cornell University Press, 1991, IX: 519–26.
20. Leader, Zachary. *Revision and Romantic Authorship.* Clarendon, 1996, p. 38 and quoting from *The Poetical Works of William Wordsworth*, ed. Ernest de Selincourt and Helen Darbishire, 5 vols. Clarendon, 1941–9, ii, p. 481.
21. Nussbaum, Felicity A. *The Limits of the Human: Fictions of Anomaly, Race, and Gender in the Long Eighteenth Century.* Cambridge University Press, 2003, p. 256.
22. See especially the discussion of 'civilization' in Chapter 1, 'Fictions of defect', pp. 42–4, and Chapter 2, 'Effeminacy and femininity', pp. 58–9.
23. Johnson is believed to have suffered from Tourette's syndrome based on posthumous studies of character descriptions by his biographer Boswell and other contemporaries, and he was widely considered to exhibit odd, abrupt mannerisms. When Arthur Shapiro published the first definitive study on the subject, he presented Johnson as the most famous example of Tourette's. Scholarship in neurobiology continues to affirm the view. See: Shapiro, Arthur K., Elaine Shapiro, Gerald Young, et al. *Gilles De La Tourette Syndrome.* Raven Press, 1978.
24. Nussbaum, p. 77 and quoting letters from Elizabeth Montagu to various others, found in Eger, Elizabeth. *Bluestocking Feminism: Writings of the Bluestocking Circle, 1738–1790.* Pickering & Chatto, 1999, pp. 159–77
25. Youngquist, Paul. *Monstrosities: Bodies and British Romanticism.* University of Minnesota Press, 2003, p. 28.
26. Youngquist, p. 36.
27. Nussbaum, p. 256.
28. See here also Youngquist, pp. 28–56.
29. David Collings's *Monstrous Society* has much to say on this connection. See: Collings, David. *Monstrous Society: Reciprocity, Discipline, and the Political Uncanny, c. 1780–1848.* Bucknell University Press, 2009.
30. Macovski, Michael. *Dialogue and Literature: Apostrophe, Auditors, and the Collapse of the Romantic Discourse.* Oxford University Press, 1994, p. 3.
31. Macovski, p. 11, quoting Abrams, M. H. 'Structure and Style in the Greater Romantic Lytic', in *From Sensibility to Romanticism: Essays Presented to Frederick A. Pottle*, ed. Fredrick W. Hilles and Harold Bloom. Oxford

University Press, 1965. Macovski brackets his claim of a vibrant, open interpretive sense of literary form and interplay with a passage from Paul Magnuson's recently reissued important work on *Lyrical Ballads* and the role the relationship of its two authors played in the discursive genre this interplay produces: *Coleridge and Wordsworth: A Lyrical Dialogue*, Princeton University Press, 1988/2014.
32. Poe, Edgar Allen. 'The Poetic Principle', available at: <www.eapoe.org/works/essays/poetprnd.htm>, p. 5 (last accessed 1 December 2016).
33. Gilmartin, Kevin. *Print Politics: The Press and Radical Opposition in Early Nineteenth-century England*. Cambridge University Press, 1996, p. 8.
34. Franta, Andrew. *Romanticism and the Rise of the Mass Public*, Cambridge University Press, 2007, p. 4.
35. On the issue of political commitment in Romantic literature, see Marilyn Butler's seminal *Romantics, Rebels, and Reactionaries: English Literature and its Background, 1760–1830*. Oxford University Press, 1982.
36. Helsinger, Elizabeth. 'Clare and the Place of the Peasant Poet', *Critical Inquiry*, 13:3 (Spring, 1987), p. 509.
37. Perkins, p. 132.
38. John Clare, 'To the Snipe', quoted in Perkins, p. 132.
39. Clare, John. 'The Old Man's Song', *Selected Poems*. Penguin, 2004.
40. Grahame, Kenneth. *The Annotated Wind in the Willows*, ed. Annie Gauger. Norton, 2009.
41. Clare, John. 'The Nightingale's Nest', in *The Rural Muse, Poems (1835)*. Whitaker & Co., 1835, ll.1–4, p. 30.
42. Clare, 'The Nightingale's Nest', ll.5–16, p. 31.
43. The first publication was in *John Clare: Poems Chiefly from Manuscript*, ed. Edmund Blunden and Alan Porter. R. Cobden-Sanderson, 1920, pp. 186–7. This version is titled 'Badger', begins with 'When midnight', and is followed by the poem 'The Fox'.
44. Clare, 'The Badger', in *John Clare: Selected Poetry and Prose*, ed. Merryn Williams and Raymond Williams. Routledge, 1987, pp. 161–2.
45. Clare (1987), 'The Hedgehog', p. 163.
46. Clare (1987), 'The Badger', ll.51–4, p. 162.
47. Clare (1987), 'The Badger', ll.1–14, p. 161.
48. Clare (1987), 'The Badger', ll.55–68, p. 162.
49. Burns, Robert. 'To a Mouse, on turning her up in her Nest, with the Plough, November, 1785', in *Robert Burns: Selected Poems and Songs*. Oxford University Press, 2014, ll. 43–8, p. 73.
50. See: Heidegger, Martin. *The Fundamental Concepts of Metaphysics: World, Finitude, Solitude*, trans. William McNeill and Nicholas Walker, Indiana University Press, 2001.
51. See: Heidegger, Martin. 'The Origin of the Work of Art', in *Poetry, Language, Thought*, trans. Albert Hofstadter. Harper, 1971, pp. 15–89.
52. Adorno, Theodor. *Metaphysics: Concept and Problems*, ed. Rolf Tiedemann, trans. Edmund Jephcott. Stanford University Press, 2001, pp. 133–4.
53. Adorno, *Metaphysics*, p. 136.
54. Smith, Charlotte. 'Beachy Head', in *Beachy Head: With Other Poems*. J. Johnson, 1807, ll. 367–74, pp. 25–6.

55. Ruskin, John. *Modern Painters*. Spottiswoode & Co., 1856. On 'affective fallacy', see: Morton, Timothy. 'The Dark Ecology of Elegy', in *The Oxford Handbook of the Elegy*, ed. Karen Weisman. Oxford University Press, 2010, pp. 251–71.
56. Poe, Edgar Allen. 'The Man of the Crowd', in *Complete Stories and Poems of Edgar Allen Poe*. The Modern Library, 1938.
57. Baudelaire, Charles. '*Paysage*/Landscape', in *Selected Poems from Les Fleurs du Mal*, trans. Norman R. Shapiro, engravings by David Schorr. Chicago University Press, 1998, pp. 156–7.
58. See: Hamilton, Paul. *Metaromanticism: Aesthetics, Literature, Theory*. Chicago University Press, 2003.
59. Available at: <www.poemhunter.com/poem/to-a-young-ass-its-mother-being-tethered-near-it/> (last accessed 1 December 2016).
60. See: Perkins, David. 'Compassion for Animals and Radical Politics: Coleridge's "To a Young Ass"', *ELH* 65:4 (1998), pp. 929–44 and *Romanticism and Animal Rights*, pp. 108–15. See also: Kenyon-Jones, pp. 68–70, 71, 73.
61. Wordsworth, William. 'There was a Boy', in *Lyrical Ballads*.
62. Dickens, *The Adventures of Oliver Twist*. Chapman and Hall, 1870, p. 76.
63. Dickens, *The Adventures of Oliver Twist*, p. 55.
64. Dickens really believed in the phenomenon, apparently, despite round rebuke from George Henry Lewes and others of his contemporaries. More interesting on the matter of Krook is that he drank bad gin constantly. Krook is a poorly organised sort and a compulsive hoarder of, what else?, documents. After his death, it turns out he had the signed legal will that solves the doomed Jarndyce case, stressing Dickens's high opinion on the arbitrary reach of not legal authority but the raw materials of the law, the papers and objects that must be assembled to establish the law at all, let alone enforce or confirm it.
65. Dickens, *Bleak House*, ed. Patricia Ingham. Broadview, 2010, pp. 64–5.
66. Dickens, *Bleak House*, p. 65.
67. Dickens, *Bleak House*, p. 65.
68. Dickens, *Bleak House*, p. 66.
69. A special nod to Jeff Fort here, who notes that this particular title reminds one of the roles gossip and hearsay play in Kafka's *The Trial*.
70. Jacques, E. T. *Charles Dickens in Chancery, being an account of his proceedings in respect of the "Christmas Carol" with some gossip in relation to the old law courts at Westminster*. Longmans, Green, 1914, p. 7.
71. Krotz, Daniel. 'Jarndyce vs. Jarndyce', *The Huffington Post*, 17 May 2010.
72. Dolin, Kieran. *Fiction and the Law: Legal Discourse in Victorian and Modernist Literature*. Cambridge University Press, 1999, pp. 83–4.
73. See: Jameson, Fredric. *The Antinomies of Realism*. Verso, 2013, pp. 66–85.
74. Dickens, *Bleak House*, p. 190.
75. See: Labbe, Jacqueline, ed. *The Old Manor House* by Charlotte Smith. Broadview, 2002, p. 7. Dickens's own preface to *Bleak House* notes contemporary suits in Chancery.
76. Dickens, *Bleak House*, p. 210.
77. Dickens, *Bleak House*, p. 752.
78. Dickens, *Bleak House*, p. 753.

Chapter 2

Meat without Animals: Outcast Objects and the Improvement of London

'Finally, he was quartered', recounts the *Gazette d'Amsterdam* of 1 April 1757. 'This last operation was very long, because the horses used were not accustomed to drawing; consequently, instead of four, six were needed; and when that did not suffice, they were forced, in order to cut off the wretch's thighs, to sever the sinews and hack at the joints . . .'[1]

The age-old meat market on the north-western fringes of the City is a site of butchery in more ways than one. Revolting peasant Wat Tyler was famously put to the sword by the Lord Mayor hereabouts, although that was more of a politically motivated murder than a planned execution. The area came to be known as something of a health hazard for anyone who disagreed with the monarch. William Wallace met his end here in 1305, via the now-familiar hanged-drawn-quartered technique. A memorial to the shouty Scot is still visited by flower-laying patriots to this day. A couple of centuries later, Smithfield was also the scene of religious executions, when Bloody Mary I condemned at least 50 Protestants to death by burning (also commemorated with a plaque). Swindlers and confidence tricksters were occasionally boiled to death in oil. Nice place, Smithfield.[2]

Harriet Ritvo summarises Darwin's intellectual outline as an 'elaborate schema in which people occupied no especially prominent position'.[3] There are myriad humiliations of the human one could consider in relation to this decentring and flattening of living communities. I will here forego some of the recent theoretical inquiries into the concept of 'life' or the insufficiency of terms like community and relations to express the various modes of coexistence fully inflecting the objects called 'alive' and 'dead', or even 'objects'.[4] But it will be worth considering what, exactly, we mean when we say 'animal' and what, then, we could possibly mean by 'meat animal'. This is addressed in the period, as animals become manufactured articles for consumption, abetted by new technologies of husbandry, management, slaughter and distribution including forms that are not even meat, but things like extracts and powders.

The contemporary animal flavours – chick'n crackers this, bacon chocolate that, ad infinitum – derive from the nineteenth-century advancements just as the veterinary sciences and the dairy industry do. Agricultural giants like Justus von Liebig, inventor of the nitrogen-fixing techniques that enabled the 'other revolution', contemporary industrial agricultural, was also the inventor of the Liebig-Oxo meat extract. Weird new foodstuffs, part and parcel of a widespread trend in food fads and body regimens, were the precursors of mass-produced meat animals in derivative post-animal products. Animals were rendered for a variety of applications, including soap, candles and various other products in which no trace of the animal was left after processing. The animal was already a disintegrated object for human consumption besides meat and dairy eating or drinking. There could be no film industry, for example, and no film at all, without the animal gelatin used in 'real' film. Some contemporary vegans suggest that, in fact, it is virtually impossible to be a 'real' vegan – one who consumes no animal by-products whatsoever, from shampoo to medicine, biodiesel to charcoal, anything with animal parts of any sort in it at any point in production or consumption.[5] Much as contemporary ecological thought considers the industrial revolution's status as the onset of the Anthropocene, the long nineteenth-century period of animal use and abuse will likely have to be considered the onset of whatever we're to call the erasure of the animal from the products and objects exploiting the former animal life in human consumption. These articulations of meat without animals rest squarely on all aspects of the technological, economic and theoretical foundations of the civilised society, and especially in the morphological specificity of London, Smithfield Market and the discourse on animals marking the long nineteenth century.

Darwin is as handy a barometer as any for the sense of categorical life and ambiguous species boundaries, and also in relation to the new modes of animal breeding in the period. In the wake of the enclosure of the British countryside under 'Farmer George', King of England, Ireland and then the United Kingdom after merger, agriculture and animal husbandry were improved to respond to food shortages.[6] English authors on the subjects of population and resources established essential threads of political economic study, which did not go unnoticed by Marx and Engels, and included William Cobbett, Thomas Malthus, and Mary Shelley's father, Mary Wollstonecraft's husband, William Godwin.[7] Malthus is the outlier of the bunch, being the conservative proponent of 'positive checks' on population, otherwise deemed catastrophes, such as war, disease and famine. In conjunction with the Poor and Grain laws in the period, theories and methods of food production and distribution also developed to address the increasing crises confronting English society. The object of this chapter is not to consider agricultural economics, however, but the specific case of animals and meat production as relating to Smithfield Market, animal rights discourse, the vilification and debasement of the butcher class, and the general shape of London public space these aspects produce.

Animal breeding is, for all intents and purposes, invented as a modern practice in the eighteenth and nineteenth centuries in the areas of horse, dog and meat animal breeding. Among the revolutions in agricultural production in the period,

> new methods of agriculture were introduced, notably the growing of root crops such as the turnip which enabled many more livestock to be fed through the winter. The most famous early improvers were 'Turnip Townsend' (1674–1738), who popularized crop rotations, and Jethro Tull (1674–1741), pioneer of farm mechanization.[8]

One improver in particular is credited as the father of British animal husbandry, as well as an important influence on Charles Darwin via the generations of breeders he inspired. Robert Bakewell, as of around 1760, was making discoveries in selective breeding of meat animals that produced more meat and better animals. From that early work, other breeders 'were increasingly able to apply their practical knowledge to the moulding of farm animals for greater efficiency and production'.[9] This notion of constructing animals for human consumption was not the true target of much animal concern and activism in the period, and yet animals were constructed precisely as such objects by the activists themselves as part of the rhetorical strategies for animal rights.

What was most commonly addressed in early animal rights debate and in the first laws protecting animals in British law, such as Martin's Act in 1822, was cruelty towards animals. Smithfield's history as London's main meat centre spans over 1,000 years, but it undergoes a radical expansion in the late eighteenth century, becoming a massive livestock centre within London before public outcry over noise, smell, public health and, most especially, animal welfare force Parliamentary debate and 1852 statutory removal of Smithfield's livestock grazing and keeping to outside London that ultimately occurs in 1855. Some of the earliest, clearest laws regarding the treatment of animals are written precisely to address the various atrocities at or on the way to Smithfield in the half century before that, and in fact Smithfield removal campaigns had begun in Parliament as part of Member of Parliament (MP) Martin's broader efforts on behalf of animals. In particular, laws regulating the 'overdriving' of animals stem directly from the Smithfield Market heyday of the first half of the nineteenth century.[10]

As Tobias Menely has written in his assessment of the 'sentimental anthropomorphism' that animal rights proponents were accused of ('exaggerated sensibility' in the words of key rights opponent William Windham), the objects of such sentimentality themselves are 'false'.[11] In this case, the false 'object' given 'personality' (this was Coleridge's complaint about animal rights claims in an 1814 letter, as Menely notes) is as easily the human as the nonhuman by the calculus of overstated humanity. Rob Boddice has written a broad review of public relationships to animals in eighteenth- and nineteenth-century Britain that surveys the primary Parliamentary debates and poses cruelty and pain as central critical targets, presents a compelling review of philosophical antecedents to animal concern and welfare positions in the period, and works them all through in a critique of contemporary anthropocentrism.[12] Boddice makes no mention of Smithfield but does evaluate other sources of the earliest animal rights laws in Britain. In particular, he credits John Lawrence's *A Philosophical Treatise on Horses and on the Moral Duties of Man towards the Brute Creation* with influencing the 1822 Martin's Act, the first anti-cruelty act of Parliament and generally regarded as the first such legal statue in modern legal history.[13] This is certainly because, besides penning a book Richard Martin MP read, John Lawrence actually collaborated with Martin in drafting the Bill.[14] Boddice evaluates the history of statutes pertaining to domestic livestock and cruelty, and provides intensive study of a number of sources for the arguments and attitudes behind animal law in the Romantic period, but it seems that what remains to be articulated is the strong connection between meat market and general animal labour issues at the time and the public concern that then leads to the formal legal defence of animals.

The suffering of individual animals and classes of labouring animals – cart horses, taxi horses, cattle and sheep driven loudly and abusively through the crowded streets of London or stored tightly and noisily at Smithfield, beaten dogs, roosters used for fighting, bait-bulls and badgers and bears – all of these maligned creatures became the cause célèbre of the humanitarian animal advocates and Parliament members like Lord Erskine and Richard Martin ('Humanity Dick' and an Irishman, let it be known). Martin's Act, also known as the Cruel Treatment of Cattle Act 1822, read as follows:

> Whereas it is expedient to prevent the cruel and improper Treatment of Horses, Mares, Geldings, Mules, Asses, Cows, Heifers, Steers, Oxen, Sheep, and other Cattle: May it therefore please Your Majesty, by and with the Advice and Consent of the Lords Spiritual and Temporal, and Commons, in this present Parliament assembled, and by the Authority of the same, That if any person or persons shall wantonly and cruelly beat, abuse, or ill-treat any

Horse, Mare, Gelding, Mule, Ass, Ox, Cow, Heifer, Steer, Sheep, or other Cattle, and Complaint on Oath thereof be made to any Justice of the Peace or other Magistrate within whose Jurisdiction such Offence shall be committed, it shall be lawful for such Justice of the Peace or other Magistrate to issue his Summons or Warrant, at his Discretion, to bring the party or parties so complained of before him . . . [15]

New periodicals like *The Animals' Friend* and *The Voice of Humanity* diligently tracked the offences Martin, and his Act, responded to.

British law articulates animal subjects in completely new ways near the beginning of the nineteenth century. What had before only been property, even when property that could be cruelly mistreated, became a protected body. Animals remained – and remain – property in specific legal scenarios such as liability, but a gradual shift to considering treatment of animals as a target of criminal charges began with these first laws. Animals that could be indirectly protected by laws curtailing human social depravity became valuable in their own right. This legal history shows how little regard had been shown toward nonhumans prior to these changes and also maintains divisive hierarchies among humans themselves through each stage of social normativity in the laws controlling human behaviour involving animals. Animals used in entertainments such as baiting or gambling games accompanied by drinking, greedy overkilling of game and abusive animal driving to market through overcrowded city streets inflicted a human social suffering, if the language in parliamentary acts is taken as a guide. But gradually, animal advocates argued for laws that protected animals from abuse for the animals' own good. Nevertheless, the language of human social improvement often accompanied even the best, most animal-focused laws in the nineteenth century. The rhetoric of animal protection rarely succeeded in presenting a stand-alone animal subject not somehow subjected anew as the equipment of human iniquity, but this, again, presumes a special status in such status.

Beginning in the late eighteenth century, British common law establishes animal rights in a form that continues to the contemporary moment. This is not at all to suggest that animal law itself, and not even animal concern and legal reform, began here. Property law had long covered cattle/chattle, and far more animals are fundamentally regarded as property by the law today in the United States and England than are treated as anything else. But property law does not cover all of the relations humans and animals engage in, and in England in the seventeenth and eighteenth centuries, laws against animal baiting and excessive gaming, as well as a variety of laws regulating Sunday observance, had already been passed. Many of these had more to do with the well-being of humans, not animals: the laws aimed to curb unsavoury human practices such as gambling and the drinking often associated with various animal entertainments. The gaming laws by and large censured greed through economic penalty while also incorporating language about the depravity of those taking more than their fill of the King's animals. Laws against animal abuses near churches, in public parts of London or during specific holiday seasons such as Easter that aimed at human welfare in this manner had a long history in English Law dating back well before 1600. The sorts of legal arguments against social depravity – 'great multitudes of the worst sorts of people resorted' to such pastimes according to a 1585 Act – would stick with animal law into the modern era. But several legislative measures, generally regarding livestock management, also concerned animals' direct welfare.

In 1635, the Irish Parliament made it a crime to work horses 'by the taile' when ploughing and pulling, and the same act also outlawed pulling 'wooll' off live sheep. The language, including 'cruelty' toward the animals and the 'barbarity of custom' and 'prejudice to' animals such cruelties inflicted, codifies animal concern precisely as the contemporary animal rights advocate might. These animals were still property, to be sure, but now the law subjected property owners to standards of comportment concerning the well-being of that property, and without reiterating the fact of property at all. Violators could be fined and imprisoned. The formal rationale for controlling this cruelty was that 'the breed of horses was much impaired in this kingdome'. Perhaps this implies a national possession, and thus reinvigorates the sense of animals as property – certainly as capital – but here the animals' health and suffering were, nevertheless, codified.

The laws of the late eighteenth century begin to address specifically urban human–animal interactions at Smithfield Market, London. The language of laws regarding cattle driving and Smithfield land use prior to this time had already accounted for the damage to property/capital poor management and insufficient grazing could inflict. In 1774, the law seems to meld human and animal welfare indelibly even when animals are merely the vehicles of 'mischief' for humans near the market. But the telling language – 'improper', 'cruel' – ushers in the intense welfare consciousness that would later influence specific laws against animal cruelty:

Driving of Cattle, Metropolis Act 1774
Great Britain Parliament
　　[14 George III. c. 87] An Act to Prevent the Mischiefs that Arise from Driving Cattle Within the Cities of London and Westminster, and Liberties Thereof, and the Bills of Mortality

> Whereas the improper and cruel manner in which cattle are driven from Smithfield market, within the city of London ... has occasioned great mischief, and endangered the lives of many of his Majesty's liege subject inhabiting therein; ... if any person or persons, who shall be hired or employed to drive any cattle within the said cities ... shall, by negligence, or ill usage, in the driving such cattle, be the means that any mischief shall be done by such cattle ...[shall] be kept to hard labour for any time not exceeding one month, or shall be publickly whipped.[16]

There is no conflation of humans and animals in the 'liege subjects' here, though many accounts of Smithfield Market at this time suggested exactly such interspecies subjection. Besides indicating how problematic the exponential increases in both animal production and human population had become for an ever-more-crowded London city centre, this law both confirms the daily proximity of animals to human life while codifying the cruelty of human animal use. This law does not specifically detail the nature of the cruelty, nor does it penalise the cruelty – the punishment was for, basically, disturbing the peace with the whips and attendant animal noise and scenes of cruelty. But built into this protocruelty legislation is the massive store of sympathy for animal suffering writers such as Defoe, on Smithfield, and Barbauld, on mice used in scientific experiment, had already expressed. More importantly, public sentiment and increasing journalistic coverage of London life had clearly established that the sights, sounds and smells of animal abuse and urban overcrowding were taking too great a toll to go unnoticed by the law. Today, one will pay a congestion charge to drive a car into the heart of London, past several congestion zones. In 1774, one would pay dearly for congesting London with excessive, disruptive cattle driving.

As discussed in Chapter 1, literary historians have focused on the connection of Romantic literature to the nascent animal rights movement in England that grows and strengthens until just before World War I.[17] Kenyon-Jones and Perkins suggest that the legislative debates of the period inflect Romantic literature with an even stronger association with the nonhuman. They often focus on Romantic literature that is not at all intent on improving human comportment toward an endangered environment but is, instead, focused entirely on animal suffering. Romantic literature articulates an inaccessible but inescapable nonhuman. Kenyon-Jones reads Lord Byron's *Childe Harold's Pilgrimage* in relation to the series of anti-cruelty measures brought before the House of Commons between 1800 and 1822, reading Byron's portrayal of a Spanish bullfights against the arguments for banning bull-baiting in England.[18]

Perkins now and then may seem to lapse into a familiar Eco-escapist model of animal concern in his book, noting a Romantic rejection of mankind when he writes that 'the cause of animals appealed to the pathologically shy, to the alienated, to the misanthropic, to those who, for whatever reason, had trouble identifying with other human beings'.[19] But to oversimplify such a Romantic environmentalism as in line with the sentimentality and sympathy mocked by Windham and Coleridge, for example, is to refuse the darker empathetic thought that embraces these anxieties and alienations (and affectless coexistences) without the overbearing sense of crisis and loss so commonly assigned by such readings. Such a dark, indeterminate sensibility is wholly appropriate to the Smithfield debates and the 'false' rhetorics of depravity and improvement, alike.

Perkins ultimately reads the Romantic period, especially in representative works like Burns's 'To a Mouse', as one defined by its focus on empathy, compassion and the improvement of humanity through a comprehensive expansion of the circle of consideration in daily life. And while the sunny outlook of such a positive, practical alteration of behaviour (think of vegetarianism or the anti-sugar and spice practices in Great Britain during the abolitionist movement) seems to fit an escapist consumerist aesthetic attitude Timothy Morton, borrowing from Hegel, has called 'beautiful soul syndrome', many of the Parliament floor arguments themselves were far worse.[20] Proponents of ending animal baiting and fighting would often openly decry the moral turpitude – the drinking, the fights amongst bettors, the betting – such entertainment engendered in the working class. The legislators argued as though they were wholly convinced that the evil reality of animal cruelty could be corrected, the evil barred for good, and they routinely based their arguments on the moral health of human subjects.

During the years 1800–35, laws were presented and eventually passed to ban uses of animals for entertainment in staged fights between dogs and bears, bulls and badgers, and some of the proposed and ratified laws included prohibitions against cockfighting. The 1835 Animal Cruelty Act, in particular, codified an intense social concern relating to domestic cattle, sheep and other species in meat production and general labour conditions. A number of arguments brought before Parliament claimed that bear- and bull-baiting threaten the morality of the poor. Kenyon-Jones notes that the debates on animal cruelty in the House of Lords were 'widely reported in the press and subsequently published as a pamphlet'.[21] Kenyon-Jones notes the humanitarian appeal of anti-cruelty measures, and she refers to Sir William Pulteney's 1800 bill introduction, highlighting passages that inveighed against the deleterious effects bull-baiting, in particular. The strongest (and most successful) opponent of the animal cruelty cause in Parliament was Windham, who, as Perkins notes, found several ingenious examples by which to argue that animal cruelty and suffering was not a fit subject of legislation and that reform 'must be left to morality and social opprobrium'.[22]

Hilda Kean has linked the animal concern of the period to the new sense Londoners had of the city and its ideal civility, drawing out especially juicy passages on the hectic scene around Smithfield:

> Screams of terrified women and children present scenes of disorder which one could hardly expect to find even in the worst regulated towns in Europe, but which are highly disgraceful to one of the largest, most populous and richest capitals in the world.[23]

The tumult at Smithfield was among the most frequently mentioned reasons to remove the market altogether.[24] Daniel Defoe had remarked on the scene, as even he could not quite believe the wonder of Smithfield. As one of his biographers presents Defoe's reaction, 'Defoe is awed by this sheer quantity: "*Smithfield* Market for living Cattle, which is, without Question, the greatest in the World; no Description can be given of it."'[25] As Dickens would write in *Oliver Twist*, this overwhelming, indescribable space overcame those near it by sheer din and danger.

Dickens's counter-sensory description is among the most often-cited sources of Smithfield critique, included in most histories of the site and excerpted as well on the incredible commemorative bench in the current-day Smithfield Square near the old Market location in London:

> It was market-morning. The ground was covered, nearly ankle-deep, with filth and mire; a thick steam, perpetually rising from the reeking bodies of the cattle, and mingling with the fog, which seemed to rest upon the chimney-tops, hung heavily above. All the pens in the centre of the large area, and as many temporary pens as could be crowded into the vacant space, were filled with sheep; tied up to posts by the gutter side were long lines of beasts and oxen, three or four deep. Countrymen, butchers, drovers, hawkers, boys, thieves, idlers, and vagabonds of every low grade, were mingled together in a mass; the whistling of drovers, the barking of dogs, the bellowing and plunging of oxen, the bleating of sheep, the grunting and squeaking of pigs, the cries of hawkers, the shouts, oaths, and quarrelling on all sides; the ringing of bells and roar of voices, that issued from every public-house; the crowding, pushing, driving, beating, whooping, and yelling; the hideous and discordant din that resounded from every corner of the market; and the unwashed, unshaved, squalid, and dirty figures constantly running to and fro, and bursting in and out of the throng; rendered it a stunning and bewildering scene, which quite confounded the senses.[26]

What recurs in descriptions of the Smithfield scene, stink and sound is the failure of rationality to account for the affective experience with all of the life in the city. The meat space of humans and animals disrupts and charges the senses, as is often said of nineteenth-century urban industrial experience.[27]

The noise is a well-known aspect of the complaints against the Market in the decades leading up to its removal. Kean's study of the activist literature in the period includes haunting passages and images from the early stages of the fight, led in part by Martin himself and the first generation of the RSPCA and mobilised in publications like *The Voice of Humanity*: 'At night the local residents could hear the animals' cries of distress as they were rounded into the pens and then they were prevented from sleeping "as the dreadful blows inflicted on the cattle are distinctly heard in their bedrooms."'[28] The activist press of the period certainly had an interest in presenting the worst view of the Smithfield atrocities they could as part of the political campaign for animal rights, but the death and gore of the site seemed to speak for itself, as well. One particularly provocative note on the killing at Smithfield Kean uncovers is also from *The Voice of Humanity*. Kean writes,

> much killing of the animals took place underground in cellars into which the animals were precipitated to a depth of several feet and 'often [had] their jaws and legs broken by the fall'. Such practices were unseen but conjured up in the evocative illustrations of the journal *The Animals' Friend*. While campaigners did not necessarily become vegetarians they were horrified about the effect meat butchered in such circumstances would have on human health.[29]

The image she includes alongside the passage is, apparently, from some ten years later, but it is certainly provocative, with ghoulish, bare-skulled Smithfield workers clubbing swarms of sheep and cattle under a fog-shrouded crescent moon and the great dome of St Paul's Cathedral. The dome is still visible from the Smithfield site in London today. The image, along with other aspects of the activist literature, suggests that all of the debauched murder and mayhem at Smithfield was happening under the watchful eyes of higher authorities who, surely, were not pleased by the lowness of it all.

Kean here highlights the invisibility but ubiquitous sense of animal death at Smithfield preceding the much larger erasure of Market removal. The startling noises and smells of the poorly ventilated basement abattoir, which would also have had little to no access to running water, heightened the fear of the butcher class and added to their urban legend status. The precipitous fall of a meat animal victim, described here in an 1827 account, is also the direct precursor to the modus operandi of Sweeney Todd with his meat human victims, dropped through the floor to their deaths in the basement for quartering and processing in mysterious meat pies, hungrily consumed by unsuspecting Londoners against the backdrop of ongoing concerns about meat sources and safety.

Smithfield would disappear as a centre of human–animal coexistence, only to shuttle the animals to a bigger, more inscrutable processing facility at Islington, The Metropolitan Cattle Market, as slaughter practices were being improved to manage the exponential increase of meat animal production arriving in the city after the husbandry advances took hold. In his study of the refinements to slaughter technique, focused primarily on the period after Smithfield's removal but still relevant to the longer process of those shifting practices, Ian MacLachlan notes that the gruesome tales of animals skinned alive or bludgeoned by 'revengeful' savages were unlikely. As butchers and meat tradesman themselves were proclaiming in their trade journals, 'Humanity and profit go hand in hand.'[30] This is in direct contrast to the stories in the animal rights journals, and MacLachlan, along with just about anyone writing on the state of slaughter and meat production in the nineteenth century, notes the general knowledge of terrible conditions and abuses surrounding Smithfield and the London abattoirs. MacLachlan then details the 'humane' innovations in slaughter technology, including slaughter masks and the captive-bolt mechanism contemporary audiences not working directly in the meat industry will recognise as the killing device used by the villain Anton Chigurgh in *No Country for Old Men*. Nevertheless, the butcher's poleaxe, likely the technology causing the terrible sounds Kean mentions, still rated as an efficient method, and rumours of drunken butchers missing their mark and causing the 'undue suffering' Martin's Act specifically warned against seem to have been further hyperbole from the effective animal rights activists.[31] Frankly, death by the poleaxe was terrible enough. As the tales of human murder addressed in Chapter 3 make clear, a clean death – even the most painless death possible of the most silent victim conceivable, such as Bartleby or the muted cow – stuns the sensibility that has lost its life object in the new, anonymous, mass metropolis. If the life that is no life suffers the death that is no death, has anything even happened at all?

Shifting legal and civic administration of meat animals in the London city centre around the Smithfield Market in the nineteenth century includes disparate city actors like the butchers' guild and the burgeoning animal rights movement, and it incorporates the various advances in animal husbandry and slaughter in the period as well as the city's growing traffic – powered by animals still. What becomes apparent through considering this dense network, as well as the extensive shifts in public awareness of and responses to disease and ecological degradation in the city, is that the primary application of animal rights law at

Smithfield was not in protecting animals' lives but in managing their efficient deaths so their meat would be best cultivated and produced. Slaughter improvement produces something like categorically 'good' deaths as meat animals, amplifying their status as somewhere in between the dead meat they were becoming and the animals they will have been after slaughter. Animals, hand in hand with animal rights and with civic improvement rhetorics, are instrumentalised and administered through legal process and civic management. These are the material facts of life (and death) at Smithfield.

Upon its removal, and in the discourse leading up to the improvement and reform of the violent Smithfield scene, the Smithfield system of animal slaughter and meat distribution became instead an erasure of the animal body from the city scene and, in the process, from the conception of meat in the consuming public. In contemporary life, one need only consider the difficulty of acquiring photographic or other evidence of the atrocities in the CAFO slaughterhouse to understand the anxiety within the industry itself about the effect of witnessing meat animal death. In London at Smithfield, there was a problem of affect in the meat space Londoners met when they arrived at the site. Dickens, Defoe, Hardy and anyone writing on the scene noted that it challenged the senses and exceeded coherent understanding. It stank, it was noisy and the mass of bodies – humans and animals intertwined and inseparable, really and truly – overwhelmed onlookers. Compounding matters, the health risks of a dirty, unmanageable meat industry, while consumption of the now readily available meat animals was at an all-time high, included rotten meat and unknown meat pie contents, all of which elicit stomach-turning responses to the Smithfield problem.

This haptic proximity only turned Londoners more against the butchers who were their final, direct link to the meat animal, especially as the issue of meat prices and quality became worse and worse:

> Since there was not a generous profit margin for dead meat, butchers concentrated on ways to mitigate the inevitable spoilage. The City inspectors fined butchers who sold 'unwholesome' meat and confiscated the offending product, some more ambitious butchers concocted ways to portray meat as fresh. . . . Butchers found that the exposure of these boxes (of meat) along with the agitation of the uneven pavement during transport degraded the meat and invited even lower profits.[32]

Butchers were left holding the bag, so to speak, on both meat quality and meat price issues, and when the Market removal debates went into full gear, they resisted because of the obvious threat to their personal business practices and livelihood. On the other hand, they were suffering from a systemic weakness at the Smithfield site that could not handle the increasing numbers of humans and animals, as shown in the conditions described in the previous passage. If anyone would have liked to see significant London improvements to roads, Smithfield traffic flows and later innovations like refrigeration, it was the butchers. As proverbial middlemen, their power had uneven application, and perhaps no trade was to suffer more than the butchers' upon Smithfield reform and removal.

While today the well-meaning animal activist can point to an accepted Big Other in the form of a capitalist meat industry, such targets in the nineteenth-century era of slaughter reform at the crest of a long evolution of meat system labour division had not yet been totally formulated. An individualist, moralist discourse still carried much more weight, as it did in calls to vegetarianism that utilised the model of temperance from religious sources. And this led directly to the demonisation of butchers and other labour groups in the Smithfield system, as it was called. What made the butchers unique in this discourse was both their obvious hand in the bloody, noisy deaths of the animals and, in a complicated turn, their dispersal throughout a teeming, intensely compact city space. On top of the animal erasure at Smithfield, the broader history of animal manufacture for various human uses parallels the city's subjection of humans to new modes of life like the deskish office existence in Poe and Melville, examined in Chapter 3.

Smithfield removal, as well as the simultaneous shutdown of the annual Bartholomew Fair located on the site, is part of the city's discipline of all life, linking the animal rights and civic reform discourses with a categorical, marginalising address of animals and working class London residents. Smithfield thus stands as a crucial emblem of the biopolitical administration of bodies and lives under the signs of civil society and public education:

> The campaign to close down Smithfield was essentially conducted on two separate but linked themes: the adverse effect on animals and the adverse effect on people, both those who carried out cruelty and those who lived or worked in the vicinity and who were obliged to see it. The anonymous pamphleteer who wrote against the 'fiend-like depravity' exhibited at Smithfield market suggested that humans were distinguished form animals by reason while the latter were creatures of instinct. But, he went on, since humans were abusing this free agency, how were humans superior except in depravity? The 'higher ranks' in society oppressed and persecuted the poor through vagrancy and game laws which led, in turn, he argued, to men in the lowest stations of life becoming the persecutors and tormentors of animals as their own inferiors. Christian philanthropists then had a duty to take a stand against the practices in Smithfield as examples of 'malignant moral distemper'.[33]

The butchers were routinely included as the abusers and depraved classes under fire in the animal rights legislature, too, and when their business practices were examined closely, it revealed other atrocities of business:

> A still more deceptive practice was that of meat polishing; the butcher would layer fat around an offending piece of meat and then rub the fat and meat with hot cloths, thus producing an even, smooth appearance. Despite the vigilance of City inspectors, techniques such as polishing allowed butchers to sell diseased or damaged meat to unsuspecting customers.[34]

Smithfield Market closed as a live cattle site on 11 June 1855 after the Smithfield Market Removal Act was passed in 1851. The debate about the city's meat industry sites – and their removal – had roots dating back well into the early modern period, including a long-standing battle between the Worshipful Company of Butchers and other city actors.

The butchers' complicated place at the heart of centuries of civic dispute becomes an impossible role as independent agents of civic management, terrible slaughterers of the suffering animals at the heart of animal concern and vivid antagonists in cultural production. They are bad humans and also the portable 'inhuman', they are the abjected nonhumans in a civic system that recognised their power and role only in order to discipline it. This produced a butcher that was really and truly horrible, stinking, bloody and crude, but also talented, skilful, intelligent, committed, organised and honest where non-craft middlemen who flocked to the Market's new economic modes like parasites were anything but. The butchers were relentlessly abused by city forces, despised and feared by the consuming public at various turns in the city's market histories, and continue on as one of the oldest guild groups in the city. It is impossible to vilify the butchers, yet they were publicly assaulted through each and every Smithfield or other market space debate. Sweeney Todd, the demon barber of Fleet Street, was a cold, bloody butcher of humans who sold his infamous meat pies in the time of dog meat 'growlers' and mystery meat pie fears. The murderers of Defoe's early stories, like the late nineteenth- and early twentieth-century murderers that made London true crime tales so famous around the world, were all known by the same name: butchers.

No single group opposed Smithfield's removal from London more forcefully, and over a longer period of time, than the Worshipful Company of Butchers. The guild has ancient roots in the city. Philip E. Jones, in his singular history of the Company, suggests that the butchers were one of the six, perhaps seven, oldest independent craft guilds recognised by the city and its Exchequer authorities. The others were the weavers, bakers, goldsmiths, pepperers, clothworkers and the saddlers. Jones writes that this last was at least on the Pipe Roll of 1179–80 with the butchers.[35] Jones goes on to say that this recognition was legal and economic, perhaps more importantly the latter as the history of London at this time includes the first Mayor of the city and an increasing reliance upon district management via wards and precincts. The butchers, then, were already crucial economic and civic forces besides being respected craftsmen. This last distinction was one the butchers thought was surely forgotten by the time of the Smithfield removal debate and the rampant violence associated with 'butchery' from the eighteenth century until present times, although to a connoisseur of meat, the butcher is the artisan, the present-day Smithfield still a venerated wholesale meat market flanked by high-end steakhouses.

The butchers also have a long history of activism and resistance to civic rule over their trade, and that history reveals a parallel history of city efforts to move and remove meat industry sites in response to shifting civic organisation needs. The butchers became notorious not only because of their trade, but also for this intensive involvement in city politics and civic design. Their centuries-long refusals to obey various reform measures related to the Smithfield Market space and other aspects of their trade made them ready targets for the city's various officials. Their defence of specific trade sites like Eastcheap, St Nicholas Shambles and Smithfield – all located within one mile of each other in the old city centre – coalesce finally in the seeming defeat of the 1852 Smithfield removal, but, as Jones writes:

> The utter refusal of the butchers to abide by restrictions imposed on the trade by Act of Parliament resulted in the punishment of the whole Company. The sustained opposition of the butchers persuaded Parliament year after year to delay the operation of a statute, an achievement which even the modern trade unions may envy.[36]

It appears that the reasons the butchers became so reviled in the city works had nothing at all to do with their horrible trade and the suffering they inflicted on animals for a significant portion of Parliament. The butchers were the most organised and effective labour unions in the city from earliest times, and their ability to resist what they considered unfair civic restrictions on their trade made them one of the city's strongest adversaries any time a new civic regulation came around. For example, in 1321, the Royal Justices of London ordered all the butchers' stalls in the well-established Eastcheap district butchers' rows be taken down. Eastcheap is only a ten-minute walk, less than a half mile, from the Smithfield site, right in the heart of the old city centre, and

Eastcheap's supplies came exclusively from the Smithfield live animal market like meat throughout the city did. The Eastcheap removal claims stated that 'the stalls were mobile and that the sale of meat within the houses might lead to fraud and deception'.[37] The butchers resisted the attempt, deeming it an effort by the Sheriffs to continue extorting unfair dues from them. The stalls in question had been numbered in 1244 for oversight and so the King could collect the owed revenue from the city's businessmen, including butchers. And so there was precedent for the practice. All of this was but one such conflict between the city and the butchers on the issue of market space and boundaries, then compounded by revenue and taxation.

The dominant trouble with the butchers, whether they were in the right or not in their various run-ins with civic management, was always pollution. Stinking Lane ran into Butcher's Alley, both right in the neighbourhood of the St Nicholas Shambles part of London south of Smithfield that was also involved in the 1321 Eastcheap dispute. Stinking Lane was so-named, precisely, as a result of its association with the smells of butchery. This is very close to the River Thames, and there were efforts to regulate the butchers' disposal of offal even in the medieval period. This area is, incidentally, directly adjacent to Paternoster Row, which was home to the early publishing industry in the city.[38] The St Nicholas Shambles area, along Butcher Lane and adjacent to Newgate Market (site as well of the notorious Newgate Prison and inspiration for the Newgate novels discussed in Chapter 3), is just south of Smithfield.

Butchers had private shops (abattoirs) not only around Smithfield, but also in many other parts of the city. Keeping animals in backyards or in smaller spaces than the massive live animal market was common practice in London even after Smithfield removal. The drivers and salesmen, who were other major targets in the Smithfield removal debates, were concentrated along traffic arteries and at the Smithfield Market site, respectively. But butchers, with their dark, dank, disgusting basement abattoirs, were in numerous city pockets. Any neighbourhood could host the mysterious, dangerous, insidious crimes of the basement killer, a trope that was exploited to great effect, commercially and narratively, in the penny dreadfuls just as it was in novel-length crime tales and horror stories across the century. So it was the case that Smithfield was by no means the only animal site in this period. It was central and singular, and had been a major topic for writers and civic actors across multiple centuries, but there is an entire city of animals, and of meat, to consider. Shepherd's Bush, a borough far west of the city centre, was known as a major pig keeping area, for example.[39] One of the major issues in the market removal debate was actually an entirely separate historical process.

This history of Smithfield Market, the butchers, and the cursory assumptions about animal concern and rights discourse in the period combine to reveal a complex political negotiation between economic actors, such as butchers and civic agents including Parliament and other planning bodies. Much of the debate between the different economic interests at Smithfield and the civic agents pushing for changes and improvement had to do with the use of public city space, which was an evolving concept through the market's height and removal periods between 1700 and 1850.[40] As Metcalfe has shown in her extensive history of the market, the public space concern melded with increasing understanding of hygiene and disease in the period.[41] London suffered an incredible string of public health crises such as the cholera outbreaks between 1832 and the notorious 1854 Broad Street outbreak. These were all the result of intense urban crowding and ineffective waste management practices that dumped the city's growing filth directly into its primary water supply, the Thames River. Smithfield was drawn into this issue, naturally, as the incredible rivers of waste from the live animals there, likewise, ran through city streets and into the same river. And one of the most gruesome aspects of this river of filth was the market effluvia from the animal slaughter practices at Smithfield and the numerous private abattoirs around the city. Smithfield thus became an emblematic object in the city's self-image and efforts to clean up its act.

Besides the waste was the incessant noise, which would go deep into the night. As Kean notes in *Animal Rights*, the noise narrative Martin and the Animals' Friend Society set in *The Animals' Friend* was at the forefront of a very successful animal rights campaign. The Society imbricated animal rights and Smithfield through sensationalist tones of intense animal suffering and the lawless, all-hours savagery. Those events also needed to be communicated to the powerful classes that didn't have to actually live near Smithfield. This drove an absent public sentiment against the Market's location and against its labourers. The animal rights debate, as it plays in the Smithfield case, contributes directly to the further demolition of the animal when the animal becomes a sterile object of mechanised manufacture (not even slaughter, really, as technological efficiency streamlines death in the public slaughterhouse). Just as troubling, the animal rights debate relies yet again upon a classist discourse that requires a bogeyman human target in its rhetorical form. The primary bogeyman in efforts to have the market removed, again, would prove to be the butcher and his associates even when they turned out to be correct about issues such as animal slaughter techniques and other practical considerations.

Slaughter reform, not only in England but also in the United States, France, Germany and elsewhere, introduced extensive new killing technologies and animal population management techniques throughout the nineteenth century. Today's antibiotics and CAFO architecture are clear results of this massive, ongoing aspect of human–animal cultural history. The nineteenth-century reforms took animal slaughter and processing out of the individual, private abattoirs and put them into the gleaming, towering new monuments to mechanised civic management and animal slaughter like the Metropolitan Cattle Market (now the Caledonian Market) at Islington. This figure of mechanised civic slaughter is the hallmark of modernity, as the new meat factories were some of the period's most anticipated and publicised civic achievements in Napoleon's Paris and in post-Smithfield London. Paula Young Lee, in her introduction to the edited volume *Meat, Modernity, and the Rise of the Slaughterhouse*, acknowledges the significant role Upton Sinclair's *The Jungle* played in public discourse around meat production, animal suffering and slaughterhouse practices. The suffering of animals was not as central in the outcry around Chicago's meat works as were the new horror of finding human parts in the consumers' meat products. Reminiscent of episodes in Frank Norris's monumental naturalist novel, *The Octopus: A Story of California*, in which the massive grain processor eats a character, Sinclair's novel features workers dying in the slaughterhouse and, likewise, being processed as meat that then goes out to customers. The novel of course also raised awareness of issues such as workers' rights and safety. She also acknowledges literature's role, in this case, in sparking political and legal change in the form of the 1906 Pure Food and Drug Act Theodore Roosevelt argued for.[42] Laws regulating slaughterhouse safety and general hygiene followed. Nevertheless, as Young Lee is quick to point out, '(n)either the misery of the workers nor the appalling conditions in which the animals were killed were meaningful factors in the political equation'.[43] The slaughterhouse machine was little changed, as far as workers' and animals' welfare was concerned. The only real impetus in any slaughter reform that did come to pass was the economic loss caused by already waning meat sales. The public had begun to consume less meat in the United States because of its generally poor, bruised or even decomposed condition and negative health impacts.[44]

This American meat machine legacy is vast. New York slaughter oversight and urban organisation led to the 1866 creation of the Metropolitan Board of Health and major slaughterhouse reforms in the latter part of the nineteenth century. Slaughter and butchery regulation had actually begun as early as 1676, and in 1806, New York City appointed a butchers' committee that would inspect the city's slaughterhouses.[45] Known problems with slaughterhouses, tanners and rendering plants, increasingly located in ever-denser urban settings through the exponential urban growth of the nineteenth century, led to widespread oversight and regulatory bodies but not to widespread enforcement. In fact, Jered Day claims that the anti-regulatory mood of the early nineteenth century in New York led to independent businessmen like butchers and tanners heavily influencing a broad economics of meat and animal processing in the city that also dictated specific geographic management. This history has strong similarities to aspects of the London situation, but does not entirely match all aspects at the same time. Some moments in slaughter reform predate London, as do reforms in Paris and other locations, but then some of the regulatory changes come later. The London Smithfield case is clearly part of a broad international meat history, and one that both American literary audiences and contemporary consumer-activists will recognise immediately from these preliminary American contexts, such as Sinclair's novel and current CAFO debates. Butchers in the New York context also have their place – perhaps Martin Scorsese's Bill the Butcher nativist from *Gangs of New York* ought to be reconsidered in this frame, for example. The British context, with its strong heritage of antecedent and resulting animal law and literatures on the nonhuman object, presents a singular study within the history of meat and civic erasure of its ideological and biological sources.

The direct relationship between literature and social organisation in the case of *The Jungle* has crucial precursors in the London case, and authors like Dickens wrote defences of the butchers in periodicals even while lamenting the squalor and chaos of Smithfield and its denizens.[46] British literature has fewer direct interventions in the meat industry than it does in the broader animal rights movement, despite extensive writings on the butchers, Smithfield and slaughter in general through the booming periodicals trade. Butchery in the penny dreadfuls, on the other hand, is a dominant trope. Butchers and butchery – meat trade labour and gruesome, heinous murder in equal parts – became one violent, bloody class of labourer. The pervasive social actor is a reminder of Poe's 'Man of the Crowd' catalogue of types, and this was also the way in which cabbies and vivisecting doctors were vilified at various points in animal rights actions in London throughout the nineteenth century. The butchers at Smithfield bear an inordinate industry burden in reform debate. A clearer sense of the role butchers played in London civic management and the public debates about inhuman urban conditions around Smithfield explicates the source of this negative trope beyond a simple notion of animal killing during a time that motivated extensive social change through the discourse of sympathy.

Butchers are one of the longest-standing organised labour groups in London, but their place in a slaughter system that was the target of major reform in the nineteenth century left them cast out of decent society, as so many diatribes against other forms of animal abuse coloured their targets. In 1624, Parliament introduced an Act to restrain butchers from grazing purchased animals in London for more than thirty days after purchase at the live animal markets, including of course the largest and most central, Smithfield.[47] The Free Butchers of London, a trade organisation, issued its Reasons against the bill.[48] The preamble begins precisely where the economic histories of American slaughter do. The butchers claim that, due to their mandatory seven years of apprenticeship learning the trade and specifically the proper pricing and selling points, they have a stronger claim to regulatory authority on aspects of meat production in the city such as city land use for animal fattening. The primary claims against the thirty-day limit are that transport over great distances (Wales and Scotland, for example) can cause the animals to lose significant amounts of weight or, in other cases, to overwork the muscle tissue that would become meat. Another concern, albeit one that could help arguments for Smithfield removal, was that it could take longer than thirty days to properly rest and re-fatten the animals since there would be competition for grazing space in the area given the heavy traffic.

This traffic in animals at Smithfield has been a known London feature dating at least back to the twelfth century, when William Fitzstephen wrote of the 'smooth field' (Smithfield was originally Smoothe-Field). Fitzstephen's account is clear: the market was already a large, bustling, varied affair with the biggest and best animals available for purchase.[49] By the early eighteenth century, when Daniel Defoe wrote of Smithfield, it was the greatest in the world. But as the Parliamentary and pamphlet histories show, Smithfield was beset by this contrast between its greatness and its unmanageable size and industry. Several different butcher groups wrote petitions to legislative changes to the Smithfield space, but there were a number of other market labour classes involved including graziers, salesmen and drivers. The graziers would have been hired middlemen who tended animals brought to the market, and as the market evolved, the butchers who would have done this part of the meat production process at the time of the 1624 pamphlet had already been split into these more specialised cogs in an expanded meat machine. The salesmen would work at Smithfield selling not to the public but to the various butchers. The drivers would have brought the cattle to market from out of town.

These different meat market classes were in direct competition with one another but also shared a Smithfield history that pitted them against other civic forces. Drovers, or drivers, were the middlemen who brought the animals into London, often from other nodes near, but still outside the main city – these were the criminal types behind the 'overdriving' of any livestock or transport animals in the early animal legislature. The most sensational target of the overdriving charge would have been the horse cabbies flogging animals in the emerging marketplace streets, which famously stunned Nietzsche. Horse floggings were a favourite anecdote of the animal rights arguments brought by upper class activists, precisely the classes that should bear witness to the most horse floggings: cab rides were expensive. The traffic congestion motivating the Smithfield debate – the clogged arteries of London – was due to meat market animal herding and storing. The savage nature of the drivers of Smithfield meat animals was legend.[50] Cabbies, drovers, butchers – the collective animal use and abuse spectacle at Smithfield turned them all into the public's whipping boys. The innards of the city works were to be kicked out, as far as public opinion was concerned.

What turned the public so adamantly against the butchers, ultimately, was not animal abuse at all but rather the increasing price of meat in a time that also saw increasing meat quality and safety concerns. Regardless of which kind of butcher one was, by the middle of the nineteenth century, the butchers were at the heart of public anger over the price of meat and blamed for all manner of commercial deceit. The jokes of the day about 'growlers' and 'meowers' – both suggesting stray pets had ended up on the butcher's block for public consumption – were based in some truth.[51] Such jokes, in stories like *Sweeney Todd* with its far more sinister meat, were actually marking the incredible public mistrust of butchers in London in the nineteenth century. The most lurid tales – and *Sweeney Todd* is certainly that – suggested an even more grisly mystery meat. Human meat, consumed unbeknownst by a ravenous public who could not get enough of the taste of delectable meat pies, was a figure that integrated the economic fears of a consuming public wary of price fixing with the justified fears of potentially harmful, diseased meat from parts – and bodies – unknown. All such fears coalesced in the figure of the butcher, who was both an economic agent and the one who slaughtered the animal in the disgusting basement abattoirs sullying local boroughs and littering the back alleys near Smithfield. That there were divisions of labour within the butchers' ranks was immaterial, and that was despite vocal opposition to Smithfield removal action brought by some butcher groups against others.

The cutting butcher dealt directly with the consuming individual.

The carcasse, or retail butcher, dealt with cutting butchers and perhaps to public houses. The killing butcher dispatched the animal. Some did all of this, some parts of it, some had other roles in the entire affair. All of these roles would be consolidated and streamlined in the public slaughterhouse, which was the city's response to an exploding population with an exploding meat consumption habit. Meat consumption in Great Britain began to exponentially increase by 1830.[52] By 1840, according to Richard Perren's calculations, Britain's per annum meat consumption crossed 1,000,000 tons for the first time. Perren notes that official records for Britain do not technically exist prior to 1867, but Perren also acknowledges that, when meat import first begins there in 1842, precise records *were* kept. Import in this case would be certainly from Ireland and from France and Germany, but then also in forms Perren does not track from later years of animal food imports such as Liebig Meat Extract, produced in Uruguay for British consumption after 1862. Perren also suggests that mere numbers of live animals or processed animal bodies would likely not suffice to account for gross production and its impact on consumption because 'imported animals did not necessarily weight the same as home-produced ones'.[53] This last point indicates that British husbandry and meat animal design had significant variations from practices and results elsewhere in Europe or in the United States, or at least that precise numbers on production via gross weight/meat output in the period 1831–1914, his focus, are hard to establish. Still, through all such qualifications of the data, Perren constructs an educated guess about meat consumption between 1831 and 1914. The per annum increase upon the 980,000 tons in 1831 (with no meat importation) hits 2,575,400 tons total by 1914, the close of his study of British agricultural and economic records, nearing a 300 per cent increase in British meat consumption, supplemented by a near even split of imported and domestic meat by 1914. Perren employs his findings in a more general statement about Britain's prosperity, claiming that the incredible increase of a number of 'the more expensive protein foods, like meat, butter, cheese and eggs' show clear improvement in overall living standards. His 'overall living standards' here of course do not include the animals' lives, but he cites the major importance of meat production to the overall British agricultural economy. Although Perren's focus is of course the human progress meat production and consumption indicate, the case for meat's essential role in Britain's total economic standing and social identity made by him and by others, such as Ben Rogers, firmly establish that this incredible period of economic development and social improvement rides, quite literally, on the backs of both animals built in and brought into the country.[54]

The changes in animal husbandry and meat production leading up to the Smithfield heyday in London both inaugurate and then respond to increasing demand for meat among the general populous. The butchers pre-exist the major advances in husbandry of the eighteenth century. The butchers also enjoy the height of British livestock production just as that peak turns into a crisis of overpopulation at Smithfield and in London as a whole. After the major population explosion heading into the nineteenth century, the butchers had a captive audience in the lower classes clamouring to partake in the good life, and British meat eating was an age-old tradition. Smithfield contributes to the city's hygiene and traffic issues in the middle decades of the nineteenth century. None of this, according to Perren, seems to curb meat consumption, and even the concerns about disease do not calm demand. Smithfield reform was a corrective measure ensuring the meat trade could continue and expand.

The butchers, as the public's primary contact with the entirety of the meat trade, end up front and centre as major targets for Smithfield opponents capitalising on the public's dearest complaint. Whether they lived near the nightly Smithfield din the animal rights activists harped on about or not, and whether they were in the same neighbourhood as the dark butchers' abattoirs of the darkest horror stories, Londoners saw the butchers as adversaries. The public blamed the butchers for the high prices, and beginning before the nineteenth century, there is a clear history of butchers themselves bringing the issue to Parliament and to the public in pamphlet form. The butchers' complaints were most often against one another. Those carcasse, retail and killing butcher specialisations within the general butchery trade also became competitors with one another.

In 1796, a committee in the House of Commons issued its report in response to a Retail Butchers' petition. The Cutting Butchers, in 1795, had submitted a petition complaining of monopolies above their station in the meat production and distribution chain.[55] The appeal frames the complaint as a service to the poor of London, and the opening also complains of unregulated price fixing these cutting butchers – the butchers who sold meat directly to the consumers after it passed through several previous agents as live animals and then as carcasses in this case – had to contend with at the market. Their argument was that they then were forced to pass on costs to the consumers. Butchers, like bakers in London at this time, were frequent targets of complaints about the high price of food in a vast, growing metropolis.[56] The Philanthropic Butcher, articulating a monopolistic but evasive supply machine of foodstuff he is subject to as much as the baker to the corn (grain) markets, cannily aligns the two supply trades within the early passages of the petition:

> The difficulty of ascertaining truth, is more conducive to the interests of the fraudulent than to the just, and operates, but too frequently, to make the innocent suffer the guilty; hence arise those ill-directed murmurings from a suffering, but undiscriminating multitude, towards the butcher and baker, which should be leveled at higher agents; it is with Smithfield Market, as with the Corn Market, where the price is not regulated by quantity of meal, but the artifices of seller.[57]

The 'base practices' of Smithfield in this petition do not relate at all to animal concern, which is no surprise to anyone not already concerned about animal concern. Accusing the butchers of sentimental humanity might still be effective, however. The terrible state of affairs at Smithfield concerning the cutting butchers, who would be unlikely animal rights activists at best, was in fact the complex retail games played by graziers, carcasse butchers and salesmen against the direct meat outlet cutting butchers. And yet the language of an 'innocent' and 'suffering ... undiscriminating multitude' in 'murmurings' under the yoke of injustice is precisely the claim of a greater humanity. Perhaps it is the economics of humanity, and not the virtue, but it is humanity nonetheless, in all its mobile affection.

The petition makes a case for prohibiting any animal slaughter within ten miles of the city; but the case has nothing at all to do with the cases that would be made in the 1852 Smithfield Removal Act that formally removed live animals and slaughter from the location. The 1795 petition wanted the slaughtering trade removed from Smithfield because the location had become home to a resale practice wherein agents would purchase live animals on one side of the market and then sell them at a price increase on the other side of the market. The market's size was about five acres, but the din and confusion of such a site, with thousands of cattle, sheep, pigs and poultry at any given time, made it seem wholly impenetrable. The Philanthropic Butcher describes the collusion of carcasse butchers and graziers in dark terms: 'The Smithfield Wickedness', 'evil agent(s)' working for the 'destruction' of cutting butchers and the public. Smithfield salesmen take advantage of outsiders and newcomers who are not 'one of the gang', according to the petition. The Philanthropic Butcher's populist appeal highlights themes of exclusivity and maliciousness in his criticism of the animal handlers and sellers at Smithfield: 'The dark cunning with which the villainy of Smithfield is pursued, renders it almost inscrutable, yet it all tends to the disadvantage of the Cutting Butcher, in the first instance, and the Public eventually.'[58]

The petition thus attempts to align the most frequent target of public complaint about high meat prices – the direct vendor, the cutting butcher – with the suffering public by blaming a sinister, inaccessible monopoly. This body afflicts London with impoverished strife while 'Society' refuses to critically examine the massive economic infrastructure of both the Corn and Meat markets the city's complaints are levied against. The Philanthropic Butcher synthesises his case, ultimately, in a clear complaint against enclosure: 'The great primary cause of this temporary misery is the consolidation of little farms into great farms, yet the calamity, as it is, might be thus reduced if not presented.'[59] The butcher's solution was surely an ill-fated suggestion: 'No person should be permitted to export corn or cattle.'[60] The Philanthropic Butcher also complains that those cattle that do make their way to Smithfield are not the best cattle, yet the cutting/retail butcher must still pay top price for these animals. This recalls the complaint of the butchers in 1624, in the petition against the bill to prohibit excessive grazing of animals owned by butchers, in which the leanness of cattle that travelled long distances from outside the city had to be mitigated by an appropriate re-fattening. Lending at least some circumstantial credence to the 1795 cutting/retail butchers' complaint of an unwieldy food production and distribution machine, 1625 language does not distinguish here between the grazier, carcasse butcher and cutting/retail butcher now pitted against each other and the consuming public. The consuming public increased roughly threefold between 1625 and 1795, and so perhaps it is only fitting that meat management staffing underwent similar multiplication.

The conclusions of the Philanthropic Butcher include a complaint about horses, which require corn (grain) that might otherwise go toward the feeding of other animals. But the complaint about horses, which would in 1795 still have been vital to general transport and farm labour, among other uses, seems particularly chosen for its relation to a broader critique of 'fashion' and unnecessary habits of consumption. The horse, according to the Philanthropic Butcher, is an emblem of the general wastefulness of an 'Epicurean' class. The carcasse butchers are unconcerned with price inflations they either can weather or do not incur themselves, and are, according to the Philanthropic Butcher, 'men of large property' many retired already, in an 'overgrown' class none challenges because of their entrenched and controlling position.[61]

None of these parties – the salesmen, graziers, carcasse butchers and higher classes feeding their useless horses – are concerned with food supply or affordable food for the public. The Philanthropic Butcher's diatribe on horses and grain in a subsection, 'The State and Management of Grain', pits food against taste:

> As the cultivation of every species of grain is materially connected with the progress and advancement of animal food, respecting both its *existence* and

its *price*, I implore the Legislature to pay some attention to the following declaration – *viz. that one third of the produce of this land, is devoured by Horses*, who consume on an average half a bushel of corn daily, and if the establishment of Horses were diminished, we should have more cows, more sheep, more veal, more bread, butter, cheese, bacon, beer, ale, soap, candles, leather, wool, &c. &c. and shall such a host of blessings be blindly sacrificed upon the polluted altars of FASHION. Good God! Is there more solicitude to keep the equipage sumptuous, then the People comfortable? – may that Epicurean perish who upholds the chilling thought.[62]

The Philanthropic Butcher then calls for a remedy to the problem of food supply in London, arguing against excesses that serve only to 'pamper, not satiate, the appetites of one or two idle, worthless sprigs of Distinction; while the virtuous and meritorious labourer is fainting at his loom for want of nourishment'.[63] The Philanthropic Butcher lists the four primary points from his 'authentic representations' of the Smithfield Market near the end of the petition:

1st. The Carcasse Butcher, causes an advance of price in the markets of the metropolis, generally speaking, of one penny, or three half-pence per pound, independent of natural necessity.
2dly. The Carcasse Butcher, by this artificial management of the markets, gives birth to all that opprobrium and rage administered by the public towards the Cutting Butcher, who is innocent of the evil altogether.
3dly. The Carcasse Butchers, have increased the number of beasts they kill, and raised their demands for all, at this precise point of time, although the idea is circulated, that cattle were never so scarce in this century!
4thly. The Carcasse Butchers, attend all the chartered markets within fifty miles of London; although those markets were established and intended for the accommodation of the Country Butchers, and not for the Carcasse Butchers of Smithfield; and it is from this measure of monopoly, more than any other, that we are to ascribe every misfortune, that has, or may arise, from the dearness of provisions. – This is an alarming and increasing evil, and must be completely done away by the government, for the preservation of common happiness and social order.[64]

The Philanthropic Butcher must be at least generally correct on the question of supply, as Perren's numbers verify. His appeal to social order matches all of the most sensible, civilised calls of the animal rights activists or any other moralising community in the new City Beautiful Syndrome – clearly, these are not the savage brutes of widespread repute. Or, perhaps more appropriately, that charge itself seeks out a vilifying animal claim where it purports animal concern and humane inclusiveness.

The offending list of pamphlets attending the Smithfield Removal Act include *Cursory remarks on the evil tendency of unrestrained cruelty : particularly on that practised in Smithfield Market*, by Elizabeth Coltman (1823), *The question of Smithfield Market fully considered*, author Clericus (1837) and *An appeal to the British public, or, The abuses of Smithfield Market and the advantages of a new central cattle market : fairly considered*, published in 1850. The 1823 text covers standard animal concern ground and reiterates ideas about the low life forms at Smithfield. This includes the dirty business dealings, the crude men labouring there, the issues with alcohol and the unsafe conditions of a writhing, stinking animal space. The 1850 text moves from these appeals to decency and public outrage to then make a clear, measured argument for what turns out to be the chosen alternative, a new 'central' cattle market. In fact, the market that replaces Smithfield is further from the city centre, not nearer, but in the context of slaughter reform, this centralisation should be read as the mitigation of sprawling, unregulated sites of slaughter and distribution in the private abattoirs around the city.

The city's argument to itself in Smithfield reform debates becomes, effectively, that a regulated meat industry will solve the public health and quality concerns, silence the very vocal anti-cruelty groups by establishing animal welfare in the mechanised meat production industry, and soothe urban traffic congestion and population impaction issues around Smithfield. The butchers became a crucial, much-maligned stand-in for all of these aspects. The unregulated abattoirs were filthy and had no running water. Their dark basement locations, wretched air and the terrible noises emanating from them fed an active urban imaginary and, thanks to the gruesome visible effluvia and offal from butchers' abattoirs, did little to quell those concerns. The butchers, lumped in with drivers and others at Smithfield and in the vicinity, were the final abusers of the animals and, on top of it all, were often perceived as drunken killers with horrible tools and skills that eventually fed an active literary imagination. Butchers were terrifying, expert disassemblers of flesh with the equipment to do the best (worst) possible job of a killing. Again, their dark alley locations, and then their dark basement workspaces besides that, did little to ease fears about inscrutable, hard butchers. And finally, the butchers' numbers, and the growing difficulty for community members at Smithfield and in butchers' shops to get a firm sense of market supply and fair rates, went hand in hand with the general increase in commercial traffic through London. Similar to the mass-produced confusion of the penny dreadful business discussed in parts of Chapter 3, meat itself had become a nonhuman object without animals and the butchers, with the rest of the Smithfield system, comprised a convoluted, anonymous but decidedly untrustworthy group.

Another treatise title shows that the major concern regarding Smithfield begins at the end of the eighteenth century with animal concern as a mere backdrop. Retail, or cutting butchers, were already bearing the brunt of public displeasure with high meat prices and market complaints, and so they organised a response in the form of parliamentary petitions that took on the whole practical economic structure of the market in an effort to shift blame to a broader target besides just themselves and, ostensibly, truly correct market woes that had made some aspects of the business less profitable and free than others: *An effectual cure for the high prices of butchers' meat : Smithfield Market, an essay: including a plan for the better regulation of drovers, the sale of live stock in the London Market, and for abolishing the trade of a wholesale butcher. With a reply to the report of the committee of wholesale butchers by Henry King and J. Edmunds. Mark now, how plain a tale shall put them down*, sold by W. Bingley, Red Lion Passage, Fleet Street, 1796.

As meat prices rose at rates similar to the bread prices that had led to widespread anger and resentment in the late eighteenth century, one curious aspect of Martin's arguments is that he represents the business interests of other businesses at Smithfield as a means of convincing his audience of his case. Presumably, the community was equally angry at the high prices in other trades. The specific animality of the meat trade was itself to blame, and thus the reform and removal actions were doubly anti-animal. Kean discusses the general public disgust at the market's live animal masses, including the resulting waste, noise and slaughter residue. But Kean also notes in the same breath that Martin circulates a petition to 'establish an inquiry into the manner in which cattle were driven and the conditions in which they were kept at the market'.[65] The petitioners also demanded investigation into the fact that local businessmen that were not in the meat trade were disturbed by the meat market's daily affairs, and especially by the noise. Local residents, particularly at night when the visible scene diminished, 'were prevented from sleeping "as the dreadful blows inflicted on the cattle are distinctly heard in their bedrooms"'.[66] Inconvenience trumped ethics.

The formal removal of the live Smithfield Market from the heart of London only re-established the divided sense of human–animal community. Kean surveys some periodicals of the day, and writers like Dickens and Hardy documented in their fiction that the city had become a dense association of animal noises, smells and bodies in the same thoroughfares humans were crammed into.[67] The sounds of animals being driven to market or of horses being flogged in the street by cartmen and cabbies completely overwhelmed Londoners while the problem of animal waste and offal in the slaughter and butchering process had become an entirely separate civic concern as more knowledge of hygiene and disease dictated the healthiest organisation of city space and waste management. Epizootic research, begun in close relation to animal slaughter in Scotland, was quickly imported to England.[68] There was also an intensive cemetery movement, discussed briefly again in Chapter 3, culminating in the Magnificent Seven cemeteries being founded around the main London city expanse to deal with the problem of dead human body storage. The stories of dead bodies floating in the Thames and of new private funeral houses in London surely added to the city's growing identification with the horror of intersecting communities of living, dead, human, animal and more. The problems needed to be solved, London needed to be improved. Humanity depended upon it.

Metcalfe suggests that the debates and removal efforts followed a general 'Victorian' trend toward a 'religion of humanity', which she borrows from Gertrude Himmelfarb's 1968 *Victorian Minds*. The arguments coming before Parliament against various forms of animal cruelty, including those practiced at Smithfield and forms of entertainment such as baiting, seem to support this view. The activism against high meat prices and monopoly seem to have been more instrumental in market removal than arguments about public health and common decency, but the 'improvable subject' tones applied in the rhetoric of anti-cruelty measures, including those related to Smithfield Market, also inform claims cutting butchers made against other market agents who damaged the meat somehow. These butchers, as the petitions show, did not trust other parts of the Smithfield labour chain such as drovers and graziers, to properly manage the livestock en route. Butchers in the 1624 petition were also the graziers. That petition sought to convince London not to impose grazing limits of thirty days upon the meat trade. The butchers were at least unified, at that time, in their opposition to regulation of their business, and their primary argument against the grazing limits was that the animals would lose weight due to the duration and the stresses of their travel. The petition also had language suggesting that the drovers might not have been as attentive to the livestock's food needs as they could have been.

By the 1795 petition, the butchers were further down the chain of purchase and exchange from the original rural animal sources. Drovers, graziers and several different classes of butcher all dealt with the live animals and their eventual slaughter and sale. The arguments about Smithfield in the nineteenth century, including the butchers' petitions, had also begun to blame the ubiquitous middlemen of the trade. These were men who would purchase animals on one side of Smithfield and then resell them on the other side.[69] Such agents, who had no skill besides price driving, were part of the general trouble with price fixing at Smithfield. The other serious charge levied by the butchers was about the seeming monopoly there, as previously discussed. Economic concerns led the charge in some significant portion of these foundational anti-cruelty laws. The decisive erasure of the basis of meat production – the living animal – from Smithfield Market, which remains to this day a cut meat market and which has seen technical advances including underground rail transport and refrigeration in the ensuing 160 years, ushers in the contemporary meat-consumer mode in no uncertain terms.

The welfarist position on humane driving and slaughter technologies and the cellophane package of red that stands in for dead animal parts to the modern consumer carry on this erasive legacy, in which the disassembly of the animal into parts or even into new weird substances and entirely manufactured food consumption overtake prior modes of interspecies community. One such weird substance, previously mentioned, was the Liebig meat extract manufactured in Uruguay starting in the 1860s. Justus von Liebig (1803–73) was a German chemist known chiefly as the 'father of fertiliser' for his work on nitrogen fixing in agriculture. But Liebig also devised a meat 'extract' process whereby 30 to 5 lb of beef could be turned into roughly one pound of 'essence', as Richard Perren terms the product.[70] One German history of the Liebig *Fleischextrakt* describes a *Brühe*, or broth, Liebig and his students made during the extraction experiments.[71] This was a soupy mixture that, after soaking meat in heated water, could be reduced to a sort of paste that was primarily meat stuff for those who could not afford actual meat. The problem was that producing the meat to reduce into meat essence was far too expensive in Europe to lead to a suitable product and cost for wide consumption – and von Liebig was indeed thinking in utilitarian terms. Production was thus exported to Uruguay.

The product he invented, and his company, changed hands and names a few times, but one can still purchase Oxo Brand meat products, perhaps most akin to what the US consumer would know as beef bouillon. The formula, however, is now a yeast extract instead of beef as of 2004. This raises all sorts of questions about the idea of meat the modern consumer is left with in the wake of the animal erasures in simply the 'real' meat production. Oxo is a bit before, but along the same lines as the Bovril 'fluid beef' invented by John Lawson Johnson in the 1870s for warring soldiers, and so its origins are intimately tied to the globalising war machine as well as the meat production industry. The Oxo Company ingeniously established its brand along the Thames via masonry despite laws against riverside billboard and other advertis-

Figure 2 OXO Tower, London. Used by permission of walklondon.com.

ing. Here's the building on the right, in recent times, across the river from 30 St Mary Axe ('The Gherkin') (Figure 2).

The distinctive container for Bovril has always had a rather bulbous profile, and Bovril advertisements from the late nineteenth century provide endless entertainment around the thinking they inspire on the question of disintegrating the animal body to then incorporate it into the human body (Figure 3). Bovril reissued a number of its early container covers in 2015 as a 125th anniversary commemoration. Searching through the various advertising campaigns and packaging slogans in the Bovril annals leads to endless cultural analysis, and some are particularly revealing. Some are curiously ambiguous on all of the intersecting animal concerns, technological reductions and disintegrations, and themes of vitality and beastliness. One original advertising image, a version of which is now part of the Victoria and Albert Museum collection, invokes the 'brother' of Coleridge's 'To a Young Ass' in a curious form of apostrophe. A weeping ox looks down upon a Bovril jar with the caption 'Alas! My poor Brother.' Other examples make the ties between national pride, duty and meat consumption quite clear (Figure 4).

Whatever the animal concern was to accomplish in the period, its ultimate, most ubiquitous product has been the welfarist-industrial subjection of animal lives to a walking death. This erasure of life from the business of food production, or this invention of meat without animals,

Figure 3 Bovril puts beef into you. Public domain.

has a parallel history in the abjection of labouring classes from the civilised society Londoners – some Londoners, at least – saw themselves as. There is a shared abjection. This time, it is not a peasant poet and a trembling mouse unified in mutual suffering, but the killer and the killed themselves united in a classist, categorical urban ideal in response to the inability to process the Smithfield scene and on the wings of the sweeping economic-industrial interests of London's upper classes.

The commemorative markers at Smithfield today include a replica of the things like the Worshipful Company of Poulters' Arms, replete with personified animal actors bowing to professional duty in holy obeisance and militant fealty (Figure 5). The commemorative bench on the Square off to the south-east corner of the current cut meat market site, which has a large Victorian-era building dating to just after removal of the animal yards, is a writhing, postmodern reminder of the city's dense his-

Meat without Animals 109

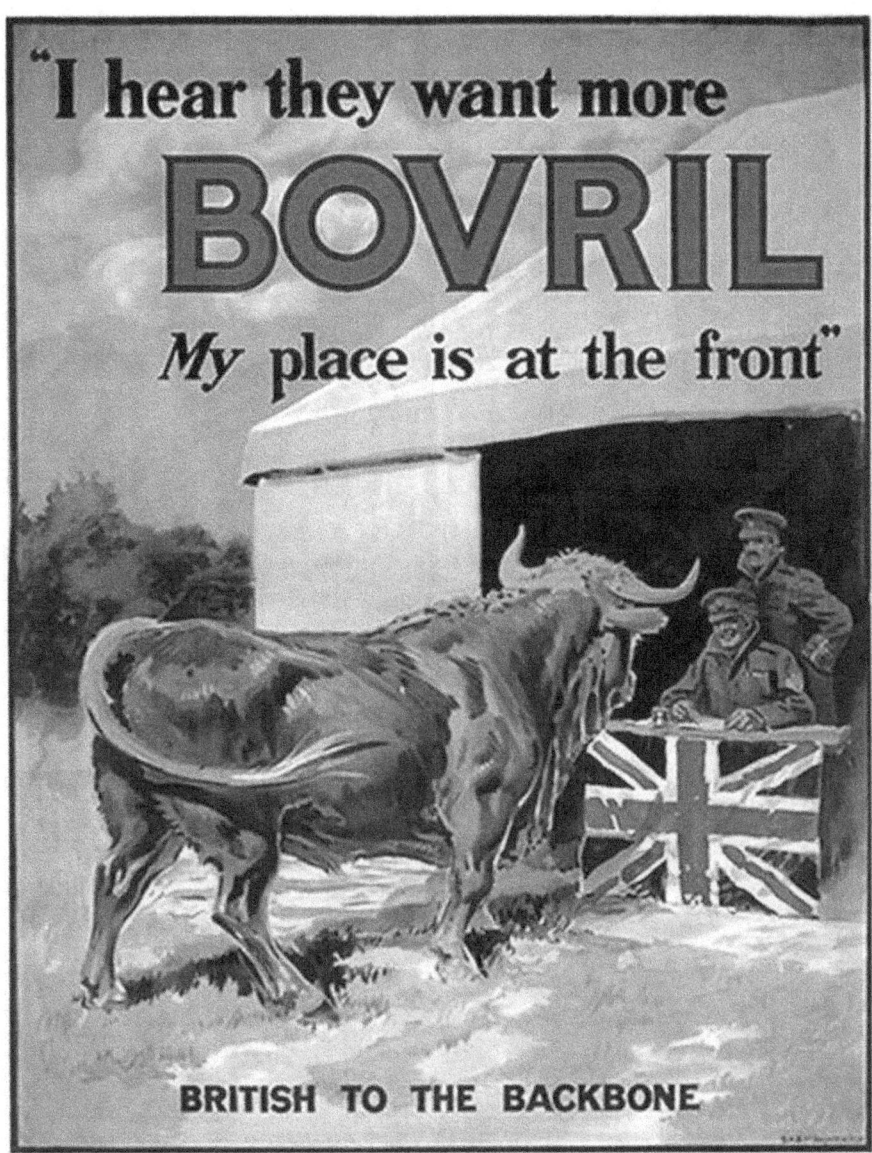

Figure 4 Bovril at the front. Public domain.

torical entanglements (Figure 6). On the bench are recognisable quotes from *Oliver Twist*, Fitz-Stephen and the animal concern movement in London through the years, staged to intersect in the barest suggestion of line and structure yet also juxtaposed along rhizomatic planes and vectors. Yet one is always sitting on the inscribed animal history of

Figure 5 Smithfield Poulters' Company Arms. Photograph by Ted Geier.

Figure 6 Smithfield commemorative bench (full). Photograph by Ted Geier.

Figure 7 Smithfield commemorative bench (detail – Smoothe-Field). Photograph by Ted Geier.

the place, as the quotes are not on the vertical axes (Figure 7). There is another London history coalescing at Smithfield in the early twenty-first century, as the venerable Museum of London will move to the site and open in 2021. Imagining a more direct sign of the London's historical production at Smithfield seems impossible (Figure 8). In contrast to the condensed, textual animal history etched into the bench, the majority of consumers post-Smithfield can easily escape the animal fact of meat. As there is no meat in the Bovril essence, there is no animal in meat once the animal has been removed from the densely civic origins of meat production, circulation and consumption, and this is Smithfield's legacy. This erasure began in London even earlier than the Smithfield removal. While, certainly, the majority of butchers' rows and the meat market itself were all within the relatively small but heavily trafficked city centre, meat purchase did not itself have to take place in proximity to the massive Smithfield site. As Dickens's 'Expedition' chapter in *Oliver Twist* neatly shows, Smithfield impresses itself upon all the senses but is but one moment of a traipse across London. And, as Dickens and Hardy later also make clear, Smithfield is not really Smithfield unless it is market day. The spectacle of high animal traffic and exchange for

Figure 8 Smithfield commemorative bench (detail – 'The bleating of sheep'). Photograph by Ted Geier.

market day is then not the routine animal encounter of the London denizen even in the Smithfield heyday. Instead, Smithfield was already a highly specialised spectacle. Nevertheless, a customer would still have gone to market to purchase some animal body part, as one still may. In the nineteenth century, however, meat canning or tinning became a standard method of preserving – not always successfully – meat for transport on, for example, British Navy expeditions.[72]

The most gruesome aspect of London's meat production was to have been the private basement abattoir, though the comparatively open-air killing stalls were no less disturbing by many accounts. Here, butchers would kill the animals they had purchased live at Smithfield, for example. The stench, particularly in summer, was total, permeating the abattoir and street spaces nearby. This bad air in butchers' quarters immediately calls to mind the oppressive fog of Dickens's impoverished London and the official, bureaucratic miasma of the texts examined in Chapter 3. The arguments for Smithfield's removal paralleled arguments for a new, more hygienic (not necessarily more humane) way to kill animals. However, the new Metropolitan Market at Islington that would replace the mass live animal market at Smithfield employed bureaucratic precision to new heights, in the process completely removing not only live animals and numerous hidden sites of slaughter from an impacted city centre, but the very knowledge of and intimacy with the animals that became meat in the new London meat architecture. In effect, the successful movement to silence animal suffering in the city centre and 'clean up' slaughter's act produced a far worse horror: meat was a clean, portable, alien object all its own with no history as an animal and no prior object status in the human community. The animal had been completely abjected from the production of meat for mass consumption quite precisely because of how horrible the entire affair had become. It was perhaps the grandest lie the contemporary urban world ever managed to sell itself.

The particularly dreadful, horrifying nature of untrustworthy and possibly sinister food supplies – specific to meat products – went hand in hand with the intensive renovation of city centre meat market and slaughter practices codified in the 1852 Smithfield Market Removal Act and the decline in private basement abattoirs as primary butchery sites after market sale of live animals and carcasses. And as the history of livestock management, meat production and slaughter in London show, the butchers operating in those private spaces were vilified and attacked for problems such as high meat prices and strains on city land through the fattening of their animals (which arrived from outside the city). As independent, identifiable vendors the consuming public had its only contact with when acquiring meat stuffs, the butchers operating out of dark, secret basement spaces with untold contraptions and cutting implements made for a particularly dense figure of public safety, health and economic strife in the period. By the beginning of the nineteenth century, the cutting butchers worked to remedy price fixing at Smithfield because they had been receiving such a landslide of public displeasure and aggression due to the very real high price of meat. Further, independent tradesmen associated with animal work, such as cabbies and butchers, would invariably be lumped together with drunk bear- and badger-baiting parties as the 'lower' class of men responsible for the animal suffering Victorian-era animal concern movements and parliamentary debate highlighted in early animal rights laws. The butcher was an especially 'lowly' professional who also was perceived to be depraved and potentially malignant. The sounds, smells and unreliable meat quality the consuming public associated with its direct suppliers, the individual butchers, contributed to a picture of the basement killer and meat food producer dominated by the insidious horror of blank, inscrutable meat products like Sweeney Todd's meat pies.

Smithfield Market in London was the site of spectacles like well-attended public executions and the Bartholomew Fair. Anxieties about untraceable meat sources and contamination at Smithfield inflected popular literature such as *Sweeney Todd*. On the eve of modern animal rights law, Smithfield Market removal from the city centre of London and advancements in slaughter technique coalesced as a target of animal rights activism, producing increased, 'efficient' livestock production, management, slaughter and distribution. This gruesome irony was all part of shifts in the geographic and spatial conception of city space as the world's leading mass metropolis articulated itself. By 1855, the Fair was ended and the live animals at Smithfield – along with their suffering – were erased from the city centre, moved to an inscrutable, out of the way, 'public' abattoir. Animal traffic was rerouted. Meat became a hygienic, humane object with no trace of the live animal on it. More animals could be killed, faster, more quietly, and thus modern meat was born hand in hand with modern urban space.

Notes

1. Foucault, Michel. *Discipline and Punish: The Birth of the Prison*, trans. Alan Sheridan. Vintage, 1995, p. 3.
2. Contemporary tourism synopsis, 'In Search of London's Execution Sites', *Londonist*, 11 January 2012.
3. Ritvo, p. 39.
4. See: Morton, 'The Mesh', in *Environmental Criticism for the Twenty-First Century*, ed. Stephanie LeMenager, Teresa Shewry, and Ken Hiltner. Routledge, 2011, pp. 19–30, and in particular pp. 20–1.
5. Websites tracking the animal-in-your-everything are by now ubiquitous and helpful for those hoping to curb some of their animal consumption. One of the stronger recent studies of this ubiquitous disassembly and 'biotic' reassignment structure is Nicole Shukin's *Animal Capital: Rendering Life in Biopolitical Times*. University of Minnesota Press, 2009.
6. See: Chambers, J. D. and G. E. Mingay. *The Agricultural Revolution 1750–1880*. Schocken, 1966; Neeson, J. M. *Commoners: Common Right, Enclosure and Social Change in England, 1700–1820*. Cambridge University Press, 1993; and Overton, Mark. *The Transformation of the Agrarian Economy 1500–1850*. Cambridge University Press, 1996.
7. Works include: Cobbett, William. *Cottage Economy: Containing Information relative to the brewing of BEER, making of BREAD, keeping of COWS, PIGS, BEES, EWES, GOATS, PULTRY and RABBITS, and relative to other matters deemed useful in the conducting of the Affairs of a Labourer's Family*. C. Clement, 1822; Godwin, William. *Of Population. An Enquiry Concerning the Power of Increase in the Numbers of Mankind, Being an Answer to Mr. Malthus's Essay on that Subject*. Longman, Hurst, Rees, Ornie & Brown, 1820; and Malthus, Thomas. *An Essay on the Principle of Population as it Effects the Future Improvement*

    of Society. J. Johnson, 1798. Marx responded to and referred to each variously.
8. Hall, Stephen J. G. and Juliet Clutton-Brock. *Two Hundred Years of British Farm Livestock*. British Museum (Natural History), 1989, p. 12.
9. Hall and Clutton-Brock, pp. 12–13.
10. Hilda Kean's chapter, 'Sight, Spectacle, and Education' in *Animal Rights* tracks Smithfield's development and the public interaction with sites (sights) of cruelty against livestock including whipping, slaughter, overdriving and overworking, and the ways in which Smithfield animal owners adapted to public concern for animal welfare by working at night and adopting other evasive means before legal reform formally censured their practices. See Kean, pp. 39–69.
11. Menely, Tobias. *The Animal Claim: Sensibility and the Creaturely Voice*. Chicago University Press, 2015, pp. 181–6.
12. Boddice, Rob. *A History of Attitudes and Behaviours toward Animals in Eighteenth- and Nineteenth-century Britain: Anthropocentrism and the Emergence of Animals*. Mellen, 2009.
13. Boddice, pp. 169–70.
14. Boddice, p. 169, and citing Shevawn Lynam's biography of Martin, *Humanity Dick Martin: 'King of Connemara' 1754–1834*. Lilliput Press, 1997, pp. 194–6.
15. Available at: <web.archive.org/web/20141030063347/http://www.animal-rightshistory.org/animal-rights-law/romantic-legislation/1822-uk-act-ill-treatment-cattle.htm> (last accessed 1 December 2016).
16. An Act to prevent the Mischiefs that arise from driving Cattle within the Cities of London and Westminster, and Liberties thereof, and the Bills of Mortality. The Seventh Session of the Thirteenth Parliament of Great Britain, Cap. 87. Eyre and Strahan, 1775.
17. Another period marker to be considered is the English Protection of Animals Act of 1911, delineating and banning specific acts of cruelty and still in force today.
18. Kenyon-Jones, p. 80.
19. Perkins, p. 4.
20. See, for example: Morton, 'Nature and culture', in *The Cambridge Companion to Shelley*, ed. Morton. Cambridge University Press, 2006, pp. 203–4 on vegetarianism as escapist consumer practice in particular. See also: Morton, *Shelley and the Revolution in Taste: The Body and the Natural World*. Cambridge University Press, 1995.
21. Kenyon-Jones, p. 80.
22. Cited in Perkins, p. 19.
23. Kean, p. 61 and quoting *The Voice of Humanity*, Vol. II, p. 2.
24. See: Kean and also Metcalfe.
25. Richetti, John. *The Life of Daniel Defoe: A Critical Biography*. Wiley-Blackwell, 2005, p. 333 and quoting Defoe, *A Tour Thro' the Whole Island of Great Britain*, Vol. II, p. 91.
26. Dickens, Charles. *Oliver Twist*. New York: Barnes & Noble Classics, 2004, pp. 188–9.
27. See, for example, the work of Georg Simmel or of Walter Benjamin.
28. Kean, p. 62, and quoting *The Voice of Humanity*, 1827, p. 27.

29. Kean, p. 62, and quoting *The Voice of Humanity*, p. 6.
30. MacLachlan, Ian. 'Humanitarian Reform, Slaughter Technology, and Butcher Resistance in Nineteenth-Century Britain', in *Meat, Modernity, and the Rise of the Slaughterhouse*, ed. Paula Young Lee. University of New Hampshire Press, 2008, pp. 111–12 and quoting Verschoyle, John. *Slaughter-house Reform*. Humanitarian League, 1903, p. 7 as well as 'Mr. E.W. Darby on Humane Slaughtering', *Meat Trades' Journal*, 351 (16 April 1896), p. 1008.
31. See MacLachlan, pp. 117–26.
32. Metcalfe, p. 38.
33. Kean, p. 59.
34. Metcalfe, p. 39.
35. Jones, Phillip E. *The Butchers of London: A History of the Worshipful Company of the Butchers of the City of London*. London: Secker & Warburg, 1976, pp. 1–2.
36. Jones, p. ix.
37. Jones, p. 75.
38. See: Raven, James. *Bookscape: Geographies of Printing and Publishing in London before 1800*. University of Chicago Press/The British Library, 2014.
39. Velten, Hannah. *Beastly London: A History of Animals in the City*. Reaktion, 2013, p. 28.
40. London after the Great Fire had no shortage of famous city planners, including Peel and Wren. Few histories of the city omit some mention of these and others, and there are a number of very readable books on the subject such as the urban historian, Leo Hollis's *London Rising: The Men Who Made Modern London*. Walker/Macmillan, 2008. Metcalf and others consider the sense of London and its space, and there are numerous studies of the changing conception of the city in the period. One excellent, relatively recent comprehensive study of nineteenth-century London city space planning that would come into conflict with mid-century population and traffic increases is: Arnold, Dana. *Rural Urbanism: London Landscapes in the Early Nineteenth Century*. Manchester University Press, 2005. David Harvey's study of Hauptmann's revision of Paris and the consequences for experience and thinking in the period is also instructive. See: *Paris: Capital of Modernity*. Routledge, 2005.
41. See in particular Metcalfe's chapter on public health and Smithfield, pp. 99–112.
42. Young Lee, p. 1.
43. Young Lee, p. 1.
44. Young Lee, p. 3, and throughout subsequent chapters by other contributors.
45. On New York City's reforms, see: Day, Jered. 'Butchers, Tanners, and Tallow Chandlers: The Geography of Slaughtering in Early Nineteenth-century New York City', in Young Lee, pp. 178–97.
46. Metcalfe and others cite the Dickens description, 'The Butcher', from Dickens, *All the Year Round*, XIX:453 (28 December 1867). Published at No. 26 Wellington Street; and by Messrs. Chapman and Hall, 193 Piccadilly, 1868, pp. 54–5. Joseph McLaughlin directed me to a separate article by Dickens on Smithfield in *Household Words*, in which Dickens

exhibits full familiarity with the humanitarian streak in cattle slaughter, whereby animals should be 'killed "comfortably."' *Household Words*, 6 (4 May 1850), p. 121.
47. *Third Report of the Royal Commission on Historical Manuscripts*. Eyre and Spottiswoode, 1872, p. 31.
48. See also: Lemon, Robert. *Catalogue of a Collection of Printed Broadsides*. The Society of Antiquaries of London, 1866, p. 62.
49. Fitzstephen, William. *A Description of London*, ca. 1174/1183. Reference here is from: *Fitz-Stephen's Description of the City of London, Newly Translated from the Latin*. B. White, 1772, p. 36.
50. See: Bosner, Kenneth. *The Drovers: Who They Were and How They Went, An Epic of the English Countryside*. MacMillan, 1970.
51. Although a longer discussion of differing cultural perspectives on meat sources is appropriate to the issue, cat and dog meat fears persist, as indicated by a March 2013 piece in the *Mirror*, 'Dog or cat in our curry: Fears over "mystery meat" in takeaway which has baffled experts'. 'Take away' food is precisely what Mrs. Lovett's meat pies were. Available at: <www.mirror.co.uk/news/uk-news/dog-cat-curry-fears-over-1789118> (last accessed 1 December 2016).
52. See: Perren, Richard. *The Meat Trade in Britain 1840-1914*. Routledge, 1978. See also: Perren, *Taste, Trade and Technology*. Ashgate, 2006.
53. Perren, *The Meat Trade*, p. 2.
54. See Rogers's *Beef and Liberty: Roast Beef, John Bull and the English Patriots*. Chatto & Windus, 2003.
55. *Monopoly. Price Sixpence. The Cutting Butchers Appeal to the legislature, upon the high price of meat: In which many of the base practices of Smithfield are exposed, and a remedy pointed out for the poor*, by A Philanthropic Butcher. H. D. Symonds, T. Bellamy, and all the booksellers, 1795.
56. See also: Barnes, Donald Grove. *A History of English Corn Laws From 1660–1846*. Routledge, 1930/2010. See also: Boyer, George. *An Economic History of the English Poor Law, 1750–1850*. Cambridge University Press, 1990. Both books include discussion of the 1795 bread riots in London. See as well: Davis, Michael. 'Bread riots, Britain, 1795', in *The International Encyclopedia of Revolution and Protest*, ed. Immanuel Nest. Wiley-Blackwell, 2009.
57. *Monopoly*, p. 4.
58. *Monopoly*, p. 8.
59. *Monopoly*, p. 10.
60. *Monopoly*, p. 10.
61. *Monopoly*, pp. 11–12.
62. *Monopoly*, p. 12.
63. *Monopoly*, p. 14.
64. *Monopoly*, p. 14.
65. Kean, p. 62.
66. Kean, p. 62, and citing Mary Dawtrey's 'Women as Food Reformers' from *Food Reform Magazine*, 1:3 (January 1889), p. 134.
67. See: Preece, Rod. *Animal Sensibility and Inclusive Justice in the Age of Bernard Shaw*. University of British Columbia Press, 2011, p. 123. Hardy

also remarked on a deplorable 'wifeselling' practice at Smithfield in *The Mayor of Casterbridge*. See also Norman Page's Appendix on the matter, and his discussion of Hardy' Smithfield reactions, in Hardy, Thomas. *The Mayor of Casterbridge*, ed. Norman Page. Broadview, 1997, pp. 378–82.
68. Perren's works are superlative on many of these issues, and Derrick Rixson's *History of Meat Trading* is especially comprehensive, covering a vast history but also offering significant detail and a full section devoted to Smithfield.
69. See: Metcalfe, 'The Smithfield System in the Nineteenth Century: A Grand Complexus', in *Meat, Commerce and the City: The London Food Market, 1800–1855*. Pickering & Chatto, 2012, pp. 33–48.
70. Perren, *Taste, Trade and Technology*, p. 46.
71. Judel, Günther Klaus. *Die Geschichte von Liebigs Fleischextrakt: Zur populärsten Erfindung des berühmten Chemikers*. Available at: <geb.uni-giessen.de/geb/volltexte/2004/1381/pdf/SdF-2003-1_2b.pdf>, p. 7 (last accessed 5 December 2016).
72. Robert Mack discusses these food practices and far more in *The Wonderful and Surprising History of Sweeney Todd: The Life and Times of an Urban Legend*. Bloomsbury, 2008.

Chapter 3

Mass Production: Impossible London's Criminal Subjects

There can be no doubt but that the love of money was the pre-dominant feeling in Sweeney Todd's intellectual organization and that, by the amount it would bring him, or the amount it would deprive him of, he measured everything.

With such a man, then, no question of morality or ordinary feeling could arise, and there can be no doubt but that he would quite willingly have sacrificed the whole human race, if, by doing so, he could have achieved any of the objects of his ambition.

And so on his road homeward, he probably made up his mind to plunge still deeper into criminality; and perchance to indulge in acts that a man not already so deeply versed in iniquity would have shrunk from with the most positive terror.

And by a strange style of reasoning, such men as Sweeney Todd reconcile themselves to the most heinous crimes upon the ground of what they call policy.[1]

The abject experience of London – in London, for London, through London, despite London, chewed up and spit out by London – ties literary culture across a very long nineteenth century to an even longer lineage in Defoe and others who remarked on its cultural habits in prior centuries. This multi-period history is likewise a cross-genre exploration in which the very grounds of the literary often factor – authorship, style, innovation and reception are but a few of the considerations. London, with its ghastly horrors, also becomes a character in its own right in works such as Poe's 'Man of the Crowd', through Dickens's works and the popular penny fictions produced in London's presses, as well as in Bram Stoker's *Dracula* and later works. This lineage shows a recurring fascination with the mysterious, dark depths of the city's condensed streets and routines. These stories were fed by a rich history of crime fiction – urban and rural – and owed a considerable debt to eighteenth-century nonfiction accounts of famous criminals executed in London like Jack Sheppard. This implicates one of the best-known figures to document Sheppard's feats and death, Defoe, in the tradition. Defoe also wrote on French murderers, culminating in one of the bloodiest tales available to the late nineteenth-century reader upon its reissue. The foremost collector of penny bloods and dreadfuls, Barry Ono, had a significant store of Defoe's bloody tales in his collection, now at the British Museum. Furthermore, the immediate precursor to the pennies, the Newgate novels published serially alongside Dickens, had a similar fascination with figures, now becoming characters, like Sheppard.

This chapter will consider many of these bloody entrails, as well as at times the vital role of plagiarism and recycled material in the pennies, and also some of the specific shifts in literary entertainment production after the advent of steam press technology and an important reduction in paper prices near the beginning of the nineteenth century. All of this must furthermore be considered against rising literacy rates among the working class and the price-point that defines the genre of the penny blood or dreadful in the first place: 'price one penny'. The technical reduction of material, production and distribution uncannily matches the meat industry while the low moral value of the pennies – their precursor, the Newgate novels, had often been censored – matches the prior legislative efforts to curb animal entertainments among the working classes. In all, the pennies reflect an abiding public interest in the gore of urban and foreign crime while amplifying the rampant, real fears coursing through the city's veins and orifices at Smithfield and other sullied sites.

The mass-produced object of public entertainment arrived in full force in London at the time of the pennies, leading to important changes in the sense of a reading public and, furthermore, of its political agency in relation to mass literacy and a print culture responding to and motivating major legislative reform. While I will not deal at length with the full breadth of penny production, I will discuss the most famous example, the Sweeney Todd story, which imbricates all of the chapter's concerns and the meaty contents of Chapter 2 in an essential expression of the nonhuman form and the London publics affected by, and affecting, that form.

In general, the question of literary value will be left aside as a concerted inquiry in this chapter. It is important to note, however, that the pennies, as shown in the quote from *Sweeney Todd* that opens the chapter, worked on many of the same themes and moods as the 'literary' works of the period. Furthermore, these works are perfectly susceptible to hearty literary analysis: one line in the quoted passage above employs free indirect discourse with the 'probably' speculation, a mode borrowed perhaps from Jane Austen, or perhaps the uncertainty that drives conjecture fits perfectly with the detective impulses of the new popular literature and its new mass audience of individual consumers and civic analysts. This gives some sense of the intersections of London serial press production, London life and bloody murder, and the complicated relationship of literature expressing impossible, damning city experience to the unshakable need to document and interrogate that city. To begin, I will consider an American work that takes up the City of London as its charge.

The narrative mode of insecurity and speculation mentioned in *Sweeney Todd* melds seamlessly with the foregrounded problem in Edgar Allen Poe's 'Man of the Crowd', in which Poe's narrator watches a parade of new professional classes and then succumbs to the haunting distortions of the new gaslights in the city, following the city's incessant activity through the visage of the inscrutable title character, who ultimately refuses to be followed in any manner that might produce understanding. 'Man of the Crowd' presents the city as an inscrutable, constant assemblage of activity and objects akin to the depravity Wordsworth presented at Bartholomew Fair. The story opens with a quote from La Bruyère's *The Characters of Man*, 'Ce grand malheur, de ne pouvoir être seul.' The quote frames the eponymous main character of the story as an afflicted soul that cannot endure solitude amidst the thronging 'sea' of 'bobbing heads' in the city. La Bruyere's *Characters*, first published in France in 1688, was both beloved and widely criticised for its cynical outlook on human behaviours and social types that well-known figures of the day thought to be based on themselves. The work fits neatly with the type cataloguing and misanthropic philosophical commentary on the appearance and characteristics of people the narrator in 'Man of the Crowd' observes.

The man of the crowd himself never stops moving and attaching himself to various groups in the story, and his great malady is his insatiable and curiously unsocial sociability. He never talks to anyone, and no one but the narrator seems to notice him, yet he is constantly amidst others and only shows affectation when he risks being alone at one point in the story. He quickly finds another group to join, and the narrator notes that the man is relieved. The narrator's description of the man is not relegated to behaviour and the final word on his identity – 'the type and genius of deep crime'.[2] But the narrator also marks that the man cannot be read, and that it will be fruitless to follow him further about the city. The narrator gives clear information on the man of the crowd at one point before concluding the inscrutability of his object:

> I had now a good opportunity of examining his person. He was short in stature, very thin, and apparently very feeble. His clothes, generally, were

filthy and ragged; but as he came, now and then, within the strong glare of a lamp, I perceived that his linen, although dirty, was of beautiful texture; and my vision deceived me, or, through a rent in a closely buttoned and evidently second-handed roquelaire which enveloped him, I caught a glimpse both of a diamond and of a dagger. These observations heightened my curiosity, and I resolved to follow the stranger whithersoever he should go.[3]

The clothing marks the man as either wealthy himself at some point or, as the dagger may suggest, a criminal who acquired high-end goods in a prior offence. The 'second-handed' item complicates matters further, perhaps even suggesting charity house donations or, worse yet, the grave robber or, in a further speculation, the charnel house denizens providing material for the new medical profession centred in London. Poe here, with the roquelaire and high quality fabric, includes the harbinger of fashion, one of the hallmarks of London fiction through the middle and later part of the nineteenth century. At the very least, Poe invokes goods consumption as a marker of status, occupation and 'character' in line with the lists of people and their appearance that populate the earlier part of the story. But the general state of disrepair the man has fallen into, even with luxury markers of possible status that so intrigue the narrator, builds a more convoluted, layered story of the man's identity and standing. He may be a criminal; perhaps he is a senile royal. He has no clear occupation to attend to, and he apparently does not need to – or at any rate, he does not – worry about the state of his attire despite its fine traces. He is weak and small, and yet he has some cunning and swiftness given his undetected, asocial, yet constant association with others. The man himself, in the narrator's ultimate surrender to illegibility, is given up as a calculable and categorised object. And this most unknowable, inscrutable, contradictory and confounding object is relegated to the grossest, deepest criminal ranks in the narrator's final, authoritative word on the matter. The man of the crowd is the unspeakable.

The inscrutability of the man denotes an aesthetic failure of the observer–narrator but not a failure of experience or reception. The failure is more an acknowledged reflective impossibility despite the narrator's verdict on the man of the crowd. The narrator perceives the man's behaviour and, in response to the uncertainty and trepidation that behaviour seems to produce in the narrator, he assigns the man the category of criminal. The story thus plays on the limited comprehension and address at the heart of Romantic concern in the works examined in Chapter 1 and produces an unreliable, or perhaps outright untrustworthy, arbiter of the social scene. The London space presented is a work-a-day drudgery of repetitious office forms, conformist and claustrophobic street traffic (pedestrian human traffic alone), and finally a weird, unsettling night space of gin-soaked depravity and organised, categorical city crime. Technological, chemical modernity fuels this aesthetic crisis of interrogation, as it turns out.

In the story, gas lighting opens the man of the crowd up briefly to the narrator's impulse to inventory. This, with the other observed behaviours of the man, is the basis for the narrator's speculation on his identity. And by the story's end, the man's resistance as a calculable object/character seems to confirm the narrator's assertion that the man of the crowd is a gross, deep horror of the city space. This is not the only time gas lighting figures in the story's interplay of observation, speculation and horror:

> [T]he rays of the gas-lamps, feeble at first in their struggle with the dying day, had now at length gained ascendancy, and threw over every thing a fitful and garish lustre. All was dark yet splendid-as that ebony to which has been likened the style of Tertullian.
> The wild effects of the light enchained me to an examination of individual faces; and although the rapidity with which the world of light flitted before the window prevented me from casting more than a glance upon each visage, still it seemed that, in my then peculiar mental state, I could frequently read, even in that brief interval of a glance, the history of long years.[4]

The city is not a space filled with people and things, partially illuminated here and there so the basically reliable status of everyone and everything can be confirmed now and then. Instead, the city is precisely these affectations and the blank, illegible non-presence that barely grazes the observations and speculations of its neurotic abjects. Bringing things into the weird, toxic light of the city only makes matters worse:

> It was the most noisome quarter of London, where every thing wore the worst impress of the most deplorable poverty, and of the most desperate crime. By the dim light of an accidental lamp, tall, antique, worm-eaten, wooden tenements were seen tottering to their fall, in directions so many and capricious, that scarce the semblance of a passage was discernible between them. The paving-stones lay at random, displaced from their beds by the rankly-growing grass. Horrible filth festered in the dammed-up gutters. The whole atmosphere teemed with desolation. Yet, as we proceeded, the sounds of human life revived by sure degrees, and at length large bands of the most abandoned of a London populace were seen reeling to and fro. The spirits of the old man again flickered up, as a lamp which is near its death-hour. Once more he strode onward with elastic tread. Suddenly a corner was turned, a blaze of light burst upon our sight, and we stood before one of the huge suburban temples of Intemperance- one of the palaces of the fiend, Gin.[5]

The gas lighting indicates the city's development. The nocturnal activity in the story is both enabled and distorted by the play of the gas lighting and the dark spaces it does not penetrate. London has become a sleepless centre of activity personified by the man of the crowd, who cannot stop moving and must always be with (though not in communication with) others. And yet, like the city partially and inconclusively illuminated by gas lighting, the man cannot be identified as readily by the narrator as the various working groups listed in the first part of the story. Not a lawyer, military man or dandy, or other category, the man of the crowd resists attempts to read him (*er lässt sich nicht lessen*, in the German Poe opens and closes the story with).[6]

Gas lighting was developed and implemented in Britain in the first decades of the nineteenth century. The Westminster Bridge had lights installed in 1813, and gas lighting was used widely throughout London within ten years. By 1840, the publication year of 'The Man of The Crowd', gas lighting would have been more or less pervasive in New York, where Poe had lived, Baltimore, where he lived in 1840, and London, the story's setting.[7] And in 1815, when the young Poe moved to London for what would be five years with his foster parents, the lighting would have been a sensational attraction, having been introduced in 1807.[8] Although Poe did not move to Baltimore until 1835, the town had been an early site of gas lighting installations in the United States in 1816.[9] Adding further intrigue, some hypotheses on Poe's death blame carbon monoxide and prolonged heavy metal exposure from gas lighting for health maladies Poe and his wife Virginia suffered. Some have interpreted his descriptions of those maladies in his letters, as well as his peculiar facial features in photographs from his later life, as signs that Poe was suffering from the symptoms of carbon monoxide poisoning due to gas lighting.[10] On the other hand, gas lighting had a directly, if not decisively positive effect on nonhuman animals.

Despite its toxicity, gas might have been a sort of salvation for land animals were there not evermore demand for meat, leather and other animal-based goods in the city. The tallow that used to be crucial for candle production was gradually phased out even before gas lighting arrived. The city of London used to have mandatory lighting of city streets in some areas, and candles were used before gas lighting and, now, electric lighting. Candle manufacture relied increasingly on paraffin by the seventeenth century. The other source that overtook tallow for candle making was of course whale spermaceti, also used in pharmaceutical and other applications. Cows and sheep were spared the candlemakers rendering, replaced by the whale. Truthfully, whale-hunting took a much larger toll on whale populations in the twentieth century, but the daily reliance on whale spermaceti in the nineteenth century was so ingrained in the public consciousness that burgeoning petroleum use

Figure 9 Vanity Fair whales ball. Public domain.

(another post-animal application) led to responses like this 1861 cartoon in *Vanity Fair* (Figure 9). All the same, even though tallow use in candle production abated in the nineteenth-century moment Poe and British authors were writing on the horrors of urban space, another product required that animal fat in mass quantities: soap.[11] So, in the end, the gas lighting doesn't quite save quite enough of anything. Electricity, naturally, will spare even less.

Poe's narrator catalogues all of the passers-by from a coffee house perch. He looks through a 'smoky' windowpane and assigns everyone their occupation while describing their foibles and gaits. The descriptions of behaviour and apparent mood or preoccupation serve as the bases for the occupation and character assessments. Yet the narrator notes the intense pace of his own reading practice, as 'the rapidity with which the world of light flitted by' precludes sustained observation. The narrator's reading is like the brief, sensational news lines he is reading on the paper mentioned early in the story. Periodicals, like window-shopping (in the reverse in this case), capitalise on rapid intensity and flashy plays upon rapt consuming agents, but they cannot be expected to withstand longer consideration if the impulse to buy is not immediately satiated. The narrator (who is a reader) has a sales job in the story. The narrator must make convincing, pithy but snap judgments on passers-by. The brief categorisation that follows must be decisive, final and total; base types of the city are the story's product. And yet this is of course its own affliction, and the lamplight is perhaps the best clue to the city's general subjection of people and lives to types and ultimately plastic surface characteristics.

Poe's narrator even invokes the physiognomy of Retzch, casting the man of the crowd as the superlative epitome of the fiend and saying that Retzch would have preferred this face to his own depictions.[12] The man of the crowd is an excessively representative case of the urban horror, the arch and inscrutable criminal named all the same as, precisely, the abject limit to both civil conduct and civil calculation. It does not permit itself to be read except as that unreadability, and unreadability is the grossest horror and the deepest criminality. Poe's narrator is disgusted with all sorts, even the 'decent' day labourers observed in the story, and this anonymous facelessness fits as well the de-individuated business classes as the hyper-individuated but indistinguishable man of the crowd. The city is legible by the lighting and organised passage ways the narrator catalogues, and its denizens are classifiable objects, as well, but the constant contact and imperative to observe and recognise becomes the city itself for the narrator. The identification game played with the others in the story does not satisfy the narrator, and seems in fact only to irritate the existing condition of needing to classify and judge everyone. People deemed 'decent' are merely 'deskish', and here Poe's narrator suggests that the bursting business class in the nineteenth century, facilitated by the lights and comprising the writhing, teeming mass of human traffic the city has become, is an unsettlingly simple-to-define monstrosity.[13]

The sheer mundaneness of London's incessant existence is its darkest horror. This mundane, deskish horror immediately recalls another American example, Herman Melville's 'Bartleby the Scrivener'. Bartleby famously declares 'I would prefer not to' whenever prompted to perform a basic task in what seems a standard office setting. The story escalates, the narrator growing more and more furious at Bartleby's immovability. The story also highlights the frustrated effort to install order and industry in the daily activity of labourers in a city space wholly devoted to business – Manhattan instead of the London thoroughfares around the business district, in this case. Giorgio Agamben, following after Gilles Deleuze in taking up the story as a philosophical byway, writes that, as

> a scribe who has stopped writing, Bartleby is the extreme figure of the Nothing from which all creation derives; and at the same time, he constitutes the most implacable vindication of this Nothing as pure, absolute potentiality. The scrivener has become the writing tablet; he is now nothing other than

his white sheet. It is not surprising, therefore, that he dwells so obstinately in the abyss of potentiality and does not seem to have the slightest inclination of leaving it.[14]

Melville's tale is worth considering in relation to the London works, and perhaps especially in relation to the Fleet Street environs of *Sweeney Todd* yet parrying off Dickens's chosen settings away from the high society and financial developments in London.

The full title of the Bartleby story is 'Bartleby the Scrivener: A Story of Wall Street'. Like the man of the crowd, Bartleby is impossible to read, and the narrator presents him in far less developed form than he does his other two scriveners, Nippers and Turkey. Of the latter and his coat, the narrator says:

> One winter day I presented Turkey with a highly-respectable looking coat of my own, a padded gray coat, of a most comfortable warmth, and which buttoned straight up from the knee to the neck. I thought Turkey would appreciate the favor, and abate his rashness and obstreperousness of afternoons. But no. I verily believe that buttoning himself up in so downy and blanket-like a coat had a pernicious effect upon him; upon the same principle that too much oats are bad for horses. In fact, precisely as a rash, restive horse is said to feel his oats, so Turkey felt his coat. It made him insolent. He was a man whom prosperity harmed.[15]

Of Nippers:

> In short, the truth of the matter was, Nippers knew not what he wanted. Or, if he wanted any thing, it was to be rid of a scrivener's table altogether. Among the manifestations of his diseased ambition was a fondness he had for receiving visits from certain ambiguous-looking fellows in seedy coats, whom he called his clients. Indeed I was aware that not only was he, at times, considerable of a ward-politician, but he occasionally did a little business at the Justices' courts, and was not unknown on the steps of the Tombs.[16]

On the other hand, the character ('figure') Bartleby arrives already foreshadowing, in his stasis and his 'forlorn' comportment, some of the later narrative events he will motivate:

> Now my original business – that of a conveyancer and title hunter, and drawer-up of recondite documents of all sorts – was considerably increased by receiving the master's office. There was now great work for scriveners. Not only must I push the clerks already with me, but I must have additional help. In answer to my advertisement, a motionless young man one morning, stood upon my office threshold, the door being open, for it was summer. I can see that figure now – pallidly neat, pitiably respectable, incurably forlorn! It was Bartleby.[17]

This is a retrospective account by the narrator, and yet the firmest speculation on Bartleby's attitude is merely the 'forlorn' countenance. The narrator is immediately pleased to have found an employee 'of so singularly sedate an aspect'.[18] This comportment is, however, merely a professional attribute:

> It is, of course, an indispensable part of a scrivener's business to verify the accuracy of his copy, word by word. Where there are two or more scriveners in an office, they assist each other in this examination, one reading from the copy, the other holding the original. It is a very dull, wearisome, and lethargic affair. I can readily imagine that to some sanguine temperaments it would be altogether intolerable. For example, I cannot credit that the mettlesome poet Byron would have contentedly sat down with Bartleby to examine a law document of, say five hundred pages, closely written in a crimpy hand.[19]

After an early period of incredible productivity, Bartleby begins to resist assignments with the infamous 'I would prefer not to.' When the narrator asks, '*Why* do you refuse?' the answer is the same as to any request of service: 'I would prefer not to.'[20] Throughout, the familiarity and perfunctory function of the social structure of the office – Turkey and Nippers, and the third employee who preceded Bartleby's arrival, the lad Ginger Nut, all fitting in, in proper form – sustains against Bartleby's inscrutable exception to the social rule:

> 'Turkey,' said I, 'what do you think of this? Am I not right?'
> 'With submission, sir,' said Turkey, with his blandest tone, 'I think that you are.'
> 'Nippers,' said I, 'what do *you* think of it?'
> 'I think I should kick him out of the office.'
> (The reader of nice perceptions will here perceive that, it being morning, Turkey's answer is couched in polite and tranquil terms, but Nippers replies in ill-tempered ones. Or, to repeat a previous sentence, Nippers's ugly mood was on duty, and Turkey's off.)
> 'Ginger Nut,' said I, willing to enlist the smallest suffrage in my behalf, 'what do *you* think of it?'
> 'I think, sir, he's a little *luny*,' replied Ginger Nut, with a grin.
> 'You hear what they say,' said I, turning towards the screen, 'come forth and do your duty.'
> But he vouchsafed no reply.[21]

Bartleby's passiveness, his 'mulishness', irritates and vexes the narrator, whose official industry is as passive and as rote but for the one fact of Bartleby's agency he cannot match: Bartleby's refusal, and his very refusal to actively refuse, violate the ethic of the office place and his docile resistance contaminates the office space. A minor rudeness in Nippers – without coffee perhaps, or almost certainly without his 'nip' of spirits early in the morning and still perhaps waiting for the nips of the night before to wear off – is calculable and ordinary. This resistance is confined to a performed conformity. He is in a bad mood, but he acts his part, fits his assignment.

The narrator makes numerous attempts to order and coerce Bartleby into action, all to no avail and producing occasional philosophising on the reasonable behaviour of human 'creatures'.[22] Curiously, despite the seeming inaction of Bartleby and the narrator's expectation of a controlled, disciplined (if routinely automatic) office space, the narrator loses track of the keys to the offices of law:

> Here it must be said, that according to the custom of most legal gentlemen occupying chambers in densely-populated law buildings, there were several keys to my door. One was kept by a woman residing in the attic, which person weekly scrubbed and daily swept and dusted my apartments. Another was kept by Turkey for convenience sake. The third I sometimes carried in my own pocket. The fourth I knew not who had.[23]

Bartleby of course has the key and is living in the office, which the narrator soon discovers. There are several more rounds of the infuriating business of asking Bartleby questions and receiving only the 'I would prefer not to' answers. Bartleby whiles away days in 'dead wall reveries' while the community of active staff members grow increasingly agitated and derisive toward Bartleby in their private office small talk.[24] In the final irony of power in the story, Bartleby refuses to quit or be moved, and the narrator moves the entire office except for the passive scrivener:

> Then something severe, something unusual must be done. What! surely you will not have him collared by a constable, and commit his innocent pallor to the common jail? And upon what ground could you procure such a thing to be done? – a vagrant, is he? What! he a vagrant, a wanderer, who refuses to budge? It is because he will *not* be a vagrant, then, that you seek to count him *as* a vagrant. That is too absurd. No visible means of support: there I have him. Wrong again: for indubitably he *does* support himself, and that is the only unanswerable proof that any man can show of his possessing the means so to do. No more then. Since he will not quit me, I must quit him. I will change my offices; I will move elsewhere; and give him fair notice, that if I find him on my new premises I will then proceed against him as a common trespasser.
>
> Acting accordingly, next day I thus addressed him: 'I find these chambers too far from the City Hall; the air is unwholesome. In a word, I propose to remove my offices next week, and shall no longer require your services. I tell you this now, in order that you may seek another place'.
>
> He made no reply, and nothing more was said.[25]

There is first the business of calling the authorities to arrest Bartleby for vagrancy. In the British context, this parallels the issue of public assembly and, more in line with Bartleby's 'symptoms', with malingering, for example, by 'motiveless' late-century asylum patients lacking in any useful occupation.[26] The asylum at the heart of much of the action in Stoker's *Dracula* should also come to mind here, and while 'Bartleby' is written a bit before the true boom in psychoanalysis and sanitaria, already the troublesome signs of modern office and urban affect are on display here in Melville's text. The crisis of occupation the narrator exhibits is parallel, in turn, to the efforts to improve the masses in England in the same period.[27]

The narrator expresses, really, two problems as one: 1. the location is too far from the seat of industry at City Hall, and 2. the air is 'unwholesome'. This issue of 'bad air' seeps in as the stifling fog and muck of London in the representative legal fiction of the British nineteenth century, Dickens's *Bleak House*, and it then becomes an even stickier existential morass later in Kafka's *The Trial*. In the civic context, 'bad air' and bad water had become real ecological concerns in London and numerous other industrial cities using massive amounts of coal and other fuels.[28] Here, however, the conflation of unwholesome air and city location reflect the city space as a disciplinary regime, wherein the expectations of central industry work automatically and Bartleby, who refuses all manner of alternative occupation offered by the narrator before this counter-eviction, is the abjected docile body. 'Either you must do something', the narrator says, 'or something must be done to you.'[29] Just as the conformist echo chamber of deskish office life makes one functioning or not, so London expects the proper cues and reference points of proper life to be upheld and obeyed while, in fact, undoing life by its very air, its very water, its very structure and ordering systems. Unkempt chaos, even destruction, might do as well.

It is at this moment that Bartleby voices a different response, no longer a refusal or a vital character's passivity but an empty figure's homogenous alienation: 'I am not particular.'[30] Bartleby from there is silent, imprisoned and does not eat – Melville writes 'I saw the wasted Bartleby.'[31] And finally: '"Lives without dining," said I, and closed the eyes.'[32] The story closes with a 'report' the narrator cannot verify – a rumour, nothing more – of Bartleby's prior occupation:

> The report was this: that Bartleby had been a subordinate clerk in the Dead Letter Office at Washington, from which he had been suddenly removed by a change in the administration. When I think over this rumor, I cannot adequately express the emotions which seize me. Dead letters! does it not sound like dead men? Conceive a man by nature and misfortune prone to a

> pallid hopelessness, can any business seem more fitted to heighten it than that of continually handling these dead letters and assorting them for the flames? For by the cart-load they are annually burned. Sometimes from out the folded paper the pale clerk takes a ring – the finger it was meant for, perhaps, moulders in the grave; a bank-note sent in swiftest charity: – he whom it would relieve, nor eats nor hungers any more; pardon for those who died despairing; hope for those who died unhoping; good tidings for those who died stifled by unrelieved calamities. On errands of life, these letters speed to death.
> Ah Bartleby! Ah humanity![33]

The notion of dead letters being dead men is of course the story's final verdict on official business, and the narrator's continued life is rendered something less than the concept ought to imply. This is Agamben's critique of the story, in part, albeit his interest in the philosophical shape of 'potentiality' and of dormancy is stronger than my own in this case; Bartleby and the narrator, as well as the three co-workers, share in the administrative potential implied through Bartleby's relocation.[34] That this relocation was among his last is incidental and, furthermore, there is no clear sense that the narrator hadn't also relocated more than once.

The narrator's subservience to the bureaucratic life is so total that Bartleby's resistance to the mode is alien to him and earns his office's reproach. None of them is particular, or particular people – particular is both adjective to the would-be subjects and preference, grammatically still the adjective. Were there an indefinite article, 'a particular' could be an individuation. This, again, is likely part of Agamben's fascination with the story, but beyond the grammatical particulars, the narrator's apostrophic throwing-up-of-hands to close can only be an insincere accounting of the burnt humans at stake in the office space. Manhattan, like London, is the centripetal interpellator. Move to the centre, impelled by business and survive or don't. Those are the only rules of the game suggested by Bartleby, a further extrapolation of the Poe tale with one key shift: the exceptional – those abjected from the norm even in radical sociality like 'The Man of the Crowd' – are deemed criminals in Poe. Bartleby is even less.

Before turning to the criminality in the pennies and the Defoe and Newgate Calendar accounts that preceded them, it will be useful to again consider the classic London novelist of social concern and urban transformation, Charles Dickens. Dickens's *Oliver Twist* is concerned directly with the criminal element around Smithfield and throughout London, and the book makes direct mention of Smithfield in the 'Expedition' chapter preceding the burglary. But in between these glaring examples of London Smithfield crime connections are multiple instances of Oliver and others associating with animals – or having their behaviour and appearance associated with animals and other nonhumans. Dickens thus builds a similar sense of the interspecies, mutual abjection the Romantic poets discussed in Chapter 1 did. Oliver is born in Mudfog, a fictional town symbolising the broader Dickens Londonscape.

When the unscrupulous Fagin takes Oliver in, he relates to him a story of a previous ward in Oliver's condition who had ratted Fagin out to the police but, in some turn of events, ended up the one hung after a trial at the Old Bailey.[35] Fagin describes the hanging in gruesome detail to make an impression on Oliver. This will prove to be prophetic of Fagin's own hanging, which I will discuss in relation to Dickens's views on public hangings in the period. Oliver, stuck in his room awaiting his captors' return, becomes part of a tremulous band of creatures in the dirty, squalid quarters:

> Spiders had built their webs in the angles of the walls and ceiling; and sometimes, when Oliver walked softly into a room, the mice would scamper across the floor, and run back terrified to their holes. With these exceptions, there was neither sight nor sound of any living thing; and often, when it grew dark, and he was tired of wandering from room to room, he would crouch in the corner of the passage by the street-door, to be as near living people as he could; and would remain there, listening and counting the hours, until the Jew or the boys returned.[36]

Oliver is beholden to the gang throughout the story, but he is not purely naive, as evidenced when the Dodger asks Oliver what a prig is, assuming he won't know. Oliver catches himself after starting off 'It's a th--; you're one, are you not?' As part of the Dodger's response, an unfortunate dog is employed in the standard anthropomorphic commentary on human behaviours, thereby normalising the criminality in question (a prig is a thief) while establishing the multispecies openness of the criminal ranks:

> 'I am,' repeated the dodger. 'So's Charley. So's Fagin. So's Sikes. So's Nancy. So's Bet. So we all are, down to the dog. And he's the downiest of the lot!'
> 'And the least given to preaching,' added Charley Bates.
> 'He wouldn't so much as bark in a witness-box, for fear of committing himself; no, not if you tied him up in one, and left him there without wittles for a fortnight,' said the Dodger.
> 'Not a bit of it,' observed Charley.
> 'He's a rum dog. Don't he look fierce at any strange cove that laughs or sings when he's in company!' pursued the Dodger. 'Won't he growl at all, when he hears a fiddle playing! And don't he hate other dogs as ain't of his breed! Oh no!'

'He's an out-and-out Christian,' said Charley.
This was merely intended as a tribute to the animal's abilities, but it was an appropriate remark in another sense, if Master Bates had only known it; for there are a good many ladies and gentlemen, claiming to be out-and-out Christians, between whom, and Mr. Sikes's dog, there exist strong and singular points of resemblance.[37]

The animal similarities here are intended not as a positive consubstantiality, however, but as a diminution of the humans in question. Dickens's inventory of depravity, inhuman poverty and an intractable, impossible London city space is thickly staged in the novel:

Beguiling the time with these pleasant reflections, Mr. Fagin wended his way, through mud and mire, to his gloomy abode: where the Dodger was sitting up, impatiently awaiting his return.
'Is Oliver a-bed? I want to speak with him,' was his first remark as they descended the stairs.
'Hours ago,' replied the Dodger, throwing open the door. 'Here he is!'
The boy was lying, fast asleep, on a rude bed upon the floor; so pale with anxiety, and sadness, and the closeness of his prison, that he looked death; not death as it shows in shroud and coffin, but in the guise it wears when life has just departed; when a young and gentle spirit has, but an instant, fled to Heaven, and the gross air of the world has not had time to breathe upon the changing dust it hallowed.
'Not now,' said the Jew, turning softly away. 'T-morrow. To-morrow.'[38]

This sense of deferral persists throughout the novel, until Oliver is eventually freed by external forces. Until the resolution of his imprisonment with the gang – a mobile imprisonment of labour and abetting – Oliver is equipment to the gang, employed in various menial support roles.

In a transformative passage, Oliver recognises his own subjection while reading, of all things, a gory, bloody account of famous criminals as would have been popular, whatever point in the nineteenth-century Dickens set the story and wrote it in:

Oliver leaned his head upon his hand when the old man disappeared, and pondered, with a trembling heart, on the words he had just heard. The more he thought of the Jew's admonition, the more he was at a loss to divine its real purpose and meaning. He could think of no bad object to be attained by sending him to Sikes, which would not be equally well answered by his remaining with Fagin; and after meditating for a long time, concluded that he had been selected to perform some ordinary menial offices for the housebreaker, until another boy, better suited for his purpose, could be engaged. He was too well accustomed to suffering, and had suffered too much where he was, to bewail the prospect of change very seriously. He remained lost in thought for some minutes; and then, with a heavy sigh, snuffed the candle, and, taking up the book which the Jew had left with him, began to read.

> He turned over the leaves. Carelessly at first; but, lighting on a passage which attracted his attention, he soon became intent upon the volume. It was a history of the lives and trials of great criminals; and the pages were soiled and thumbed with use. Here, he read of dreadful crimes that made the blood run cold; of secret murders that had been committed by the lonely wayside; of bodies hidden from the eye of man in deep pits and wells; which would not keep them down, deep as they were, but had yielded them up at last, after many years, and so maddened the murderers with the sight, that in their horror they had confessed their guilt, and yelled for the gibbet to end their agony. Here, too, he read of men who, lying in their beds at dead of night, had been tempted (so they said) and led on, by their own bad thoughts, to such dreadful bloodshed as it made the flesh creep, and the limbs quail, to think of. The terrible descriptions were so real and vivid, that the sallow pages seemed to turn red with gore; and the words upon them, to be sounded in his ears, as if they were whispered, in hollow murmurs, by the spirits of the dead.
>
> In a paroxysm of fear, the boy closed the book, and thrust it from him. Then, falling to his knees, he prayed Heaven to spare him from such deeds; and rather to will that he should die at once, than be reserved for crimes, so fearful and appalling. By degrees, he grew more calm, and besought, in a low and broken voice, that he might be rescued from his present dangers; and that if any aid were to be raised up for a poor outcast boy who had never known the love of friends or kindred, it might come to him now, when, desolate and deserted, he stood alone in the midst of wickedness and guilt.[39]

The trouble for Oliver, as for multiple London characters, is seeing his way clear of the precarious criminal existence he is subjected to while his character or soul is preserved in its good will. On the night of the burglary, when Oliver's fate as innocent or criminal is potentially in the balance, Dickens makes London the dangerous, criminal antagonist via obfuscation and confusion:

> It was now intensely dark. The fog was much heavier than it had been in the early part of the night; and the atmosphere was so damp, that, although no rain fell, Oliver's hair and eyebrows, within a few minutes after leaving the house, had become stiff with the half-frozen moisture that was floating about. They crossed the bridge and kept on towards the lights which they had seen before.[40]

The noun choice for Oliver's status in the crime achieves its object while the ironic 'dark lantern' with which to accomplish the deed violently illuminates matters:

> 'Now listen, you young limb,' whispered Sikes, drawing a dark lantern from his pocket, and throwing the full glare on Oliver's face; 'I'm a going to put you through there. Take this light: go softly up the steps straight afore you, and along the little hall, to the street door; unfasten it, and let us in.'[41]

Object is not bad enough, however, and Oliver's suspended vitality punctuates the sudden visibility and legibility of the scene; Sikes has Oliver at gunpoint:

> 'Take this lantern,' said Sikes, looking into the room. 'You see the stairs afore you?'
> Oliver, more dead than alive, gasped out 'Yes.' Sikes, pointing to the street-door with the pistol barrel, briefly advised him to take notice that he was within shot all the way; and that if he faltered, he would fall dead that instant.[42]

Oliver is shot, not by Sikes but by the residents of the house, who then turn out to be his safe harbour when he returns to the front door of the house, in his worsened state, later that night. He had intended to dart up the stairs to warn them but dropped the horrible light and alerted them to the burglary. The Dodger and Toby ditch Oliver in a gutter. This entire turn of events is precisely the volta toward Oliver's redemption and salvation – Oliver's progress turned on the lowest abjection, left for dead when already more dead than alive, and returned to those he would have saved in the first place.

When he recounts events in the safety of the boarding house later, it is amidst tones of magnanimous society and mutual 'humanity' uttered by characters like Mr Giles. Giles worries he'd injured a 'fellow-creature' and the discussion of criminals undertakes not dramatic rebuke of criminality but reverent appreciation for the law, reasonable explanation and the spirit of charity. Only the poor family dog is left out in the cold, as it were, from the warm sentiment of Society on display:

> With the next morning, there came a rumour, that two men and a boy were in the cage at Kingston, who had been apprehended over night under suspicious circumstances; and to Kingston Messrs. Blathers and Duff journeyed accordingly. The suspicious circumstances, however, resolving themselves, on investigation, into the one fact, that they had been discovered sleeping under a haystack; which, although a great crime, is only punishable by imprisonment, and is, in the merciful eye of the English law, and its comprehensive love of all the king's subjects, held to be no satisfactory proof, in the absence of all other evidence, that the sleeper, or sleepers, have committed burglary accompanied with violence, and have therefore rendered themselves liable to the punishment of death; Messrs. Blathers and Duff came back again, as wise as they went.
>
> In short, after some more examination, and a great deal more conversation, a neighbouring magistrate was readily induced to take the joint bail of Mrs. Maylie and Mr. Losberne for Oliver's appearance if he should ever be called upon; and Blathers and Duff, being rewarded with a couple guineas, returned to town with divided opinions on the subject of their expedition: the latter gentleman on a mature consideration of all the circumstances, inclining to the

belief that the burglarious attempt had originated with the Family Pet; and the former being equally disposed to concede the full merit of it to the great Mr. Conkey Chickweed.[43]

The tone hardly lets up from there, as Oliver's salvation from the dark, evil depths of London criminality progresses:

> Oliver told them all his simple history, and was often compelled to stop, by pain and want of strength. It was a solemn thing, to hear, in the darkened room, the feeble voice of the sick child recounting a weary catalogue of evils and calamities which hard men had brought upon him. Oh! If when we oppress and grind our fellow-creatures, we bestowed but one thought on the dark evidences of human error, which, like dense and heavy clouds, are rising, slowly it is true, but not less surely, to Heaven, to pour their after-vengeance on our heads; if we heard but one instant, in imagination, the deep testimony of dead men's voices, which no power can stifle, and no pride shut out; where would be the injury and injustice, the suffering, misery, cruelty, and wrong, that each day's life brings with it!
>
> Oliver's pillow was smoothed by gentle hands that night; and loveliness and virtue watched him as he slept. He felt calm and happy, and could have died without a murmur.[44]

Oliver is a tragic animal figure, and also one subjected to English law. He is made pathetic: 'the feeble voice of the sick child recounting a weary catalogue of evils and calamities which hard men had brought upon him'. Oliver and the suffering child class he stands in for invokes deep social concern – the extrapolation of the sympathy movement that incorporates social reform logics into the designed emotional content. This is a rational calculation of care, and Oliver can hardly even narrate the circumstances himself; that there can be an implied audience to the narration of social abjection and calculable recuperation marks both Oliver's social abjection and his narrative impotence. Oliver is a diminished subject, an inoperable object. At the same time, he is possessed of a good will, giving second chances and half his inheritance away to those who do not deserve his kindness. He is saved by a beneficent other, much as Dickens's Esther is in *Bleak House*. The resolution of the story is complete on another important count, as Fagin is to be hanged after a time in the famous Newgate prison.

True to London form, a large crowd gathers for the public hanging, to which Fagin goes ignominiously and without any of the stoic courage of the criminal Jack Sheppard in the other crime novel published in *Bentley's* at the same time as *Oliver Twist*. Dickens's setting matches this action – public executions remained extremely well attended events into the middle of the century. Execution history is a particularly well-catalogued archive, and it is a subject that has translated very well to the famous

London walking tours, several of which may include execution sites or grisly murder tales and additional drippings from the execution spectacle to add a little juice to the exercise. The Museum of London also has an impressive store of scandal and intrigue such as the 1824 execution of Henry Fauntleroy, Esq. a prominent banker who had defrauded the Bank of England. One hundred thousand people showed up to watch the 'gentleman' hang. If one would like, reproductions of the broadside for Fauntleroy's execution can be purchased for £25 (and viewed free of charge) on the Museum of London website. Horace Bleackley's 1905 compendium, *Some Distinguished Victims of the Scaffold*, kept the entertainment in print circulation by including the Fauntleroy broadside and others, trial coverage documents and so on. His preface notes Wordsworth and Coleridge for their fascination with Hadfield, and points his Victorian readers back to the *Newgate Calendar* for a clear description of London history in the eighteenth century. The broadsides for Fauntleroy's and other executions kept the pulse of the gallows beating, even after the end of the live public hanging entertainment that Dickens wrote against. Execution culture is a multimedia affair.

Ten years after the publication of *Oliver Twist*, Dickens attended a public hanging and wrote a letter of complaint to *The Times*. In *Oliver Twist*, Fagin's fate is to be revelled in, though he is made pathetic. Of the 1849 execution he witnessed, however, Dickens would write the following:

> I believe that a sight so inconceivably awful as the wickedness and levity of the immense crowd collected at that execution could be imagined by no man, and could be presented in no heathen land under the sun. The horrors of the gibbet and of the crime which brought the wretched murderers to it, faded in my mind before the atrocious bearing, looks and language, of the assembled spectators. When I came upon the scene at midnight, the *shrillness* of the cries and howls that were raised from time to time, denoting that they came from a concourse of boys and girls already assembled in the best places, made my blood run cold. As the night went on, screeching and laughing, and yelling in strong chorus of parodies on negro melodies, with substitutions of 'Mrs. Manning' for 'Susannah,' and the like, were added to these. When the day dawned, thieves, low prostitutes, ruffians and vagabonds of every kind, flocked on to the ground, with every variety of offensive and foul behaviour. Fightings, faintings, whistlings, imitations of Punch, brutal jokes, tumultuous demonstrations of indecent delight when swooning women were dragged out of the crowd by the police with their dresses disordered, gave a new zest to the general entertainment.[45]

The reaction is identical to the arguments against animal abuse in the Parliamentary debates, and Dickens's own Smithfield criticisms echo loudly here as well. Dickens, canny as his works are on the issue of ambiguous characters and shifting narrative perspectives in a work like *Bleak House*, is ever the moralist here.[46] Dickens would go on to base the character of Mademoiselle Hortense in *Bleak House* on one of the hanged individuals, Marie Manning. The hanging took place at the Horsemonger Lane Gaol that, despite the name, is not near Smithfield but in Southwark (across the Thames from the city centre, for those unfamiliar). The resulting picture of things from Dickens's study in crime is a complicated nexus of Sikes using public hanging's sensational effects as a disciplinary measure against Oliver, only to be punished horribly himself in a fitting administration of poetic justice, and concluding in Dickens's admonishing city officials and the media for continuing the practice a mere ten years later.

Sweeney Todd, one of the best-known penny fictions, capitalises on public fears about deep criminality as well as the gathering concerns about mystery meat products in the slaughter reform era. It is an uncommonly precise melding of public/private disciplinary regimes, civic anxieties, and foodways in the Metropole. Its bureaucratic critique is easily overlooked: the story's grisly works depend upon the urban erasure of solitary travellers – the demon barber's victims were business travellers in the new business centre of the world, perhaps even market drovers, and certainly the deskish types who would yet not be missed amidst the new anonymous city. *Todd* is so mundane as to be haunting in its technological fascinations with the rank abattoir form. The double-barber's chair is a killing invention akin to the innovations of the slaughterhouse, a mechanism for dispatch no less effective than the office life that is no life, clean in its execution and skilfully terrible. This, however, is not the sole mode of penny horror.

Once Stoker read another penny fiction, *Varney the Vampyre*, he had the ideal supernatural spectre through which to express a gathering fear of disease and biological permeations of the body, and he also capitalised on concerns about foreign blood arriving to contaminate London. His fusing of scientific rhetoric and rational analysis, often in the form of journalistic *verité*, also reflected the period boom in daily journalism covering all issues of the city's business. This association of Stoker's novel to journalistic impulses is not quite as neat as it could be, for the more ubiquitous documentary techniques in the novel are phonograph recording and journals. The trouble with any notion of documentary reliability, as the novel plays on for some of its most gripping tensions, is that all of the materials recording the purported events have been catalogued and indexed by one of the characters who is afflicted during the story. Furthermore, the perspective of the characters is routinely unclear or unreliable.

The trouble with narration in *Dracula* has even become a defence of the vampire himself. Nina Auerbach, perhaps the most important *Dracula* scholar to date, discusses this in her book, *Our Vampires, Ourselves*, in which she turns to another key *Dracula* scholar, Carol Senf, to get at the matter:

> Senf claims that *Dracula* is dominated by a series unreliable, even criminal narrators who suppress their vampire, victim: 'Dracula is *never* seen objectively and never permitted to speak for himself while his actions are recorded by people who have determined to destroy him and who, moreover, repeatedly question the sanity of their quest.'[47]

In this case, Stoker's book may shed more light on the trouble with Poe's 'Man of the Crowd' and its narrator than it does on *Sweeney Todd*. In attempting to establish an authoritative order on the city's perceived threats, each of these narratives fit into a London genre that may even require the abjection of narrators in order to sustain a reliable, ordered sense of urban reality that does not overwhelm and 'confuse the senses' as Smithfield does Oliver in Charles Dickens's novel. Dickens himself was a prolific journalist, besides his clear role in the lineage of London urban literatures negotiating increasing population impaction, social divisions and the burgeoning critique of technologically abetted modern labour and living conditions in the megalithic city space. Documenting the horror remained an aspirational act of recovery.

A word here about the broader nonhuman form articulated in the London literatures. None of these urban preoccupations, nor the decisive shift in the material form and price, if not value, of literary output after the reduction in paper costs and the 1810 innovation of the steam press in London, should distract from the intense preponderance of nonhuman thought in British cultural production that links Romanticism, realism and modernism with parallel period popular print forms. In fact, the apparent gap between popular pulp forms – like the pennies and the new journalistic output – and the canonical works of Romanticism or Dickens's novels (published in serial form themselves) is as misleading as the apparent animal concern of the period is on the issue of the amplified erasure of the animal that this concern enables by promoting the Smithfield removal agenda. What arises in the new mass media, abetted by rapid technological advances as well as successful education reform – the city and its citizens *were*, certainly, improved per the agenda of the day – is a blurred and impossibly vast cultural reservoir of print that both documents and articulates a vast audience.

Media, in general, has also been discussed in relation to the articulation of life in the period. For example, Margaret Linley's essay on

Frankenstein and technology, including print technology, interrogates recent biopolitical theory on exclusion and bare life, drawing primarily on Foucault, Agamben and on Judith Butler's critique of media and politics. Linley writes that,

> [a]ccording to Butler, the very conception of the human is elaborated among inequalities illegible from within the framework established by the human, for the human is born on the basis of a 'norm of exclusion' which helps ensure that the violent conditions of its emergence remain unintelligible.[48]

Linley's claim is that 'media creates a predicament for any assertion of life, since exceptional or bare life forms must have a means through which to be recognized'.[49] Linley goes on to discuss the cholera outbreak panic attending the First Reform Act of 1832, during which '[m]edia intensified the scale of dread which would underwrite the infectious disease as both a population concern and an object of political discipline'.[50] The Act in fact marked the third attempt to pass the Bill in Parliament, and so the build-up presented ample opportunities for the press, including the penny presses, to argue for passage via cartoons and other means. As Louis James notes, the press saw its printing capacity triple between 1801 and 1831 in London even with the old, heavy taxation system in place.[51] Nevertheless, media and print succeeded in meeting a huge new 'public' described at the time as 'for the first time becoming a *reading* population, actuated by tastes and habits unknown to preceding generations, and particularly susceptible to such an influence as that of the press'.[52]

On the one hand, 'print' here implies The Press, which congratulated itself on the victory of the 1832 Reform Act Linley discusses. From an August 1832 celebration of the June passage of the Act, at Derby:

> Intellect and Justice have triumphed over Ignorance, Corruption, and misused Power. The Reform Bills have passed. The Land rejoices. In that joy the printers of Derby – the men who exercise the glorious art of the PRESS – the art by which man communicates with man, and by which political truths, the strength and wealth of the public mind, the force of public opinion, are at once diffused and concentrated – unite with unreserved transport. . . .
> THE GREAT ORGAN OF MENTAL STRENGTH IS
> The Press[53]

There has been some attention paid to the role of the new, cheaper press and increased literacy rates in political activity, such as the Chartist movement, and on general reading habits in relation to the sense of an administrative 'public', as also discussed in relation to Andrew Franta's work in Chapter 1.[54] As the backlash against Newgate novels featuring sympathetic criminal characters showed, the public's exponential increase and, in turn, its exponentially increased access to literatures such as the emergent popular press works, was a problem to the civilised society types Dickens can rightly be grouped among given his moralising tendencies. At the same time, Dickens's own social aims – his politics and economic critique – group him squarely with the radicals on other counts.

The development of the pennies, on the other hand, includes the issue of taste: 'dreadfuls' and 'bloods' were terrible works full of nothing but gore and misdeeds, and certainly with no redeeming attributes. On the issue of public affect and conditioning via the readership of new popular literature, which eclipsed even the numbers attending executions, Louis James summarises his discussion of *Sweeney Todd* thusly:

> Apart from its horrific theme, the story sustains the reader's interest, and is occasionally relieved with gentler passages of description ... The story is bound up in itself, and does not impinge on the reader's sense of reality. A reader can enjoy the monstrosity of Sweeney Todd's adventures and, unless he has some mental distortion that makes it real to him, be none the worse ...
>
> While I doubt whether the most unsophisticated reader would be tempted by *The String of Pearls* into a taste for cannibalism, the author added to the fun by setting the story firmly in London: Londoners were invited to think, as they passed St. Dunstan's Church, of the congregation convulsed with the rising stench from Todd's abattoir.[55]

This concern with literature's redeeming aspects and social effects dominated public discourse around the popular fiction of the day while, simultaneously, the pennies were built on plagiarism and mass production. Their basement prices and the ready consumer in the newly literate workingman required rapid and voluminous production to turn a profit.

Before turning to my full discussion of the penny dreadful and popular literature's London production and audience, which will connect as well with other London industries of mass production like the traffic in animals and their multiple uses, I would like to focus on a precursory work by Daniel Defoe. While its publication in 1723–4, on the one hand, rules out any overblown claims that nineteenth-century London is an exceptional host to the bloodthirsty reading public, Defoe's journalistic interest in brutal murders of English business travellers in France – the same Defoe who would write on the terrible immensity of Smithfield, as discussed in Chapter 2 – and his rendering of the tale for the British audience reveal a critical historical context for the development of popular fiction in London as it melds with the mass productive modes under investigation here. As mentioned in Chapter 2, Defoe had a well-known take on Smithfield. Defoe had also written a story about a Colonel Jack that was recycled, as penny material typically was, in a nineteenth-century penny edition. In Colonel Jack one will find, incidentally, another reference to Smithfield Market and to Bartholomew Fair – they pick pockets and rob gentlemen, as one naturally does at Bartholomew and at Smithfield.[56]

This concern for the Defoe story is not incidental, but an archival necessity. The edition of this Defoe work contained in the greatest penny bloods and dreadfuls collection in the world, Barry Ono's, is an 1869 edited volume – the reception of Defoe's crime journalism and narratives enjoyed a revived London heyday under the sign of the post-Smithfield urban malaise.

The Ono Collection includes Defoe stories alongside the highwayman adventures and bloody dreadfuls such as *The String of Pearls*, the serial that Sweeney Todd's human meat pie horrors appeared in. Ono was the most famous and important archivist of penny fiction. His collection is the British Library, and thus perhaps is the Ono Collection is something like the official representation of the genre. The Ono Collection has recently been part of a massive task of digitising and cataloguing an impossibly vast, unruly and incomplete body of works from the nineteenth century. We do not know even what we might be missing in cases where the catalogue is blank and the materials lost. His collection is a signal of the pennies' audience in general, which has also been discussed by James and others. The pennies fed a ravenous London audience, lovers of savage cruelty and bloodshed, marauding adventurers, and imperilled women and murdered children. The Defoe story is a particularly gruesome assemblage of true crime journalism passed along to the ravenous reading audience.

The primary difference between Defoe's early eighteenth-century tale and the pennies' cultural significance to nineteenth-century London has much to do with price and accessibility. The cost of paper shifts dramatically near the time the steam press revolutionises the mass production and distribution of reading material in London, and this boom in journalistic output and the much more affordable (than even the widely available Dickens) penny fiction is hand in hand with a major spike in public literacy rates. As such, the 'taste' for bloody murder is of course a much older proclivity than the appetites of the unwitting cannibals in *Sweeney Todd*.[57] What is especially provocative about Defoe's story as a critique of audience tastes and experience, however, is its basis in the events of the day. Furthermore, a closely related account of the life and execution of the most famous London criminal of the early eighteenth century, Jack Sheppard, was part of an even larger public audience phenomenon. Sheppard's execution was one of those many public executions at Smithfield and at Tyburn Tree, the gallows on Hyde Park right along Holborn/Oxford Street – the busiest central vein of the city dating centuries back. If anything, making too much of literary tastes for blood and offal in the nineteenth century would only further repress the lingering effects of the quite real, visceral blood entertainments the city's populous had long supported.[58]

Defoe's accounts of Sheppard and of Cartouche, a French criminal of even bloodier exploits, foreshadow the London crime fascinations and terrors, as in the case of Jack the Ripper for example. Reminding the contemporary reader perhaps of Truman Capote and *In Cold Blood*, which Capote wrote based on prison interviews of the two killers in a sensational crime that gripped national attention in the United States as it violated any presumptions of a quiet, good, Midwestern simplicity, Defoe's journalistic enthusiasm (he went immediately to Newgate prison to inspect after one of Sheppard's escapes in 1724) drew the admiration of Sheppard, who knew Defoe in fact as 'Mr. Applebee', editor of *Applebee's Original Weekly Journals*.[59] What is more important, however, is the office of Cartouche's victims. The Cartoucheans, as Cartouche's gang was called, had taken to killing businessmen and lawyers on the roads outside urban centres. Not only did this cause commercial losses, it also pitted organised crime of unknown, powerful numbers against a still-organising European law enforcement body. In London, in fact, police forces, like most of civic management, would undergo significant reform and revision during the nineteenth century. The Metropolitan Police Force (Scotland Yard) was founded in 1829 by Robert Peel, and the separate City of London force would be established ten years later. It would truly arrive as a city centre institution in response mostly to new traffic needs during and after the Smithfield removal period, incidentally, and would become notorious, by ineffectual association, thanks to the Jack the Ripper case in 1888.[60]

Defoe, and the public, seemed to have been especially drawn to the Cartouche execution and its aftermath. Cartouche identified hundreds of his associates, leading to law enforcement's grand victory over the mysterious, bloody marauders terrorising international business classes. This abuse of the business classes would be precisely the stuff of *Sweeney Todd*, where the Fleet Street barber 'polished off' lone travellers in London for financial and, more than likely, a good deal of animal trafficking to Smithfield and the butchers' shops just off the famous Fleet Street address for Todd's shop. As public literacy rose in the nineteenth century, so too did ideals of escaping the abject poverty Dickens documented alongside the harrowing tales of Sheppard's crimes and escapes in *Bentley's*. The mass public identified more with the poverty-stricken young Sheppard, feared the authorities, and, sure enough, when Defoe was tracking Sheppard relentlessly, the public was especially inspired and enthralled by the criminal's resourcefulness in eluding the authorities they considered to be more their own oppressor than their ally against his crimes.[61]

The scandal of Englishmen being murdered while abroad in France was, of course, always the scandal of an English gentleman being murdered, as no others would be able to travel or be murdered under such circumstances as Defoe's accounts details: middle class and above would have been the sort with the most money or possessions worth robbing. Contrast this with the intense public pleasure taken in the hanging of the gentleman banker, discussed earlier in the chapter. As William Lee writes in his 1869 volume of Defoe's works, this aspect was sensationalised to sell copies. Defoe's second pamphlet on the Cartoucheans was entitled 'A Narrative on the Proceedings in France for Discovering and Detecting the Murderers of the English Gentlemen'. Lee also notes the popular appeal of Sheppard and even suggests that he ought not to be associated with the inhuman depravity of Cartouche at all. Lee is at pains to communicate the evil savagery of the French criminal before his largely apologetic account of Sheppard. Defoe took his account of the Cartoucheans from an English victim of the crimes who recovered, a surviving servant to one of the murdered gentlemen. Defoe's role in sensationalising Sheppard's exploits, and criminal celebrity more broadly, is well known. From Lee's account of Defoe's Cartouche reports:

> Before his death, this great robber had confessed the names of a large number of his followers, and the crimes they had committed. The horror produced by these revelations gave such an impulse to the course of justice, that several hundreds of these villains were shortly afterward executed. The confederacy being thus broken up, some of the members became leaders of smaller parties, marauding separately, but sometimes together. On the 21st of September 1723, John Lock, Esq., and English Gentleman, returning from Paris, was robbed and murdered within a few miles of Calais by one of these gangs, and a few minutes afterward three other Englishmen, Edward Seabright, Esq.; Henry Mompesson, Esq., John Davies, Esq., and their servants, being on their way to Paris, came to the spot, and were also robbed and murdered by the same miscreants . . .
>
> Although Cartouche occupies a high place in the annals of crime in France, a name so stained with the blood of his fellow-creatures can scarcely be mentioned without execration. Nothing of this kind attaches to the name of John Sheppard, whose brief but wonderful career of infamy produced at the time a degree of public excitement, that might be fitly termed a popular mania; whose sad fate never ceased to be pitied, even by the virtuous, – and

whose acts of ingenuity and daring courage, have invested his character with as much of admiration, as could be bestowed on so great a criminal.[62]

The connection of Defoe to the pennies is of course stronger than simply a contingent inclusion of a bloody document of French murders among the papers of a pennies collector.

Defoe's account of the notorious English criminal Jack Sheppard was one of the most popular pieces for the eighteenth-century reading public captivated by Sheppard's deeds, and the later penny genre made great use of those 'literary accounts'. Defoe's account was featured in a relatively popular periodical, *Applebee's Original Weekly Journals*, published in 1724 as *The History of the Remarkable Life of John Sheppard, Containing A Particular Account of his many Robberies and Escapes*. Sheppard famously approved of Defoe's accounts at his execution. He was hung, but of course, on Tyburn Tree in Hyde Park. As the story goes, what remained of his body, having been assaulted by thronging masses, was buried at St Martin's-in-the-Fields. According to reports, as many as 200,000 of London's roughly 600,000-person population attended the spectacle.[63]

Sheppard was the subject of a very popular Newgate novel in 1839–40 by William Henry Ainsworth, when it ran alongside Dickens's serial, *Oliver Twist*, in *Bentley's Miscellany*. The Newgate or Old Bailey novel was, for all intents and purposes, the predecessor of the penny blood. Ainsworth wrote several of these, including works that included another major penny character, Dick Turpin. The novels hold an especially vexed place in literary-cultural studies because, perceived as they were at the time to glorify, or at least revel in the acts of their criminal protagonists, they were the target of legal censure and general ridicule in various literary magazines and even an occasional direct satire by William Makepeace Thackeray. Although not as roundly rejected on literary grounds as the pennies would be, the Newgate novels were deemed lowbrow. At least one of the Newgate authors, Thomas Peckett Prest, would become directly involved in the penny business: he was the co-author, with James Malcolm Rymer, of *Sweeney Todd* and *Varney the Vampyre*. So it is that Defoe, via his work on the real Jack Sheppard that would inspire such a robust afterlife in popular cultural expression including plays, songs and other works, is linked indelibly to the business of the pennies and, as such, is a perfectly logical author for Barry Ono to catalogue alongside his more pedestrian texts. Defoe published in *Applebee's*, and Applebee had also been the primary publisher of crime literature as well as the overseer of the precursor Newgate press preceding the *Newgate Calendar* of criminal trial and execution accounts that Sheppard and others populated.

The account of the Cartoucheans showcases criminal terror on business travel routes in horrible, brutal detail. This poses these liminal criminals in a gruesome didacticism. *Oliver Twist* also traded in the educative potential of an abject criminal environs. The mass readership of crime accounts, like the attendees of sensational executions, however, suggests that nothing terribly edifying was afoot. As I've written elsewhere, Kafka's 'In the Penal Colony' suggests a similar disconnect between the scene of punishment and disciplinary affect.[64] The account begins with an inadvertent connection between horror and entertainment:

> As the robbery and murder committed in September last, on the persons of four English gentlemen and their servants, near Calais, justly filled the world with a kind of uncommon surprise, so France seemed more than ordinarily touched with it. The whole nation entertained the relation of it with horror, as if, however innocent, it had reflected upon the very name of the French, and that it had been a fact so cruel, and so outrageously vile, that nothing like it had ever been committed but in France . . .
> But such a piece of savage cruelty as this was, in murdering the gentlemen without mercy, after they had peaceably delivered their money into their hands, filled everybody with an inexpressible horror and amazement.[65]

The criminals under investigation may have inspired Dickens to articulate the small time initiatory circles in *Oliver Twist* that surely lead, eventually, to the unspeakable class of criminality in Poe:

> He says that this Joseph Bizeau acknowledged he had used the trade long before Cartouch was heard of; that the said Cartouch was at first but an underling, a poor low-priced street-runner, a kind of shop-lifter, or pick-pocket, and knew nothing of the matter, being only a disbanded foot-soldier, naked, and almost starved, when, merely for his bold, audacious spirit, he was taken in, upon his humble petition, into the great society of gentlemen, as he called them, meaning the gang of highway robbers, who acted in a higher sphere of thievery, and had, for some years, plied the forest of Orleans, the great road to Italy, and the woods about Fountainbleau, where they robbed with security, as well as success, and were seldom attacked, and never overcome.[66]

These transcendent criminals – their inscrutable, supernatural criminality is established from square one – are called throughout the narrative a 'bloody gang'. Their butchers' work is 'horrid murders', and they 'mangle and cut in pieces the bodies of those they kill, so that they may not be known, throwing body parts in the Seine in the aftermath'. The city 'was a constant scene of blood and rapine' and the acts' cover of night meant that 'no man was safe in going abroad after candlelight'.[67] The objects stolen were almost always stock receipts – papers that were the only evidence that money had been spent on stock shares. The narrative notes that these were not 'ear-marked', and so they could be transferred without procedural intervention via gift or, in this case, theft. Possession was all that was required to claim the monetary share, and so the paper was as good as gold:

> The sum of the matter is this, that, in a word, this circumstance of the papers was the encouragement of the robbers, and the raising the fame of Cartouch and his company, for now, to get the paper of a stock, was to get the stock, let it amount to what sum soever; to pick a pocket, and draw out a pocket-book, was to get an estate, and it was a frequent thing to have some gentlemen in the crowd whose very pocket-books were worth many millions.[68]

The Cartoucheans then sold the papers quickly for ready money and, rather than committing one great final score, established a thriving business model of their own to rival the staid office productivity in 'Bartleby'. While they could have left the realm of justice with the money, never to be traced or apprehended, they did not. The criminal that takes shape in this narrative is the total outlaw who also populates the business and financial world as a rich thief who cannot be tracked or punished, a savage appendage of the roads themselves. Defoe writes that these criminals had office positions as 'setters' and 'winkers' who watched the market and knew who bought or sold stock, and then the gang's leader could set the gunmen to rob them on the road. The business afoot was a bloody traffic in paper:

> In most, or all these cases, they seldom executed their designs without blood; for the booty they had in pursuit was generally so great, and the method of coming at it was naturally so violent, that there was no remedy but to murder the persons they attacked, and they were, indeed, almost obliged to this butchery by necessity; for that there was too much difficulty in coming at the prize, if the person had life left to struggle for it, or a voice to cry out, which, in a city so populous as that of Paris is, would not fail to bring help instantly about them; they were therefore obliged either immediately to cut the person's throat or to throw a handkerchief about his neck, or, at one blow, to knock him down, and then dispatch him, or they would be surrounded with people; and the soldiers, who were appointed, on that extraordinary occasion, to be always patrolling in the streets, would be upon them.
> These things made Paris, indeed, be a dismal place to live in; nothing but known poverty was a protection, nothing but broad daylight and the open street a security, so that, after some time, those who were charged with great sums transacted nothing but in private, made no bargains in the Quincampoix but by whisper, and, as it were, in secret, or by appointed retirement to proper places; in a word, a general wariness possessed mankind, and they seemed to be afraid of everyone they met; they seemed to take everybody that did but look at them to be a thief, and to clap their hands immediately to the

pocket where the letter-case lay, if any man that they did not know came but near them.[69]

These tropes of blood and of butchery mount in the narrative, and also make up the visceral, gruesome stuff of the later pennies.[70] Other crimes against humanity committed by the gangs include the robbery of a 'whorehouse', replete with 'lewd acts', some of them unspeakable for the benefit of the readers' imaginations, as in the case of prostitutes 'tied naked to fiddlers in position not fit to be named' and more:

> The story is embellished by our author with some lewd pranks they played also with the gentleman's mistress, who they had caused to lie stark naked before them all the while they were plundering him and the matron of their money; but those things, as too gross for our relation, we purposely omit, our business being of a more serious nature.[71]

And then, the narrative begins to introduce the moral account of these acts, employing its apparent limit concept rhetoric of criminality. It matches the still-to-come nineteenth-century animal rights, Smithfield removal and anti-butcher rhetoric discussed in Chapter 2:

> [T]his is certain, that they carried on their trade of robbery, both before and after, more like savages and butchers than men born among Christians, and, as our author relates things, nothing has ever been acted with so much barbarity and unnatural cruelty in our age.[72]

Defoe's account notes that they deserved their punishment, much as Fagin surely deserves his hanging in *Oliver Twist*, suggesting also that they are perhaps even more to be feared and punished by virtue of their professional office, their practiced craft:

> Of this horrid race of men, and thus introduced, these two, whose execution has been so justly severe, and who we are now speaking of, are produced; and if the author, from whom these facts are thus published, had made a true collection, they have had a great length of time to practice their villainies . . .[73]

The report of the murders, transcribed supposedly from a survivor of the gang, is dominated by words relating to butchery: 'Who was butchered next I cannot tell', 'Mr. Mompesson took notice in the night, that he thought the rogues were but indifferently paid for the drudgery of butchering so many', 'This inhuman butchery soon spread its fame over the whole country; and as it filled the ears of all that heard it with horror', 'the butchery rogues', 'bloody disposition' and so on.[74] The other terms

– barbarity, inhuman murder, massacre – all echo the complaints from Smithfield and the demonisation of butchers that come in the century after these accounts. As discussed in Chapter 2, the Butchers' Guild in London had a long and troubled civic history and Defoe was among the public authors who noted the atrocity of the Smithfield space. Likewise, the techniques he employs to communicate the Cartoucheans' atrocities – their 'barbarous massacre' – play on the question of civilised society: the 'coup de grace' is so 'horrible' it 'cannot be heard by Christian ears'. It was 'inhuman murder' all around.[75]

Curiously, however, Defoe also includes the social determinant of the atrocities. The gang is comprised of sutlers. Sutlers, technically, were salesmen and merchants who provided various wares or soldiers via moving stores on the warfront. Defoe's account includes further information: This 'barbarous race of people', including boys and women, was a species of body strippers who followed the camp with no employ, taking things off dead bodies and finishing off not-yet dead bodies on the battlefield:

> Of this wretched gang what could be expected but a crew of ruffians, who, being early – from their very childhood – drenched in blood, and hardened against the cries and entreaties of the miserable – deaf to all the most moving expostulations, and strangers to pity and compassion, were ripened up for all manner of cruelty, and the more bloody any undertaking was likely to be, the more suitable to their nature and inclination.[76]

The conditions of war meant people tolerated these nonhumans, with their inhuman acts and bloody depravity. And yet when they were left without a job to do, post-war (or at least interwar), they turned their comportment and their skill in liminal 'priggery' to the business classes travelling in an increasingly cosmopolitan and financialised Europe that could not comprehend (or 'hear') their acts, let alone mitigate them:

> But this gang, who sheltered on the frontiers, being, as is observed, the refuse and outcast of the army, the brood of sutlers and blackguard boys, their usage was so bloody that nothing seemed to be attempted by them without it; and, as our author writes, murder was their element, and they delighted in it; nay, even they killed people when no danger of discovery, no difficulty of escape, or any other necessity, pressed them to it.[77]

This is the sort of criminal that Ono and the nineteenth-century penny fiction aficionado would fall madly in love with. This was the 'type and genius of deep crime' that was not merely clever, deceptive and evasive. The criminal element being proffered in popular narrative – the public hanging, the journalistic press, the midrange Dickens serial or the dreadful cheap mass market presses – had to be wholly expunged from the human ranks in order to galvanise the desire for civil society in a time of sweeping abjection in the London streets, in particular, and at a time of intense participation of the working classes in social organisation in mid-century London.

London's population increases to 1,000,000 around 1810, making it the first true metropolis of the modern world. Also in the nineteenth century, literacy rates among the working class skyrocket throughout Britain. David Mitch and others have examined the causes for this increase, and Mitch considers both the national elementary education system and an increase in popular demands for education in his work, *The Rise of Popular Literacy in Victorian England: The Influence of Private Choice and Public Policy*. Mitch tracks the literacy rates via several statistical studies including the increasing instances of marriages confirmed by actual signatures instead of simple marks such as 'X' by the marrying parties. Mitch and others note at least a doubling in literacy rates between 1840 and 1900.[78] Another evaluation of literacy in the period by Martyn Lyons considers the rise in literacy not just among working class populations but also among all children and all women. Lyons claims that 70 per cent of the male population of England was literate by 1850, which seems at first a potential contradiction to the numbers of Mitch and others, if they are to double by 1900, but Lyons also notes that rates varied dramatically between town and country.[79] Literacy within massive London was, before 1850 even, high and rising.

To answer the insatiable demands of this massive reading public, popular presses began to produce in earnest. The stamp tax reforms had put cheap paper in the hands of both radical and improvement publishers, and a boom in periodicals put reading into the daily lives of Londoners.[80] Into the second half of the nineteenth century, in response to growing popular demand for this newly accessible mode of entertainment, not merely information and education, other publishers began to produce short, cheap, lurid tales of adventure, murder and supernatural mystery. These works would cost a penny, sometimes even a mere halfpenny, and enterprising readers would often trade and circulate one copy among multiple readers. The penny dreadfuls, or penny bloods, were thus read by more individual readers than the works of even the very popular Charles Dickens or other canonical nineteenth-century British authors.[81] This comparison has become the gold standard by which to show the popularity of penny literature. Dickens, published in serial form as well, was still overpriced for much of Britain. Louis James, in *Fiction for the Working Man 1830–1850*, makes such claims and also tracks popular fiction by yearly consumption.[82] The penny periodicals that arrive shortly after 1820 and the invention of the steam printing press begin a continuous growth in popular literary production and consumption to match the rising literacy rates. And most importantly, as one reviewer of James's book, Patricia Thomson, notes, the widespread consumption of such works presents an essential view on British society in the period that the social novels by Dickens and others in fact may distort. Thomson summarises: 'The social novels of the 1840's convey an aura of working-class plain living and high thinking which does not stand investigation.'[83] This rehearses and old claim about highbrow/lowbrow tastes and trends, but in the case of the pennies, there is sheer, simple consumption to contend with just as the period's historic animal law achievements attend the massive increase in real meat consumption.

There was also an American tradition of penny literature, published independently of the British series by American publishing houses and dominated by boys' tales of adventure and heroism that fit well with the frontier wilderness of the young US terrain. The British pennies could, as in *Sweeney Todd*, be an urban affair, defined by the intense proximity of unknown others, the strange, inescapable dangers punctuating even the most familiar city spaces with dark alleys and hidden basement abattoirs, and the growing sense of health and social risks that invaded homes and bodies without the victim ever being aware of contamination. This bred a permanent condition of fear, bringing the bad sorts and depraved criminals who terrorised the liminal open road between familiar cities in highwaymen pennies right into the city space. Something – one never knew what, but *something* was surely amiss – lurked around every corner, in every dark alley or perhaps even in one's own home. But a vast number of these works also took place outside city spaces on the high seas or in remote caves and woods. Many were set in prior centuries, before widespread mechanisation of life and transportation. There seem to be more horses in penny dreadfuls than in Dickens, for example, and rarely is the horse riding a casual entertainment or unremarkable travel at a country estate. The stories investigated escape – from the city, from the present – and facilitated the fantasy of conquest that urban work life could hardly produce.

Londoners, alienated and displaced by the massive industrial city, could not stop consuming the abjection that was the pennies' stock and trade. This was also the strongest and most consistent mood of now-canonised literary authors such as Poe and Baudelaire, but the sheer form and circulation of these comparably mass-produced works hit right at the core of the urban critique these authors expressed. The pennies excepted, horrible villains exploited perfectly the blank inhumanity of the human and animal condition in London, while their low status was so certain that it is now difficult to even find a number of the works given the physical insignificance of the very materials they were produced from and the total disregard nearly everyone paid them as objects. The pennies both were and were not 'collector's item' literature, echoing comic trading and other practices while not holding the same precious appeals to originality given the plagiarism and anonymity of its author ranks. Perhaps they were the nineteenth-century version of repurposed clickbait online, sensational and convenient relative to those costly subscription substances, down and dirty like a fast food quick fix.

The name 'penny dreadful', once again, itself indicates both the material fungibility of the works and their perceived literary value. They would be bought and recycled, shared amongst a readership group within a neighbourhood or work community, so that they could be consumed – quite literally 'used' up' – via excessive handling within one serial edition run. The pennies could disintegrate before their serial lifespan had even passed, given enough hands processed them. Ono's collection is missing an undetermined number of its original items due to a basement flood and casual disregard for the materials after his death. The works hardly seemed important. Now, this crucial reflection and propellant of the pervasive moods of urban abjection in nineteenth-century London shares the material insignificance it exploited so effectively for the popular literacy that, ironically, was produced to consume and be consumed in urban industrial London. The objects themselves are as vulnerable and fungible as the cheapest physical materials and as disposable as the most replaceable, easily consumed and prurient narrative material. The stories themselves were often sensational, condensed narratives. The earliest ones favoured highwaymen and tales of frightening travel outside city walls, as in *The Cartoucheans*. The open road and open country dissolved social regulations, and the most popular stories often featured outlaws – bandits, primarily – acting not as virtuous Robin Hoods but as outright mercenaries of self-interest. All of this reflects disintegrating forms of life and daily occupation in the city space and the vast meat space that both saturated and exceeded civic borders.

The period in print publication history after 1810 includes an incredible increase in production for a combination of reasons. In 1810, in London, Friedrich Koenig first employs automatic printing techniques to mass-produce texts. Before his steam press innovation, all presses had to be turned by hand. This severely limited the quantity of production. Once Koenig's steam-driven press was implemented in other London publishing houses, the sheer volume of print material positively dwarfed the prior output. This would be the beginnings of the mass production, distribution and circulation of literatures of any sort – literary, popular, journalistic, any type at all. *The Times* of London would be the first to purchase the new technology in 1814.[84]

This does not happen precisely in 1810. Rather, the true explosion in print production would come about ten years later once paper production for this purpose catches up to the technology and can consistently produce paper of uniform, larger sizes. The shift to machine paper manufacture instead of hand-pressed pulp techniques is developed during the first two decades of the nineteenth century, mostly in England and in France, and is quickly taken up in the United States and elsewhere after 1820.[85] Paper in the first two decades of the century had become exorbitantly expensive, contributing directly to a severely diminished publishing industry and high book prices. Paper-making technology had been developed already, but only around 1820 was machine paper manufacture finally employed across the industry. Once this was the case, paper prices dropped steeply. What follows from this combination of technological advances and adaptations is a bustling popular press industry.

Pinpointing the origins of the demand for the new mass production is a trickier business, but that demand among a new public is a crucial dynamic. Discussing claims by Leigh Hunt and William Hazlitt around this time about printing's remarkable new power in public discourse, Andrew Franta, in *Romanticism and the Rise of the Mass Public*, writes that

> neither printing nor its widespread dissemination were new in the nineteenth century ... Hunt's and Hazlitt's claims have less to do with technological innovation than the effects of the emergence of the mass reading public. Their point, in other words, is that while print technology was by no means new, it took the appearance of new classes of readers to realize print's full potential.[86]

However, there is significant reason to believe that, in fact, no such mass public pre-existed the new print mechanisms and their advancement. Historians of the literary consumption in the period often note that the prior century had seen expansive public education programmes and, on top of this, enclosure and other forces had driven a new mass public to cities like London in the proverbial droves. This explosion of the public was unprecedented, and with a higher rate of literacy among all classes in the metropolis, there is at least some explanation of a reading public fit to consume the sheer volume of literary output from the new mass presses. The development of mass print culture was, thus, as rapid as London's population increases in the period were. Beginning slowly in 1810 and exploding by around 1820, the amount of literature available skyrocketed alongside an incredible increase in literacy.

London was the world's first million-person city as the nineteenth century began. The 1801 census recorded 1,096,784 people living in London. By 1815, the number was 1.4 million. By 1860, there were 3.2 million inhabitants.[87] This meant London had the largest reading public in one concentrated metropolitan area ever. The print industry quickly learned to keep up with the demands of this massive public. This mirrors the Smithfield scenario and its meat supply role for the same consuming public. Furthermore, as James Raven notes in his geographical study of London publishing histories (albeit the period immediately preceding 1810), the publishing industry itself is housed in much the same area of London as Smithfield.[88] But on the issue of nineteenth-century print culture alone, there is a clear and massive increase due to a specific historical technological circumstance borne of the gathering demand for this increase. The people were hungry. There were a lot of people.

Once the texts were more ubiquitous, their individual prices came down in some cases. This was true, generally, across the spectrum of publication, but there was still a firm sense of literary status, or at least of the value of fame, and some paper cost more than other paper; prolific London authors like Dickens saw the prices for their novels, even in serial form, stay much higher than prices for the exploding cheap paper serial trade. Another key development in the nineteenth-century print trade was the lowering of taxes on paper and, in 1861, the outright abolition of the paper tax. The newspaper trade grew even more after 1861, as did the print industry in general.[89] The increasing demand led to tensions between the publishers and the government, and in line with the 1810 steam press innovation came a previously unheard-of access to cheap paper for mass literary production. And so the first part of the penny dreadful moniker has to do with price. A penny dreadful cost one penny. Contrast this with the production cost of 'penny-a-liners' like Dickens, paid as the expression suggests.[90]

Even a penny could be too rich for some workers in London, and this was why they would often share one copy amongst several readers in a neighbourhood area. This is one issue that makes determining the precise readership of any penny dreadful extremely complicated. But circulation numbers suggest that these were the most commonly read literature of the nineteenth century. Besides this, there is a significant archive problem in tracking penny dreadful history: it's often impossible to know who the actual authors were.[91] On top of this, it can be difficult, sometimes impossible, to determine even which printer ran a particular penny dreadful. Other times, publishers might have existed only to publish one series. Other times, the same story may have several publishers associated with it. And further still, even those publishers that are reasonably well known and clearly associated with particular serials seem to have kept terrible records during their existence that have become no better through the passage of time since.[92] This all amounts to a jumbled, bloody mess. The material history of these texts resists cataloguing in ways the era's fascination with natural history and taxonomy would seem to have surely ruled out. Nevertheless, tracking these texts and their multiple versions and editions, and getting clear information on actual authors while wading through myriad pen names and constant plagiarism stands as a monumental task with no guarantee of successful completion. The trouble with the history of penny dreadful, really, could not match the city's general problems with cacophonous, untraceable overcrowding and intersecting influences at Smithfield any better.

Besides the confusion caused by such archival challenges, the serials themselves troubled notions of precise literary value thanks to their rampant plagiarism, and the incredible reduction in price literature undergoes in the nineteenth century amplifies the question of literary value in yet another sense. Charles Dickens, wildly popular despite still being inaccessible to large sections of the population due to the cost of his works, was also a wildly popular victim of penny press plagiarism. The penny fiction reign of terror as London's most accessible and popular literary form begins essentially with Thomas Pickett Prest's plagiarism of Dickens's *Pickwick Papers* as *Penny Pickwick*. The penny press thus made literature available to the newly massive reading public in a form of discount recirculation. There were original stories and series, to be sure, but the pennies also made the works of famous authors available to a ravenous reading public. Dickens, for example, was typically available in monthly instalments at one shilling per issue. One shilling was twelve pence. Thus, one weekly series in a penny edition was one third as expensive as Dickens, and there would be, by the close of the nineteenth century, a number of halfpenny editions on the market. The economical alternative is clear, and the general accessibility a penny promised is matched in the price of a shave in the most notorious penny serial of all. Sweeney Todd's barbershop, with its white and red pole, boasts the window advertisement: 'Easy shaving for a penny, As good as you will find any.'[93] The alternative to the shilling monthly serial, for those who wanted to read Dickens, was a library subscription. Those typically cost forty-two shillings, or more than five hundred pence; a reader could get ten different penny serials per week at such rates. Publishers that made Dickens and other works available to the working classes at the penny rates thus not only met an existing demand, they fomented that demand by levelling the cost of literature. Readers found other ways to stretch their money, often sharing penny editions amongst neighbourhood communities of readers who then split the cost even further.[94]

There are other aspects of nineteenth-century serial publication that highlight the unruliness attending early mass production of popular culture. One is the case of boys' magazines, a primary mode of serial fictions that included highwayman suspense stories and tales of adventure, the former being a more direct precursor to the penny dreadful and urban murder tale. There were massive numbers of different publications with titles including the word 'boys' in some form. The narrative and material quality of these publications was apparently not important. The same storylines could show up in multiple different series, characters killed in prior editions could be suddenly alive and well in later issues with no explanation at all, and general typographical errors were all common. Nevertheless, these boys' tales and the broader serial fiction of the day enjoyed a voracious readership. The publishers had no trouble satisfying that demand, as they could borrow liberally from prior publications and from more established literature including the works of Dickens and other canonical writers of the period. Dickens was wildly popular, but his works and other literary works remained out of the price range of the new, massive reading public in London. But copyright law was still developing, and so individual publishers could plagiarise to their heart's content with little consequence.[95]

The pennies also challenge notions of authorship and celebrity relative to material cultural consumption. Dickens himself was serialised, and his notoriously prolific output (similar to Sir Walter Scott) included pervasive media activity. During his lifetime, Dickens was a well-known author of city journalism, a serial fiction writer, a legal reporter and so on. But even though his output was ubiquitous and he was serialised per the period's trends, Dickens was still Dickens. He was famous in the manner the personalities of Romanticism were. The authors of penny dreadfuls were often unknown. There are clear exceptions, such as Thomas Pickett Prest and James Malcolm Rymer, the authors of *Varney the Vampyre* and *Sweeney Todd*, though Rymer is generally also considered the primary author of *Todd*. But in general, the pennies were mechanised, anonymous and even surreptitiously written works. Some writers had multiple aliases to protect their identities as aspiring serious authors. The early forerunner to the gig or sharing economy, these occupations highlight the developed forms of disassembled labour in nineteenth-century literary culture. They would ghost write these lurid, cheap stories and often recycle narratives from prior works or proper authors like Dickens. The penny dreadful was the processed meat of literary production, the amalgamated sausage of narrative. Penny authors were invisible, nameless drones.

The inscrutable provenance of these mostly unremarkable narratives and the cheapness of their material composition seem almost too harmonious with the canonical example of the genre. The Sweeney Todd episodes are also especially pertinent to the gruesome state of London meat products and general anxieties about human food contamination and consumption. Published serially from 1846 to 1847, the series features the eponymous Sweeney Todd, the 'demon barber of fleet street', whose modus operandi is to collect his victims from his own barber chair. Published by the most prolific penny publisher of the era, Edward Lloyd, *Sweeney Todd* is a textbook example of the penny dreadful's recycled, or reassembled, processed meat mode – there are multiple versions of the story. Although there were earlier stage versions and multiple printed versions – or perhaps, as a result of all of this overlap – the story became very popular, very fast.[96] *Sweeney Todd* would be a simple enough story about a serial killer but for the horrible aftermath: Todd's victims end up in meat pies sold to unsuspecting customers. This is not the first version of such a food horror.

Charles Dickens portrayed a meat pie salesman who put cats into his meat pies in *Pickwick Papers*. This information is part of a general advisory to urban dwellers that they educate themselves on the source of their foods, and relates more broadly to urban legends about alien meat pies and other products made outside London but consumed by Londoners. Perhaps reflecting some of the same anxieties that produced earlier highwaymen penny dreadfuls, this urban mistrust of dark, unknown, disordered rural foodways in fact recurs in Dickens's later novel, *Martin Chuzzlewit*, when the narrator remarks on 'the dens of any of those preparers of cannibalistic pastry, who are represented in many country legends as doing a lively retail business in the metropolis'.[97] The city was during this time host to myriad programmes to clean up streets and rectify social ills, many of which led to intensive architectural and street renovations coinciding as well with expansive rail development.

Sweeney Todd proceeds as a series of these food production murders, basement butcheries, assembly-line pie manufacture and then sale at the (unsuspecting) public market. In the stories, Todd pulls a lever in his shop and the customer/victim plunges into the dark basement abattoir below. The victims are often killed by the fall when they fracture their neck or crack their head open, which was a common means of dispatching livestock around Smithfield as well. If the fall does not kill them, Todd heads downstairs to finish the job with his gleaming straight razor, 'polishing them off' with a clean slit of the throat. Todd's barber chair is a technologically intricate revolving 'double chair', with two barber's chairs that can be flipped by the press of a button so a body is turned upside down and erased from existence while, up in the barber shop, a clean, empty chair betrays no crime. Next, the corpse is processed into unidentifiable meat, which then, through another ingenious mechanism, passes through cabinet shelves in the wall and into an adjoining basement where a young man is being held prisoner. His charge is to make the meat pies for Mrs. Lovett to sell at the market. These grisly assembly-line pies were eagerly anticipated by a voracious consuming audience much as the *String of Pearls* stories themselves were by the reading public of London.

As Robert Mack has discussed in his work, *Sweeney Todd*, the victims of Todd's violence are solitary, anonymous travellers 'lost' into belly of London. Mack does not draw the connection to the sutlers of Defoe's tale, but he notes that '[t]he clothes, possessions and unusable body parts of Todd's former customers are hidden both within the barber's house and within the increasingly noisome and overcrowded vaults of the neighbouring church of St Dunstan's in the west, also on Fleet Street'.[98] As London became a buzzing business centre, it also drew travellers from all corners of the world, and those travellers were often males travelling alone in pursuit of their fortune. Fleet Street would also have been the metonym for the newspaper industry and the press.[99]

What are most alluring in the *Todd* story are its associations with the meat industry – and the host of London anxieties therein reflected – discussed in Chapter 2. In Thomas Peckett Prest's version of the story, for example, a magistrate attempting to crack the case poses as farmer who had brought beasts from out of town to market. This seemingly incidental note in fact implicates Smithfield Market directly in the narrative as the most likely destination for any live meat animals brought to London from outside the city. Mack's introduction includes a dazzling overview of other attending meat topics, such as the fact that, by the beginning of the nineteenth century, the Worshipful Company of Butchers was letting just about any kind of meat be sold in the city as a result of suburban competition: '"every kind of shoddy or mouldy flesh could be purchased," Ackroyd observes of the period, so that the "unchecked reign of commerce" involved with the sale of meat became itself a kind of "symbol of city life"'.[100] There were even 'penny pies' to be had, as a result, aligning indeed the penny press with the meat trade in London. Mack's review of London malignancies and the gathering anxiety about 'perfect' murders committed by invisible criminals like those already discussed in this chapter, includes authors from De Quincey to Orwell.[101] He also considers other atrocities such as rumoured cannibalism at sea (a fear Stoker may have also had in mind for the ship travel in *Dracula*) and the tinning of meat as a means to mitigate humans falling from their humanity under duress.[102]

Mack compiles all of the juicy bits of the London meat space with all of the gruesome urban fears and historical developments in place: 'burkers' tracking vagrants and killing them for dissection experiments by the 'sawbones' doctors exploring anatomy in the early London medical schools. And the poet John Clare hearing from an acquaintance of the hysteria surrounding travel in London as 'unwary walkers in the great metropolis routinely disappeared into trap-doors connected to a subterranean network of tunnels' robbed, murdered, thrown into boiling cauldrons, bones sold to doctors.[103] There are then the grave robbers in Dickens's *Our Mutual Friend* (Mack references *A Tale of Two Cities* instead). As Mack writes,

> Such macabre tales of flesh, bones, and body parts were naturally of a piece with the gossip related to similar stories of unspeakable desecrations in the heart of an increasingly mythologized London after dark – a London of gas-lit, yellow streets, and deep, impenetrable fog. The so-called 'gas-light ghouls' of the Victorian era, at least, appear to have been all the more ghoulish when they confessed to feeling a bit peckish.[104]

It is the London of Poe, of Dickens and even of Defoe's French butchers. Mack's work bridging the meat-eating culture of nineteenth-century London with the *Sweeney Todd* concludes with an accounting of some of the all-time great terrible, huge, alien meat pies of English culinary history. To a one, they stink and offend.

In the story itself, which has offensive crimes and a drawn-out narrative arc befitting the pennies' disposable status and the crime tale's sensational figures, takes place in the environs immediately off the butchers' stalls and known icons of the Smithfield-era meat industry even when off the Smithfield track a bit. The magistrate posing as drover tells Todd he is staying at the Bull's Head Inn, which was at the important meat space of Clare Market, right off Fleet Street.

Clare Market had tons of butcher's shops and was known, definitively, as a meat market specialising in cut meat and not the Smithfield live animal store. However, it was also an active slaughter site in the private butchers' abattoirs, which were discussed in greater detail in Chapter 2. Among other incidental Bull's Head details: Hogarth and his artists' group used to meet at the Bull's Head, and it is now roughly on the spot of the London School of Economics.

A visit to modern-day London will confirm the anxieties the story and the others reviewed in this chapter present: narrow winding alleyways.

Heavy traffic. Proximity but anonymity, even for regular travellers. There would have been an itinerant market class besides the butchers and grocers themselves, involving all of the barren occupations and fixations of the middle classes and the sordid abjections thereby inflicted, bettering any Dickens could have imagined for the poor if not for the bare fact that, still, they had money. On this note, the Bull's Head block would have been rundown and poor, but the victim has money on him all the same. Todd buys it all in the story's resolution, though the story seems implausible at best and suggests Todd is 'slipping'. Readers sense the game is up as well, as the meat delivery mechanism has by this point been revealed. The only remaining event is for the law to witness the killing apparatus, the two-sided chair performing automated slaughter and erasure under the cover of the doubled assigned seat of the customer–victim. Clare Market was renovated at end of the century, erased in a similar flick of the civic administrative straight razor as discussed in Chapter 2. The final, staged victim is the empowered agent of the law and the wizened city denizen. His story is that he consorted with drovers and butchers, meat industry figures who were as disposable for the city as were the animals it ate. Their fate was as peripheral and unimportant as any of Todd's travelling piefolk, the lowest life forms in city, yet also at the heart of profiteering complaints and suspicions of corruption and secret wealth.

If the story is not gruesome enough, the bloody geography of the space can be made clearer: near the butcher shop is Chancery Lane and the court in *Bleak House*. A bit further north, Smithfield Market, the great heart of the meat industry refracted by the mystery meat pies Todd and Lovett sell to the city – the imported and the foreign unwittingly consumed even amidst the rampant anxieties about the meat-industry risks to the new mass public. The area, like all of London at the time, also included stinking churches, with the dead returning from under the floorboards. The city's new, massive population still had to die, and there was yet another unscrupulous yet enterprising business to be had in taking on more bodies (and the fees charged for disposal) than could reasonably be buried. Horrid stacks of the dead interrupted church services regularly in the city centre and elsewhere until the 1852 civic act on burial, right as the Smithfield Removal Act was in process. This is the source of a popular tourist attraction: the seven great Victorian cemeteries, including Highgate at Hampstead Heath, site of Lucy's white lady on the Heath, eating children (no matter what a current-day tour guide may say to the contrary). The City Beautiful improvements weren't simply the organic result of a civilised society. Parishioners went to church breathing in the bad air of decaying corpses: life with death, throughout the city and threatening its denizens at every corner.

An urban legend such as the one Dickens employs with the 'growlers' and 'meowers' and the foreign meat fears reiterated an urban/rural animosity that *Todd* carries on. This furthers the general sense of urban anxiety and reactive complaint about uncontrollable but intimately felt economic and health woes smuggled into every crevice and pore of the human in London. This subjection was total and oppressive in the form of fogs, smells and foods. *Sweeney Todd*, as a popular serial on the eve of the major London slaughter and general civic reform, inculcates the economic and media identifier of London – Fleet Street – and the burgeoning service consumption industry – barbers for hire – with the abjection of urban anonymity and the administered atrocities and forms of life discussed earlier in this chapter. Humans purchased all goods and were subject to the quality and price set by uncontrolled, potentially malicious and unknown forces. Humans themselves end up becoming the meat the city consumes as fodder for its mechanised workings. The penny dreadfuls of the mid- and late-nineteenth century form a coherent expression of this London malaise, which is articulated in the other literatures here under review as bureaucratic routines juxtaposed with unspeakable, undefined horrors of bloody murder, impossible city experience and the exclusionary, abjective logics of the improving society.

Notes

1. Mack, Robert L., ed. *Sweeney Todd: The Demon Barber of Fleet Street*. Oxford University Press, 2007, p. 141.
2. Poe, Edgar Allen. 'The Man of the Crowd', in *The Complete Tales and Poems of Edgar Allen Poe*. The Modern Library, 1938, p. 481.
3. Poe, 'The Man of the Crowd', p. 479.
4. Poe, 'The Man of the Crowd', p. 478.
5. Poe, 'The Man of the Crowd', p. 481.
6. Poe, 'The Man of the Crowd', pp. 475, 481.
7. Night shopping and window-shopping were new, popular pastimes in the early reign of Victoria as gas lighting made the London city space at night accessible in new ways. See: Nead, Lynda. *Victorian Babylon: People, Streets, and Images in Nineteenth-Century London*. Yale University Press, 2000. See in particular Part II, 'Gas and Light', pp. 83–148.
8. See: Tomory, Leslie. *Progressive Enlightenment: The Origins of the Gaslight Industry, 1780–1820*. The MIT Press, 2012.
9. Beadenkopf, George. 'The Centenary of the Introduction of Gas in Baltimore', *The Baltimore Gas and Electric News*, 5:6 (June 1916), p. 243.
10. Mackowiak, Philip A., MD. *Postmortem: Solving Histories Great Medical Mysteries*. American College of Physicians, 2007, p. 251.
11. In a typically scandalous irony attending the Smithfield reforms, the

nineteenth-century soap boiler's works comprised a particularly noxious site of stink, effluvia and public health threats. See: Metcalfe, pp. 99–103.
12. See: Retzsch, Morris. *Retch's Series of Twenty-Six Outlines, Illustrative of Goethe's Tragedy of Faust*. Boosey and Sons, 1820. Referenced in Poe, 'The Man of the Crowd', p. 478.
13. Besides the nineteenth-century renditions, London as monstrosity dominates accounts of the city in the eighteenth century, too. Defoe stands in as the voice of London here once again, calling it 'this great and monstrous thing'. See further: White, Jerry. *A Great and Monstrous Thing: London in the Eighteenth Century*. Harvard University Press, 2013.
14. Agamben, Giorgio. 'Bartleby, or On Contingency', in *Potentialities: Collected Essays in Philosophy*, ed. and trans. Daniel Heller-Roazen. Stanford University Press, 1999, p. 253. See also: Deleuze, Gilles. 'Bartleby; Or, The Formula', in *Essays Critical and Clinical*, trans. Daniel W. Smith and Michael A. Greco. University of Minnesota Press, 1997, pp. 68–90.
15. Melville, Herman. 'Bartleby the Scrivener: A Story of Wall Street', available at: <www.bartleby.com/129/>, par. 11 (last accessed 1 December 2016).
16. Melville, par. 11.
17. Melville, par. 15.
18. Melville, par. 16.
19. Melville, par. 19.
20. Melville, pars. 33–4.
21. Melville, pars. 41–9.
22. Melville, par. 84.
23. Melville, par. 85.
24. Melville, par. 166.
25. Melville, pars. 172–4.
26. See, for example: Chaney, Sarah. 'Useful members of society or motiveless malingerers? Occupation and self-injury in late nineteenth-century British asylum psychiatry', paper presented at *Therapy and Empowerment – Coercion and Punishment: Historical and Contemporary Perspectives on Labour and Occupational Therapy*, 26–27 June 2013, St Anne's College, Oxford.
27. Not to be confused with social concern and resistance to the improving classes attempting to discipline the unruly, threatening working masses. See: Engels, Friedrich. *The Condition of the Working Class in England*, ed. David McLellan. Oxford University Press, 2009.
28. There is no shortage of discussion on the Romantics' sense of ecological damage, for example. Among the representative commentaries on specific literary works responding to coal pollution, deforestation and other concerns, see again Bate's *Romantic Ecology* and McKusick's *Green Writing*, as well as: Hutchings, Kevin. 'Ecocriticism in British Romantic Studies', *Literature Compass* 4:1 (2007), pp. 172–202; McKusick, 'Ecology', in *Romanticism: An Oxford Guide*, ed. Nicholas Roe. Oxford University Press, 2005, pp. 199–218; and Morton, 'Environmentalism', in Roe, *Romanticism*, pp. 696–707.
29. Melville, par. 197.

30. Melville, par. 200, and repeated thereafter.
31. Melville, par. 245.
32. Melville, par. 247.
33. Melville, par. 250–1.
34. Agamben, 'Bartleby, or On Contingency'.
35. Dickens, Charles. *Oliver Twist*. Barnes & Noble Classics, 2004, p. 162.
36. Dickens, *Oliver Twist* (2004), p. 164.
37. Dickens, *Oliver Twist* (2004), p. 166.
38. Dickens, *Oliver Twist* (2004), p. 179.
39. Dickens, *Oliver Twist* (2004), pp. 181–2.
40. Dickens, *Oliver Twist* (2004), p. 196.
41. Dickens, *Oliver Twist* (2004), p. 198.
42. Dickens, *Oliver Twist* (2004), p. 200.
43. Dickens, *Oliver Twist* (2004), p. 271.
44. Dickens, *Oliver Twist* (2004), pp. 257–8.
45. 'Mr Charles Dickens and the execution of the Mannings', reprinted from *The Times*, 13 November 1849. British Library. Available at: <http://www.bl.uk/collection-items/mr-charles-dickens-and-the-execution-of-the-mannings-reprinted-from-the-times> (last accessed 21 December 2016).
46. Several works address Dickens's moralising tendencies, including: Gold, Joseph. *Charles Dickens: Radical Moralist*. Oxford University Press, 1972. See also: Hardy, Barbara. *The Moral Art of Dickens*, 2nd edn. Bloomsbury, 2002. J. Hillis Miller was famously dismissive of Dickens's 'fear of a moral life of breadth, imagination, or novelty. Dickens sometimes seems to believe that only with this narrowness is the moral life likely to be successful.' Hillis Miller, J. *Charles Dickens: The World of His Novels*. Harvard University Press, 1970, p. 221.
47. Senf, Carol A. '*Dracula*: The Unseen Face in the Mirror', *The Journal of Narrative Technique*, 9 (1979), pp. 160–70 and reprinted in Carter, Margaret, ed. *The Vampire and the Critics*. UMI Research Press, 1988, p. 95. Quoted in Auerbach, Nina. *Our Vampires, Ourselves*. Chicago University Press, 1997, p. 204, n. 32.
48. Butler, Judith. 'Afterword. The Humanities in Human Rights: Critique, Language, Politics', *PMLA* 121.5 (October 2006), pp. 1658–61. Referenced and quoted in Linley, Margaret. '*Frankenstein* Revisited: Life and Afterlife Around 1831', in *Media, Technology, and Literature in the Nineteenth Century*, ed. Colette Colligan and Margaret Linley. Ashgate, 2011, p. 264.
49. Linley, p. 264.
50. Linley, p. 275.
51. James, Louis. *Print and the People 1819–1851*. Penguin, 1976, p. 17.
52. *Society for the Promotion of Christian Knowledge Minutes*, 21 May 1832, pp. 284–5, quoted in James, *Print and the People*, p. 18.
53. Reprinted in James, *Print and the People*, p. 16.
54. See: Gilmartin, Kevin. *Print Politics: The Press and Radical Opposition in Early Nineteenth-Century England*. Cambridge University Press, 1996. See also: St Clair, William. *The Reading Nation in the Romantic Period*. Cambridge University Press, 2004. On the political press, see especially:

Haywood, Ian. *The Revolution in Popular Literature: Print, Politics, and the People 1790–1860*. Cambridge University Press, 2004.
55. James, Louis. *Fiction for the Working Man 1830–1850*, p. 164.
56. Defoe, 'Colonel Jack', in *The Novels and Miscellaneous Works of Daniel De foe, With Preface and Notes, Including those Attributed to Sir Walter Scott*. George Bell and Sons, 1904, pp. 310–11.
57. On the matter of Victorian cultural blood thirst, Rosalind Crone's *Violent Victorians* is definitive. Crone tracks developments from public executions to popular stage works and, ultimately, to the pennies and *Sweeney Todd*. See: Crone, Rosalind. *Violent Victorians: Popular Entertainment in Nineteenth-Century London*. Manchester University Press, 2012.
58. There is no shortage of historical accounts of London's history of executions, and much has been written on the eighteenth-century trouble with mobs and public disciplinary displays. Regulations on public assembly attempted to mitigate the former, and ironically put Speaker's Corner, for a time the only location public audience assembly for political and other debate was allowed, right where Tyburn Tree gallows had been on Hyde Park, all in the shadow of the Marble Arch. See: Shoemaker, Robert. *The London Mob: Violence and Disorder in Eighteenth-Century England*. Continuum, 2004. See also: White, Jerry. *A Great and Monstrous Thing: London in the Eighteenth Century*. Random House, 2012, and in particular pp. 456–66, '"Low-Lived, Blackguard Merry-Making": Public Punishments'. See also: Linebaugh, Peter. *The London Hanged: Crime and Civil Society in the Eighteenth Century*. Verso, 2003, and in particular chapters on Jack Sheppard (pp. 7–41) and Tyburn (pp. 74–118).
59. Lee, William, ed. *Daniel Defoe: His Life, and Recently Discovered Writings, 1716–1729*. John Camden Hotten, 1869, pp. 384–5. On the contemporary 'nonfiction novel' and the true crime genre, see: Capote, Truman. *In Cold Blood*. Vintage, 1994. Capote established a strong bond with Perry Smith, one of the killers, that has been the subject of much speculation and conjecture since; Sheppard wrote to Defoe, 'This with my kind love to you ... your humble servant' at one point nearing his final days (Lee, p. 385).
60. For more on the history of London police forces, see: Taylor, David. *The New Police in Nineteenth-Century England: Crime, Conflict and Control*. Manchester University Press, 1997. See also: Emsley, Clive. *The English Police: A Political and Social History*, 2nd edn. Routledge, 2014. For the hundred-year period between the public executions such as Sheppard in 1724 and the Victorian period, see especially: Reynolds, Elaine A. *Before the Bobbies: The Night Watch and Police Reform in Metropolitan London, 1720–1830*. Stanford University Press, 1998.
61. By the nineteenth century, stories about Sheppard would be censured and banned because of copycat crimes, but the notion that Sheppard, Cartouche and even Todd represent threats to private business interests and not public safety has been discussed elsewhere. On the former view, see: Brantlinger, Patrick. *The Reading Lesson: The Threat of Mass Literary in Nineteenth-century British Fiction*. Indiana University Press, 1998, pp. 71–2. Brantlinger also discusses the intersecting roles of Dickens (*Oliver Twist*) and Ainsworth (*Jack Sheppard*) in the debate on

romanticised crime Thackeray instigated. On the latter, see: Seymour, Benedict. 'Notes on the Last Days of Jack Sheppard: Capital Crimes and Paper Claims', *Mute*, 2:13 (August 2009).
62. Lee, p. 383.
63. For one particularly entertaining account of Sheppard's life and execution, see: Moore, Lucy. *The Thieves' Opera: The Riveting True Story of 18th-Century London's Most Notorious and Active Criminals*. Harcourt, 2000.
64. See: Geier, *Kafka's Nonhuman Form*.
65. Defoe, Daniel. *An Account of the Cartoucheans in France*. J. Roberts, 1724, p. 1. Included within *Popular Literature in 18th and 19th Century Britain, Parts Three-Ten: The Barry Ono Collection of Bloods and Penny Dreadfuls*, British Library. Accessed via Nineteenth Century Collections Online, Gale Group. Hereafter: *Cartoucheans*.
66. *Cartoucheans*, p. 5.
67. *Cartoucheans*, pp. 5–7. The mention of 'after candlelight' also periodises the piece nicely against the gaslit London of Poe's story.
68. *Cartoucheans*, p. 7.
69. *Cartoucheans*, p. 8.
70. Crone tracks the development of this taste for blood and the spectacles of suffering in her chapter, 'From Scaffold Culture to the Cult of the Murderer', in *Violent Victorians*, pp. 75–123.
71. *Cartoucheans*, p. 11.
72. *Cartoucheans*, p. 11.
73. *Cartoucheans*, p. 19.
74. *Cartoucheans*, pp. 14–15; 20–1.
75. *Cartoucheans*, p. 24.
76. *Cartoucheans*, p. 12.
77. *Cartoucheans*, p. 14.
78. Mitch, David F. *The Rise of Popular Literacy: The Influence of Private Choice and Public Policy*. University of Pennsylvania Press, 1992.
79. Lyons, Martyn. 'New Readers in the Nineteenth Century: Women, Children, Workers', in *A History of Reading in the West*, ed. Guglielmo Cavallo and Roger Chartier. University of Massachusetts Press, 1999, p. 313. Another, longer history of public literacy suggests that 46 per cent of country residents who married could sign their own names by the mid-eighteenth century. See: Laqueur, Thomas. 'The Cultural Origins of Popular Literacy in England 1500–1850', *Oxford Review of Education*, 2:3 (1976), pp. 255–75. Laqueur, setting up the popular contemporary imagination of nineteenth-century English culture early in the article, presents bear-baiting and St Monday drunks as cultural markers that might belie an extensive public literacy. Both issues played large roles in public discourse and parliamentary debate on social improvement and animal rights during the first half of the nineteenth century.
80. On the early political impetus for popular literature, including surveys of pamphlets by Paine, Chartist, liberal and other didactic literatures, see Haywood, *The Revolution in Popular Literature*.
81. Haining, Peter, ed. *The Penny Dreadful*. Victor Gollancz, 1976, pp. 14–16. Haining's example is *Jane Eyre* instead of Dickens.

82. James, *Fiction for the Working Man 1830–1850*.
83. Thomson, Patricia. Review of *Fiction for the Working Man 1830–1850*, *The Review of English Studies*, 16:61 (February 1965), pp. 92–4.
84. Lee, Alfred McClung. *The Daily Newspaper in America, Volume 1*. Routledge, 2001, pp. 114–15.
85. See Munsell, John. *Chronology of the Origin and Progress of Paper and Paper Making*. J. Munsell, 1876, pp. 55–72. For further discussion on the London machine patent and technical evolution, see James, *Fiction for the Working Man 1830-1850*, pp. 10–11.
86. Franta, *Romanticism and the Rise of the Mass Public*, p. 137.
87. London makes its historical census information available to the public via a governmental website. Available at: <data.london.gov.uk/dataset/historic-census-population> (last accessed 6 December 2016).
88. Raven, James. *Bookscape: Geographies of Printing and Publishing in London before 1800*. University of Chicago Press/The British Library, 2014.
89. See: Barker, Hannah. *Newspapers and English Society: 1655–1855*. Routledge, 2000, pp. 37–9. See also: Gray, Drew D. *London's Shadows: The Dark Side of the Victorian City*. Continuum, 2010, p. 97.
90. James, *Fiction for the Working Man 1830–1850*, p. 154.
91. Marie Léger-St-Jean, of Cambridge University, has established the definitive online resource on the pennies, Price One Penny. One of the most useful aspects of the site is its consolidation of the few known narrative histories of penny production and statistics, including references to all known bibliographies or notes to future inclusions not yet incorporated. Available at: <www.priceonepenny.info/index.php> (last accessed 1 December 2016).
92. The bibliography at Price One Penny is again definitive here. Louis James's *Fiction for the Working Man* is a crucial source of these details, as is the excellent narrative introduction to the Ono Collection by Elizabeth James and Helen R. Smith.
93. Rymer, James Malcolm. *The string of pearls: or, The Barber of Fleet Street: a domestic romance*. E. Loyd, 1850, p. 2. Included within *Popular Literature in 18th and 19th Century Britain, Parts Three-Ten: The Barry Ono Collection of Bloods and Penny Dreadfuls*.
94. Léger-St-Jean, available at <www.priceonepenny.info/notes.php> (last accessed 1 December 2016).
95. For a general sense of copyright and related issues in England during the nineteenth century, see: Alexander, Isabella. *Copyright Law and the Public Interest in the Nineteenth Century*. Hart, 2010.
96. There is to date no better history of the narrative and its myriad contexts than Mack's *The Wonderful and Surprising History of Sweeney Todd: The Life and Times of an Urban Legend*. See also the critical introduction and other prefatory materials in the Mack-edited edition of *Sweeney Todd: The Demon Barber of Fleet Street*, pp. vii–xxxviii.
97. Dickens, Charles. *Martin Chuzzlewit*. Oxford University Press, 2009, p. 495.
98. Mack, *Sweeney Todd*, p. xvii.
99. White, Jerry. *London in the Nineteenth Century: 'A Human Awful*

Wonder of God'. Vintage, 2007, Section VIII, 'Fleet Street: City of Words'.
100. Mack, *Wonderful and Surprising History*, p. 12, and quoting Ackroyd, Peter. *London: The Biography*. Verso, 2000, p. 316.
101. Mack, *Wonderful and Surprising History*, p. 23.
102. Mack, *Wonderful and Surprising History*, p. 38.
103. Mack, *Wonderful and Surprising History*, p. 41.
104. Mack, *Wonderful and Surprising History*, p. 44.

Conclusion: Post-meat

Animals and other nonhumans course through literature long before the British Romantic and Victorian periods of British literature, but literary works through the long nineteenth century take as their frequent task an articulation of nonhuman forms marking increasingly abjected modes of modern life and negotiating the attending anxieties through the ambiguities of Romanticism. This includes experimentation with narrative authority, irony and fragmented forms that veer often into apparent poetic failure – certainly their themes dwell on human failures, at least – in a broad project on the human being as a concept. This turn to literary form and to philosophical rumination on the status and prospects of the human responds directly to the historical conditions of industrial modernity, but then it also attempts to resist such decisive triangulations of a condition; history, science and narrative each imply some frame of coherence that Romantic authors are highly suspicious of. A broken narrative voice would thus be capable of performing an ethical or political abjection such as Burns's speaker and the mouse upturned in 'To a Mouse', but then only as an indicator of the historical situations in question.

Romantics were associated with radical traditions resisting infringements on the rights of marginalised classes, which also must have some relation to a sense of individual freedom such as the Romantic poet's creative spontaneity.[1] Coleridge's political projects with Robert Southey and he and William Wordsworth's early alliances in *Lyrical Ballads* on the heels of the new Poor Laws show a coherent and principled political commitment during a period that has often been studied for its incarnations of radicalism, populism and general political activism. This suggests that the literary works, which frequently engage political issues directly alongside recurring themes of human fragility and inconsistency, attempted a precise form of address that does not submit to the very nonhuman conditions that seem to motivate them. As Chapter

1 suggested, literary works mitigate those conditions even where they suggest an incommensurable divide between history and subjects, science and life, society and individuals. The form by which they attempt to do so, however, is generally an individuated voice or agent failing, in various ways, to resolve the conflict or circumstance a poem or novel constructs.

As naturalism and realism react against this individual mode and become dominant genres later in the nineteenth century, the task of literature has already succumbed entirely to the facts of society, science, economy, history, humanity and, finally, animality. Dickens's long novels describe and present the immense decay, but also the profound joys, of London society. In Dickens, there is still a society to be rescued from its increasing velocity and mechanisation, if only those who don't know how the other half lives would realise the full scope of modern life. Dickens's novels often suggested that middle class social concern, which includes animal concern although Dickens does not explicitly engage in that discourse, could itself be a ridiculous performance with no relevant purpose. His lasting expression of the horror of such encasings only reiterated, yet again, the basic despair of a saturating, total nonhuman form.

Nineteenth-century London urban history has multiple, complex vectors, but its total revolution in meat, the very idea, has proven to be both materially disastrous for animal life and historically decisive in the context of general shifts in animal use and consumption. The British meat economy evolves rapidly through advances in animal husbandry producing 'manufactured articles', and revised market slaughter management in response to increased production and consumption culminated in the 1852 Smithfield Removal Act. But the Act also came on the heels of intense complaints and formal parliamentary petitions by butchers about unfair market price fixing. Market removal was also motivated by an increasingly annoyed public crammed into tighter urban spaces with loud, smelly and suffering animal bodies. This combination of factors produced both an animal and a human that accomplished a total, technical administration of life but then demolished all sense of individual, meaningful, valuable life in the end. The debates between the butchers and other civic entities, in particular, shed new light on the matter.

To focus only on the moralist arguments for removal or on the Smithfield case's important role in the foundations of animal rights is to avoid the broader civic management issues and to risk yet another erasure of the resulting nonhuman condition. Metcalfe's important history of the market offers the most comprehensive account to date of the primary motivations for and debates surrounding Smithfield removal and civic space use, and instead of presenting the Smithfield case as an animal rights issue, as one might, she proceeds in a more complex archival mode through the interconnected economic and political history of the 1800–55 removal conceptualisation, planning and execution. Reminiscent of the thick historical assessments of British animal use by Ritvo, Metcalfe's study draws together the civic negotiations and select examples from cultural production of the day (Dickens, for instance) to argue that the Smithfield case was a matter of community space and sanitation. Metcalfe's issue is not, then, the concept of nonhumans, but she does consider the role of the Worshipful Company of Butchers and other groups in the removal debate, and thus presents clearly the general absence of animal concern besides economic investment in a 'quality' meat object threatened by untenable traffic and storage options in an ever-more-crowded London city space.

London reacts to this horror in law and in intense civic planning to remove animals from the site (and the sight) of human industry in the city centre. The killing, no longer done at Smithfield, moves to the shiny new Metropolitan Cattle Market a bit further north of the city centre in Islington, and achieves a more hygienic and orderly meat production process. This plan, which responded to rampant public health concerns among the exploding London population as much as to any concern about the killing (or suffering) of animals, drew inspiration from the incredible success of similar moves to public abattoirs in France just a short time ahead of the Smithfield revisions. Nevertheless, critics including Dickens, who used Smithfield more than once in his novels as a site of depravity and filth in juxtaposition to the goodness of characters like Oliver, defended the Market and its denizens against the more unsavoury sorts in Parliament and in British business interests. Dickens eschewed the French system some Londoners were infatuated with in their arguments for market removal, on the grounds that Paris could hardly fathom the greatness of a place like Smithfield. He was not alone. Defoe, about a hundred years earlier, had also remarked on the wonders of Smithfield. Its massiveness, in the heart of the most massive city the world had ever known by 1850, for Dickens, certainly left an impression. But ultimately, the public resentment of the Market's health and moral implications, resentment Dickens helped along in literature even where his journalism argued for its maintenance (he was also a major proponent of the butcher classes), won out and the Market was removed.

What remains at the old site is still an impressive and very large working meat market in a Grade II protected Victorian building, but there is no live animal traffic along major arteries any more and the place is often quite empty relative to the current sites of commerce nearby. One can get up very early some days of the week to observe the functioning market at peak hours, and it is well worth it, but the place is cavernous and vacant, even dead silent, throughout much of the day. This is an eerie remnant not 500 feet from the current noise of the Farrington/A201 renovations and general bustle; Fleet Street, Chancery Lane and the Royal Court of Justice – the sites of much of the literature examined in this study – are all within exactly the same neighbourhood near the city centre. The strange, vacant silence of contemporary Smithfield is really too much of a success for the nineteenth-century civic reformers. One would never even know what had come to pass here.

Smithfield removal, despite its gruesome outcomes, still realised the intent of modern animal concern reflected also in later public commemorations of animal suffering from the brown dog statue at Battersea Park to the present Smithfield Market site.[2] Today, the commemorative bench in the Smithfield Market park in downtown London incorporates quotes from the animal welfare debates in Parliament, noted literary passages on Smithfield Market din and atrocities, and even a nod to the site's long history as a religious and political execution site known as Smoothe-Field back to medieval times. The water fountain in the park, one of many spots in present-day London in which one can see a particular aspect of interspecies utilities history 'in the flesh', was placed there by the Metropolitan Drinking Fountain and Cattle Trough Association. That organisation, founded in 1859 and changed to include cattle in 1867, exists today as merely the Drinking Fountain Association. There are of course no more cattle troughs in London, though perhaps there are dog-watering sites. Smithfield thus remains a dense comparative node in London's nineteenth-century civic development and cultural history, including the first major animal rights laws, waste and water oversight, livestock and animal labour management, and broad literary histories.

One must admit that animal welfare in the British meat trade had, at least for a time, or at least cosmetically, been dramatically improved as a result of the evolution of meat animal traffic and meat object processing efficiencies. But of course, this all amounts merely to a traffic rerouting and not to, if one extends the metaphor, an eradication of the offending modes of transportation altogether. The meat still courses through the city, moving in fact only more easily, at greater speeds and in greater quantities. Not incidentally, animals suffering in and around Smithfield, as well as the larger metropolis, supported the city's primary transportation energy source before the full arrival of railways, which also have a precise connection to Smithfield. Smithfield was among the very first central railway points in London's nineteenth-century design. The trains were directed through Smithfield specifically to facilitate meat trade and simultaneously ushering in the age of meat refrigeration.

This nonhuman, but all-too-human condition is not at all lost on Londoners or historians of the city and its animal history. The commemorative bench at Smithfield is a decidedly modern affair, a winning design by students at the University of Edinburgh installed in 2006. That the most recent addition to the West Smithfield Garden Rotunda, as the commemorative square is called, is on the subject of animal suffering and market removal is both fitting and also surprising confirmation of the place of animal concern in contemporary thought. Smoothe-Field has a long and gruesome past as a major site for political and religious executions dating well back to medieval times, and its connection to St Bartholomew's Hospital is, likewise, long-standing.[3] Those histories are also documented in various forms at the present site and amply in literature on the history of Smithfield. Its dense iterations of animal and labour history connect animal concern, cruelty and rights debates in a mutual history of civic reorganisation and social concern. The next step, as the postmodern commemorative bench at Smithfield suggests, is to address the fuller lineage of nonhuman thought and the critique of institutional forms the literary examples in this study, like the bench in the West Smithfield Garden Rotunda, wage well after revisiting the basic, though important, tenets of conventional animal concern and rights discourse.

British interspecies cultural history, marked at all points in both canonical and other literary forms, presents the clear origin of contemporary animal concern and ecological consumerism while also suggesting modes of thought that deserve to be reiterated as possible solutions to the problems caused by pre-packaged, artificial concentrations of that thinking. The period, from Romantic through Victorian, wages clear thinking and negotiations of coexistent horror. The sense of human life Smithfield communicates, and that is represented both on the floor of Parliament and in key cultural products of the day like the works of Dickens, thus forced immediate action both on practical terms and in terms of philosophical premises about evolved human society. These tropes of human decency and right sentiments, both having strong origins in the popular literatures of the preceding century, were routinely mobilised in the Smithfield debates in an intense collaborative history of animal rights discourse and London civic planning as pertains to animal slaughter and market traffic. Smithfield was a morphologically profound problem for the members of decent human society of London confronted with their own increasing anonymity outside replicable, fungible roles in a social totality. The mass spectacle at the site of undeniably technological reproduction of animal bodies, such that the question of 'life' was rendered irrelevant altogether outside the requisite meat animal gestation and extraction timelines, was a sublime threat to humans' self-image in an age of increasingly scientific, taxonomic logics of species and evolutionary theories that animal husbandry and genetic understandings only reinforced. Humans were not so special, on the one hand, and yet were genetic terrorists on the other: life was far too easy and too impossible to manage.

One urban geographic irony in Dickens is that Oliver and the company travel from a more traditionally hard scrabble, working class part of London to a tonier area well south of the city centre. Of course, the market and attendant cattle removal (and Thomas Hardy is yet another author to chronicle the market in negative tones) goes the other way, potentially inflicting the atrocities of market space so effectively lamented in Parliament on the poor working class citizens most aligned with the nonhuman condition at the market.[4] But in fact, removing the market to such locations alongside revising slaughter and management forms to the new systems of efficient invisibility meant that civic reform ensured the classes most likely to have an aesthetic moral response to the fact of animal killing for meat would be far less likely to ever remember that the meat came from somewhere in the first place. And rather than align some anonymous, suffering poor class with some anonymous, suffering animal class, Smithfield removal only further ensures that the upper classes can shield themselves from London's horrors. Their 'pure' and ascetic dietary abstention from meat products attempt to mitigate the encroaching horror of interminable nonhuman community with organisms, objects and masses through escapist denial that merely promotes the evolution and entrenchment of the original horror. Meanwhile, a logic of automatic consumption reproduces itself at and after Smithfield.

Smithfield stands now as a lasting monument to the anthropocentric trends Romantic and Victorian literature responded to by suggesting animal suffering and interspecies community, and the animal meat market has lasting literary traditions in other contexts as well, perhaps most famously in the case of Upton Sinclair's *The Jungle* and associated US legislative work. Smithfield's interspecies history of total annihilations of life to bare forms shows that removal did not ease but merely erased mass animal suffering, quelling middle class animal concern but further mechanising mass slaughter and disassembly. Removing live animals and private abattoirs – the pervasive sites of slaughter that continued to feed a vivid urban imaginary of murder and unknown terrors in the pennies through the middle and latter parts of the nineteenth century – from impacted city centres shattered a prior intimacy with meat animals, producing a far worse horror.

Modern London sold itself a capital lie: meat became a clean, portable, alien object fuelling the human world but without any trace of animal history. This removal rhetoric's classist improvement arguments made villains out of working classes – stations and occupations, as addressed in Chapter 3 – like butchers and the other men who used animal-baiting for entertainment. Some labour groups were more reviled than others, such as cabbies and other jobs with horses for goods and people transport. Individual retail butchers, who in fact did not always kill the animals they sold as meat at Smithfield and other locations, were an especially frequent target of animal rights activists. Meanwhile, Charles Dickens and the butchers themselves made strong cases for their expertise and their quite sober, calculative eye when it came to meat procurement and dispensation.

The primary causes for market reform, which was not always presented as removal, were explicated by market actors themselves as issues of market efficiency and, increasingly, of meat quality. Long transport of live animals damaged meat animals through a variety of problems such as weight loss, bruising and illness. The earliest resistance from the butchers, in the early seventeenth century, was to new grazing laws restricting a practice the butchers depended upon to get the best prices for their meat. Animals driven from the country to Smithfield Market would lose considerable amounts of weight, they argued, and limiting re-fattening to thirty days once butchers purchased live animals at Smithfield would further reduce their profit while all other market agents saw the same rate of profit as always. The history of butchers and animals at Smithfield crosses a number of such entangled concerns. The intense urban population explosion and cultural interactions between species and new organisms, as well as the growth of medical understanding and mechanisation of commerce and transport, not to mention objects as seemingly wondrous and harmless as gas lighting, were converging in all aspects of cultural life and literary production as an ongoing interrogation of the strange, alien nature of mutually vacant yet inescapably coexistent lives in nineteenth-century London. But the London butchers and meat tradesmen were in the crosshairs of relatively unfettered, direct practical conditions that, in a spectacular fit of irony, made butchers the bad guys because they did the killing that the rest of the meat system simply wanted more, and more reliable, capitalised control over.

The butchers still remain as the Worshipful Company of Butchers, with offices at present-day Smithfield and with their famed old hall still nearby. But one aspect of the Smithfield case that fits well with the experiments in paradoxical, petrifying horror in the literatures here examined is the fate of butchers as both culturally slaughtered objects of public aggression, as in penny dreadfuls like *Sweeney Todd* and a variety of other forms examined, and as economically reduced, rendered agents in the expansion – and thus, concentration and minimisation – of capitalist networks in the London meat market system. The butchers, for lack of a better term, get butchered in multiple arenas. The spectacle of this butcher execution satisfies several consuming publics.

The public suspicions about 'growlers' with cat or dog meat in them or about foreign meats from unknown origins, and the unknown meat pies in *Martin Chuzzlewitt* and *Sweeney Todd*, condense the various horrors of the dreadfuls and the broader horror tradition including *Frankenstein* and *Dracula* to investigate, or simply capitalise upon, a deep and constant urban anxiety at anonymous and total coexistence with things that no longer support frames of the human, to be sure, but also a frenzied uncertainty about all consumption exchanges in an increasingly unsanitary, dangerous city space. This coexistence is not simply being in the same places as or suffering the same fates as each other. It is a complete intermingling of all that must be separated first in order to determine identity. Epizootic viruses and bacteria transgress any hard boundaries between species, but epizootic outbreaks are only one variation of total coexistence. The even more disorienting and destabilising issues of the period were the increasingly pervasive permutations of layers of coexistence such as animal use, collective waste, water sources and the diseases then plugged back into consumption channels like the cholera outbreaks.

Stoker attempted to import some of the dense horrors preceding him, and also the penny dreadfuls he himself consumed, but he also attempted some of the authoritative, realist management of those horrors in a documentary fictional mode. This also realises the cultural forms of the day in an objective, articulate administration of factual presentation and nonhuman reproductions of reality. Stoker considered the fetishisation of documentary fidelity through the case of the phonograph and typewriter technologies in the novel, both supposed to be more accurate and reliable as observers of the story's manifold violations of some physical, biological reality, and yet neither inviolably so in the novel's development. The penny dreadfuls rarely engaged in such intertextual explorations, but their production in fact relied precisely on the technological machinery of mass extraction and (re)production, and their primary audience was the massive, newly literate London working class population. This voracious urban working class readership ensured that the community continued to consume its own abjection as a form of mass entertainment. The stories of urban murder and unwitting cannibalism, highwaymen marauders and 'butchers' in terrible bands of robbers, and other popular horrors, made use of the day's lived dangers and fears but solved many of these stories or featured prototypes of the twentieth-century superhero who fought off all manner of threat to decent society and community safety. Chapter 3 examined this reader/ spectator figure and the demand for both literary and civic supplies of such narratives and themes in the pennies and in the public spectacle of executions.

Across this lengthy cultural history of bloody London, there is a manufactured object that troubles prior concepts of that object – literature and meat – but also at least partially erases that prior status in the process of production. Literature becomes serial parts of varying quality and unknown origin. Or, the origins may be known plagiarisms of other pennies. At the risk of a trite, tired metaphor, these cobbled-together scraps are something of a 'Franken-text', and there is a decided literary cannibalism circulating through the penny press period. Meat, and the animals manufactured to produce it, is likewise a streamlined but ambiguous affair. Meat City, the vast meat machinery in London and elsewhere, was not only about animals. Or rather, animals did not stop at the live stock sold explicitly at physical meat markets.

This is perhaps the most lasting legacy of the Smithfield Market removal of 1852. The morphological specificity of meat production and distribution processes in the seething urban centre leads directly to today's contemporary CAFO-market efficiency model. Post-Smithfield animal management erases the known horror of animal use and slaughter and inaugurates the invisible, alien meat form. Authors like Poe, Stoker and Dickens explore the horror such organising principles and administrative consequences bestow – Poe in the anonymous cacophony of urban work classes, Stoker in the insidious permeation of boundaries and blood, and Dickens in elaborate presentations of the dingy squalor of London. Dickens even addresses London's incredible problem with dead bodies in the period in *Our Mutual Friend*, which responds in turn to the incredible cholera outbreaks and Thames River water pollution issues of the day.[5] Many of the weird, uncanny new boundary seepages, health risks and contaminations influence reform of, but also arise from the dominant biotechnological modes of, meat–animal production, construction and distribution. The result is an intensification of bureaucratic and administrative forms instead of a mitigation of the nonhuman forms of modern urban life.

Conclusion: Post-meat   177

This is not to imply that such a mitigation either ought to be desired or could be accomplished. What is clearly at stake in the Smithfield case – and this is also the reason that it so directly informs and refracts the literary modes of the nineteenth century and beyond – is the same impulse to conceal the workings of social organisation in order to maintain precisely the social hubris of perfectible subjects (reform); correctable crimes (justice); and reliable identities (species). What the Smithfield case materially exposed in its public health, morality and commercial intersections is the same nonhuman condition the literatures of the day expressed across species and trades, and thus the apparent solution to the Smithfield question was in fact only a deeper ossification of its origins.

The cultural heritage of nonhuman form passes through the proverbial 'meat grinder' of nineteenth-century urban life. The legal conundrums produced through British laws of enclosure, grain regulations and governing the poor in the new civic spaces spiralled into the sincere, but also sincerely flawed, animal rights movement in nineteenth-century England. What Romantics express about nonhuman life – whether an animal or a human that experiences it – is that nothing can salvage anything from the violent abjection of categorical divisions like the labour class mutations the butchers undergo through the history of Smithfield or the refinements in manufactured articles meat animals suffer during the same period. At times, the Romantics directly engage livestock and labouring animals such as the young ass of Coleridge's poem or Clare's badger. But Mary Shelley approaches the same trouble with flesh and 'corpsing', to borrow a modern apocalyptic figure from Beckett's *Endgame*, by articulating a nonhuman deprived of, yet defined entirely through, the human. The creature lives, yet cannot live, and Victor dies, yet cannot properly die because the performed sublime of his life sublimates his aesthetic recognition of experience. The creature explodes Victor's world yet Victor cannot access this expression of suffering. Victor is inhuman and the nonhuman cannot instruct him in human ways despite apparent expertise. These narrative and philosophical circumstances are expressed in the framing structures of the novel and the repeated play upon iterative subject positions such as 'I' and 'the creature' that began this book.

The Romantic nonhuman form gives way, by the 1821 implementation of the steam printing press and the progress of animal rights in relation to the trope of sympathy and the upper class narrative of improvement, to the further demolition of literary individualism even as the cult of authorship and the 'complete' great work, the novel, comes into fullness. If Romantic literature is often held up as a defence of individual expression against the encroaching homogeneity of urban anonymity and mass population, it then falls mightily to the burgeoning popular pulp literary culture Dickens himself fought in the courts, by virtue of the encroaching literary economies that did not pay him properly and also plagiarised him so successfully. That popular literary culture, which rides the wings of a massive increase in public literacy that ironically leads to the mass consumption of cheap literatures with uncomplicated narrative structures and poor production value, ultimately inculcates a nonhuman form both in mass, untraceable and fungible anonymity at the level of authorship and at the level of material production. On top of this, the shallow narrative forms, although gripping and sensational as suspense narratives with conventional denouements, are saturated with gore and the horrors of bloody marauders, dark urban murderers, supernatural nonhumans and the infamous supplier of cannibalistic fare, Sweeney Todd.

At the same time, the tradition of spectacle in London, including the immensely popular public hangings of the very same criminals who would be immortalised in the penny fiction, suggests that these gruesome tales were as entertaining as they were terrifying. Whatever real anxieties they expressed, about meat insecurity or about new urban dangers to the rural traveller or anyone else, the public had a very strong stomach for it all as evidenced by the sheer volume of consumption. The demon barber of Fleet Street, harvesting the meat of replaceable, travelling, business class visitors in London's increasingly labyrinth urban centre, realises the darkest horrors of the uncontrollable city, but it then also deputises the evolution of dulled urban sensibilities.

Dickens's immense, singular London realism, with its myriad flourishes belying a strict realist tenor and coupled with his journalistic output, ultimately fails to present London as it is because it succeeds so very well in presenting it and succumbing to it, as in Esther's self-effacement. When Krook is finally consumed in a spontaneous combustion like so much candle tallow, it is the consummation of the absurd, abjective urban space and the trappings of administered modern life as well as the legal consumption of both common experience and the individual. Just as London eats itself in *Sweeney Todd*, so does it finally burn itself up in *Bleak House*. Esther's narrative position matches the Romantic ambiguity of narrative authority perfectly. Esther does not burn up in a sensational self-consuming spectacle. Esther *writes* herself into abjection as an appendage, a dependent and apparatus of civic managerial existence. The narrative arc that consumes the object and purpose of the legal case at the heart of the novel achieves Dickens's critique of the mass society in London.

Bleak House does not deal in squalor and atrocity in the way *Oliver Twist*, with its disgusting, overwhelming passage on Smithfield, must. Instead, Dickens shifts his attentions to the far more destructive administrative forms of middle class, aspirational class and upper class consumption habits. The broad consumer class born in nineteenth-century London culture and buttressed by its raging legal structures – the same structures that would defend the suffering animal objects at the heart of fashionable consumer class animal rights activism – eats everything, from everywhere, and perfects the systems of domination and extraction that produce the essential extract of meat, like Bovril, and perfectly mechanise animal slaughter for the perfectly rendered, anonymous, invisible meat objects the consumer class, necessarily, had to erase all animal traces from with Smithfield removal. Meat *had* to be cleaner, *had* to be quieter, *had* to be more 'humane'. This was what the market demanded, though it pursued a mythic, perhaps a *mise en abyme*, humanity.

These myths attended the domination and irrevocable abjection, and the parallel totality and futility of social structures. Harriet Ritvo, in a dazzling material gesture, named her seminal text *The Animal Estate: The English and Other Creatures in Victorian England*. The 'animal estate', or the nonhuman behemoth of Jarndyce and Jarndyce – London and social structuration – is a similarly interminable affect for its subjects but a definitively terminal condition. The animals produced *as* produce, like the heirs trafficked to an alienating London to be shuffled about in productions of domesticity like Esther with her wonderful husband, and like the famous creature tracking the entire globe in Mary Shelley's text, all languish in their efforts to articulate themselves and address interlocutors. The legal protection of animal bodies in the metropolitan meat works produces an individual object, a substantive subject of law, but erases any animal livelihood from legal articulation. The human meat commodities Sweeney Todd manufactures in intricate, professionally innovative technologies and 'breakneck' rates, realise the full potential of the urban meat production system in a grisly business metaphor.

All classes succumb to nonhuman forms of administered life in the meat market. The pulp serial press, the urban-business quotidian and the legal structure of society refining itself in intense, exponential strides throughout the nineteenth century inaugurate this biopolitical figure, produce the critique in the material forms of life and its management. London has not stopped its development of city life, and today's Smithfield Market, once the site of vibrant animal rights activism as well as riveting social critique, is a quiet space a bit off the main drags of London traffic. The commemorative square is a soothingly circular, silent, shady enclave with a precious view of St Paul's dome housing a writhing postmodernist bench installation. It also has a key post-Smithfield, post-cholera outbreak clean water source, a remnant of the sedimented London livestock history commemorating the site's animal welfare importance.[6] And so it is that nonhuman forms, if they aspire to shake free of human forms, never quite do, but then the other side of the coin is as gravely imprinted. That is the claim of much recent work on the animal and on post-human, post-biopolitical inquiry. Neither post, human or nonhuman, sufficiently grounds committed comportments toward an alternative coexistence. All suffer and flourish in unison. Only coexistence remains.

Notes

1. Consider Wordsworth's Preface to *Lyrical Ballads*: 'Poetry is the spontaneous overflow of powerful feelings: it takes its origin from emotion recollected in tranquility.'
2. The Battersea monument commemorates mid-century animal rights activism in relation to early medical experimentation on a specific test subject, a little brown dog the gallery claimed was twitching and moving violently during a demonstration, not at all 'out' from anaesthetic. The monument itself was immediately vandalised by pro-medical centre individuals angered by the public censure of the developing medical profession. The current statue is a replacement after the original was destroyed, and it was placed in what was originally an out of the way corner of Battersea Park, just southwest of the city centre across the Thames. The site's general vicinity is perhaps most famous now for the Battersea Power Station, whose smoke stacks will be immediately recognisable to any Pink Floyd fan who has seen the cover of their album, *Animals*. The site is now being repurposed, among other uses, as luxury apartments and Apple offices.
3. St Bartholomew, not incidentally, is the patron saint of butchers.
4. Rod Preece has written in several works on Hardy's reaction to witnessing the Smithfield cruelty, and Hardy's works include frequent remarks on animal suffering and market spaces. See: *Animal Sensibility and Inclusive Justice in the Age of Bernard Shaw*, p. 123.
5. The popular tourist attraction, Highgate Cemetery, home to the grave of Karl Marx (among others) and near the very same Hampstead Heath Lucy/the White Woman traverses at night, stealing babies in *Dracula*, is the direct result of hygiene programmes to manage the increasingly stinking, massive piles of corpses underneath city centre church floors and in the River Thames. Highgate is one of the 'Magnificent Seven' cemeteries opened between 1832 and 1841.
6. Dickens, naturally, had an entry on the city's new drinking fountains in his *Dictionary of London*. See also: Kean, *Animal Rights*, and 'Animals and War Memorials: Different Approaches to Commemorating the Human-Animal Relationship', in *Animals and War: Studies of Europe and North America*, ed. Ryan Hediger. Brill, 2013, pp. 237–62.

Index

Abrams, M. H., 39
Adorno, Theodor, 6, 8, 33, 48–9, 55
Agamben, Giorgio, 33, 126
Ainsworth, William Henry, 145
Animal Cruelty Act (1835), 84
The Animal's Friend, 16, 82, 93
Animals' Friend Society, 93–4
Applebee's Original Weekly Journals, 143, 145
Auerbach, Nina, 139
Auschwitz, 49
Austen, Jane, 120

'Badger', 28–9, 43–7, 177
Bakewell, Robert, 79
Bank of England, 137
Barbauld, Laetitia, 83
Bartholomew Fair, 3, 27, 36–8, 89, 114, 142
Bartleby the Scrivener: A Story of Wall Street, 4, 6, 60, 68, 87, 126–31, 147
Bate, Jonathan, 29
Battersea Park, 171
Baudelaire, Charles, 54, 151
Beckett, Samuel (*Endgame*), 177
Bellenger, Georges, 1
Bentham, Jeremy, 40
Bentley's Miscellany, 144, 145
Bill the Butcher, nativist, 95
Bingley, W., 104
Blake, William, 27, 47, 51–4, 67
Bleackley, Horace (*Some Distinguished Victims of the Scaffold*), 137
Bleak House, 2, 8, 26n34, 60–73, 130, 136, 138, 160, 178–9
Bloomfield, Robert, 42
Boddice, Rob, 80
The Book of Thel, 27, 47, 51–4, 67
Bovril, 20, 21, 106–9, 111, 179
British Library, 4, 142
British Museum, 42, 120
Broad Street outbreak (1854), 93
Brummel, Beau, occasional pea-eater, 69
Bruyere (*Characters*), 121
Bull's Head Inn, 159–60

Burns, Robert, 8, 10–12, 17–18, 20, 27–8, 38, 42, 43, 47–52, 58, 84, 168
Butcher Lane, 92
Butcher's Alley, 92
Byron, Lord George Gordon, 23, 28, 42, 51, 83, 128

Caledonian Market, 94
Capote, Truman (*In Cold Blood*), 143
Carroll, Lewis, 10, 11–12
The Cartoucheans, 143–52
Chancery Court, 62–73
Chancery Lane, 160, 171
Chartists, 140
Chigurgh, Anton, 87
A Christmas Carol, 64–5, 67
City Hall (New York), 129–30
Clare, John, 28, 29, 42–7, 50, 159, 170
Clare Market, 159–60
Clericus, 103
Cobbett, William, 78
Coetzee, J. M., 5
Coleridge, Samuel Taylor, 27–8, 29, 30, 32, 50, 54–8, 80, 84, 107, 137, 168, 177
Coltman, Elizabeth, 103
Concentrated Animal Feeding Operation (CAFO), 5, 88, 94, 95, 175
Corn Laws, 32, 78
Corn markets, 99–102
Cowherd, Reverend William, 23

Darwin, Charles, 6, 77–9
De Quincey, Thomas, 158
Defoe, Daniel, 7, 21, 70, 83, 85, 88, 90, 96, 119–20, 131, 141–9, 158, 159, 170
Deleuze, Gilles, 126
Dickens, Charles, 2, 3, 4, 6, 7, 8, 11, 14–15, 20, 21, 22, 37, 38, 60–73, 85, 88, 95, 104, 111, 112, 119–20, 127, 130–8, 139, 141, 142, 143, 145, 146, 149, 150–1, 154, 155, 156, 157, 159, 160, 161, 169, 170, 172, 173, 174, 176, 178–9, 180

Dolin, Kieran, 65–6
Dracula, 19, 51, 57, 119, 130, 139, 159, 175
Driving of Cattle Act (1774), 82–3

Eastcheap, 91–2
Edinburgh, University of, 172
Education Acts, 65
Erskine, Lord Thomas, 80

'Farmer George', 78
Fauntleroy, Henry, 137
Fitzstephen, William, 95, 109
Fleet Street, 37, 90, 104, 127, 143, 158–61, 171, 178
Foucault, Michel, 6, 8
Frankenstein, 1, 6, 8–10, 20, 27–8, 30, 33, 51, 52, 55–7, 140, 175
Frankfurt School, 4
Franta, Andrew, 40, 140, 153
Free Butchers of London, 96

Gangs of New York, 95
The Gherkin, 107
Gilmartin, Kevin, 40
Godwin, William, 78
Grahame, Kenneth, 43
Great Expectations, 60, 69

Hamilton, Paul, 55
Hampstead Heath, 160
Hardy, Thomas, 7, 8, 88, 104, 111, 173
Haymarket, 36
Hazlitt, William, 153
Hegel, G. W. F., 84
Heidegger, Martin, 17, 48–9, 55
Helsinger, Elizabeth, 42
Highgate Cemetery, 160
Highland Clearance enclosure, 17
Himmelfarb, Gertrude, 105
Hogarth, William, 159
Holborn Street (High Holborn), 5, 143
Horsemonger Lane Gaol, 138
House of Commons, 83, 99
Household Words, 62
Hunt, Leigh, 153
Hyde Park, 143, 145

'In the Penal Colony', 146

Jack the Ripper, 67, 143
Jacques, E. T., 65
James, Louis, 140–1, 160
Jameson, Fredric, 66–7
Jenners v. Jenners, 69
Johnson, John Lawson, 106
Johnson, Samuel, 36
Jones, Phillip E., 90–2
The Jungle, 94–5, 173

Kafka, Franz, 1, 130, 146
Kean, Hilda, 8, 15, 85, 86, 87, 93, 104–5
Kenyon-Jones, Christine, 43, 50, 58, 83–4
King George IV, dandy, 68
Knackers Act, 5
Koenig, Friedrich, 152

Labbe, Jacqueline, 69
Lawrence, John, 80
Leader, Zachary, 35
Lee, William, 144
Levinson, Marjorie, 29–30, 41
Liebig, Justus von, 4, 20, 78, 106, 118
Liebig Meat Extract, 4, 20, 78, 98, 106
Linley, Margaret, 139–40
Lloyd, Edward, 157
London Museum, 63
London School of Economics, 159
Lyons, Martin, 150
Lyrical Ballads, 28, 29, 32, 168

Mack, Robert, 158–9
McKusick, James, 29
MacLachlan, Ian, 87
Magnificent Seven cemeteries, 105
Magnuson, Paul, 39
Malthus, Thomas, 78
'Man of the Crowd', 2, 40, 54, 60, 72, 95, 119, 121–7, 131, 139
Manning, Marie (138)
Marcovski, Michael, 39–40, 42, 48
Martin, Richard ('Humanity Dick'), 10, 15, 80, 86, 93
Martin Chuzzlewit, 157, 175
Martin's Act, 4, 10, 15, 79–80, 87
Marx, Karl, 4–5
Marx and Engels, 78
Meat City, 23, 176
Melville, Herman, 4, 89, 126–31
Menely, Tobias, 80
Metcalfe, Robyn, 8, 16, 93, 105, 169–70
Metropolitan Board of Health (New York), 94
Metropolitan Drinking Fountain and Cattle Trough Association, 171
Metropolitan Meat Market at Islington, 7, 16, 87, 94, 97, 112, 170
Metropolitan Police Force (Scotland Yard), 143
Mile End, 69–70
Milton, John, 52
Mitch, David, 150
Montagu, Elizabeth, 36–8
Moore, Alan, 31
Morton, Timothy, 84
Muir, John, 29
Museum of London, 111, 137

Napoleon, 94
Newgate Calendar, 131, 137, 145

Newgate Market, 92
Newgate novels, 92, 120, 140–1, 145
Newgate Prison, 92, 136, 143
Nietzsche, Friedrich, 97
No Country For Old Men, 87
Norris, Frank (*The Octopus: A Story of California*), 94
Nussbaum, Felicity, 36–8

Old Bailey, 64, 132, 145
The Old Manour House, 69
Oliver Twist, 2, 60–73, 85, 109, 111, 131–9, 145–6, 148, 170, 173, 179
Ono, Barry, 120, 142
Orwell, George, 158
Our Mutual Friend, 159, 176
Oxford Street, 143
Oxo, 4, 19–20, 21, 78, 106–7
'Ozymandias', 30–1, 33, 36, 42, 57

Paternoster Row, 92
Peel, Robert, 143
Perkins, David, 28, 42–3, 50, 58, 83–4
Perren, Richard, 98–9, 102, 106
The Philanthropic Butcher, 99–102
Pipe Roll, 91
Poe, Edgar Allen, 2, 4, 6, 19, 21, 40, 54, 60, 72, 89, 95, 119–26, 131, 139, 146, 151, 176
Poor Laws, 28, 32, 78
The Prelude, 27, 32–5, 37
Prest, Thomas Peckett, 19, 145, 155, 156, 158
Pultney, Sir William, 84
Pure Food and Drug Act (1906), 94

Raven, James, 154
Reform Act (1832), 140
Removal Act, 29
Retzch, Moritz, 126
'The Rime of the Ancient Mariner', 27, 54–7
Ritson, Joseph, 21
Ritvo, Harriet, 77–9, 170, 179
Rogers, Ben, 98
Roosevelt, Theodore, 94
Royal Court of Justice, 91, 171
Royal Society for the Protection of Animals (RSPCA), 5, 7, 15, 86
Ruskin, John, 54
Rymer, James Malcolm, 19, 138, 145, 156

St Bartholomew's Hospital, 172
St Dunstan-in-the-West church, 158
St Martin's-in-the-Fields, 145
St Nicholas Shambles, 91–2
St Paul's Cathedral, 86, 180
Scorsese, Martin, 95
Scotland, 17
Scott, Sir Walter, 3, 65, 70, 156

Senf, Carol, 139
Shakespeare, William, 52
Shelley, Mary, 6, 9, 20, 27, 42, 52, 55–7, 67, 177, 179
Shelley, Percy, 22, 30–1, 33, 36, 42
Shepherd's Bush, 92
Sheppard, Jack, 21, 67, 119–20, 136, 142–5
Simpson, David, 32–5
Sinclair, Upton, 94–5, 173
Singer, Peter, 60
Smith, Charlotte, 36, 51, 57, 69
Southey, Robert, 57, 168
Southwark, 138
Spitalfields, 69
Stinking Lane, 92
Stoker, Bram, 19, 67, 119, 130, 138–9, 159, 175–6
The String of Pearls, 141–2, 158
Sweeney Todd, 3, 4, 14, 20–1, 37, 41, 67, 86, 90, 97, 113, 119–21, 127, 138–43, 145, 151, 155–61, 175, 178, 179
Swift, Jonathan, 7

'Tam o'Shanter', 27, 50
Thackery, William Makepeace, 145
Thames River, 92–3, 105, 106–7, 138, 176
'There was a Boy', 17–18, 30, 58–9, 76
Thompson, E. P., 17
Thompson, Patricia, 151
'To A Haggis', 10–12, 24
'To A Mouse', 17–18, 27–8, 38, 43, 47–51, 58, 75, 84, 108, 168
'To A Young Ass', 27, 28, 57–8
The Trial, 1, 130
Tull, Jethro, 79
'Turnip Townsend', 79
Turpin, Dick, 145
Twain, Mark, 3
Tyburn Tree, 153, 155
Tyler, Wat, 77

Uexküll, Jakob von, 48
Uruguay, 20, 98, 106

Vanity Fair, 125
Varney the Vampyre, 19, 138, 145, 156
The Vegetarian Society, 22–3
Victoria and Albert Museum, 107
The Voice of Humanity, 81, 86

walklondon.com, 107
Wallace, William, 69, 77
Watchmen, 31
Westminster Bridge, 124
Whitman, Walt, 23
Williams, Merryn and Raymond, 44–5
The Wind in the Willows, 43
Windham, William, 80, 84
Wolfe, Cary, 6
Wollstonecraft, Mary, 6, 78

Wordsworth, William, 7, 17–18, 27–8, 29, 30, 32–9, 58–60, 61, 121, 137, 168
The Worshipful Company of Butchers, 22, 90–1, 158, 170, 174–5
The Worshipful Company of Poulters, 108

Young Lee, Paula, 94
Youngquist, Paul, 37

Zola, Emile (*Pot-Bouille*), 1–3

EU representative:
Easy Access System Europe
Mustamäe tee 50, 10621 Tallinn, Estonia
Gpsr.requests@easproject.com

www.ingramcontent.com/pod-product-compliance
Lightning Source LLC
Chambersburg PA
CBHW051117230426
43667CB00014B/2620